KINGDOM CHURCHES

New Strategies For A Revival Generation

2nd Edition

MARK PERRY

Cameo
BOOKS
ARROYO GRANDE, CALIFORNIA 93421

KINGDOM CHURCHES

Cameo
BOOKS
ARROYO GRANDE, CALIFORNIA 93421

ISBN - 13: 978-1484002865 / ISBN – 10: 1484002865

Unless otherwise indicated, Scripture quotations are taken from:

The Holy Bible, New International Version. Copyright © 1978 by New York International Bible Society.

New American Standard Bible. Copyright © 1978 by Thomas Nelson, Inc. © The Lockman Foundation, 1960, 1962, 1963, 1968, 1971, 1972, 1973, 1975, 1977, La Habra, California.

The Amplified Bible. Copyright © 1965 by Zondervan Publishing House and The Lockman Foundation.

The Holy Bible, New Living Translation, copyright © 1996. Tyndale House Publishers, Inc., Wheaton, Illinois 60189. All rights reserved.

Cover design by DSD Creative Group
Printed in the United States of America

Endorsements

"Finally! An excellent book that will cause you to see the church as Jesus intended it to be! If you think the church is not relevant and essential today, then be ready for an exciting, empowering and enlightening discovery! I've seen people raised from the dead but this book will literally bring the dead church to life!"

Mel Tari
Revivalist, Speaker, and Author of *Like a Mighty Wind*

~ ~

"I knew at Mark's opening comments that I would enjoy his book. Building by focusing on the person of Jesus Christ sounds as though it should be so obvious that it doesn't need to be said again, and yet it so clearly does. Not only that, it has been *well said* again by Mark.

I am actually at a loss to pick one theme to focus on in endorsing this book. There are literally dozens of themes and quotes that are very dear to my heart. Mark has, I believe, managed to write a book about kingdom church growth without minimizing the beauty and role of the church and without limiting the potential of kingdom. Mark hasn't resorted to balance--which in my view is somewhat neutral--but he has succeeded in articulating and holding many themes in healthy tension.

This book is undeniably Christ-centered and yet practical. Mark acknowledges a major shift and, at the same time, challenges a shift to continue: 'This radical shift of attention from works to the person of Jesus changes everything.' It does, and this book will guide you to put as you this into action. I commend it to you not just to read but to put into practice."

Paul Manwaring
Director, Global Legacy
Author, *What On Earth Is Glory* & *Kisses From A Good God*

~ ~

"Mark Perry is carrying a new wineskin for what kingdom culture looks like. I believe we are living in a epoch season where the church is being reformed into a presence driven community that brings abundant life. For decades Mark has said "Yes" to God to build His Church and has discovered instrumental keys to bring his Kingdom. I would strongly encourage you to read, study, and implement in your personal life the book *Kingdom Churches*. You will never be the same and you'll be forever changed to bring Heaven down to earth!!"

Chad Dedmon
Global Legacy Pastor

"Mark has had a hunger for finding keys to growth, supernatural, and community for years. How does the kingdom power fit into emerging churches of the 21st century? This book is the result of not just theory, but a sincere effort to demonstrate and activate kingdom principles. Your thinking will be challenged, your perspective may change, and your life and personal ministry may be transformed!"

Steve Witt
Senior Leader, Bethel Cleveland

"The Body of Christ is in a monumental season of transition. From the exalted mega-church pastor to the humble house church minister, every leader I am aware of seems to be searching for a more authentic and effective way of doing church and being The Church. In his groundbreaking book, *Kingdom Churches*, Mark Perry offers a valuable contribution to this discovery process by lovingly identifying the weaknesses of the existing church and providing fresh solutions that are both soundly biblical and extremely practical. Having been a senior pastor for over 25 years, I cannot recommend this book highly enough. I only wish it had been written a couple of decades earlier."

Michael Brodeur
Pastor and Author

"*Kingdom Churches* falls into that rare category among Christian books of being both fresh and timeless simultaneously. As most in church leadership are aware, there is always a plethora of new books on church growth, style, and innovation. Many seem to very much be merely a restating of either the call for reformation or fresh innovation. Mark Perry, however, has excelled at combining fresh perspectives of church together with the timeless values of the Bible and the Kingdom of God along with a compelling sense of the prophetic.

God is a God of the 'both/and'. For example, He gave the Hebrews, fresh out of Egypt, both very practical instruction for camp life but also led them supernaturally by His presence. Recognizing that God is often 'both/and' it is both refreshing and insightful to read within the same volume a call for prayer, anointing, and the prophetic joined with a call for Christ like character and intentionality of purpose amongst leadership. It is extremely helpful to read that the Kingdom of God is a kingdom of power and miracles but it is also a kingdom whose citizens are not exempt from suffering. I especially appreciated the insights regarding 'greenhouse culture, contexts, and catalysts' being found within a book that also stresses the need for being a people living out of God's consuming fire.

Thank you, Mark, for this gift to church leaders who desire to truly bring forth kingdom fruit that will stand the test of time."

Marc A. Dupont
Founder, Mantle of Praise Ministries

~ ~

"Mark Perry is a treasured friend whose understanding of current church issues springs from the grace of God in his life as he has diligently pursued his calling as a church leader over many years. I stand behind his many rich and valuable perspectives, and I especially commend this book and its spiritual DNA to Western pastors everywhere. He is first of all preoccupied with God, and his forward path is always lower still. For us in Iris Global his writing is a trusted guide to seeking first the kingdom of God through church leadership."

Rolland Baker
Founding Director, Iris Global

~ ~

"Mark is a wonderful friend and partner in ministry whose insights on leadership are valuable for any church leader today. In *Kingdom Churches*, he addresses an important paradigm shift in the way we do church. When a family of laid down lovers come together to worship the King, the Kingdom is naturally released all around us. He also recognizes that lower still is a true key to walking in the footsteps of Jesus. He calls for a fresh baptism of fire that will cause us to burn with intensity for Jesus. He rightly says that '*Intensity in pursuing the Person of God releases intimacy in the Presence of God.*' I gladly recommend *Kingdom Churches* and pray it inspires us all to forever burn with the fire of God and to realize that family is at the heart of the Father."

Heidi Baker, PhD
Founding Director, Iris Global

Dedication

I dedicate this book to Papa Rolland Baker and Mama Heidi Baker who have modeled revival in our generation and who have been building kingdom churches for decades. You are amazing and I love you both so much.

CONTENTS

Acknowledgments   i
Preface   ii

1   Kingdom REVOLUTION   1

2   Kingdom CULTURE   17

3   Kingdom PRIORITIES   27

4   Kingdom INTENSITY   48

5   Kingdom PRIESTS   69

6   Kingdom BUILDERS   90

7   Kingdom LEADERSHIP   108

8   Kingdom MEMBERSHIP   129

9   Kingdom GATHERINGS   150

10   Kingdom ADVANCEMENT   172

Acknowledgements

This book would not have been possible without the consistent support and encouragement of my wife Cheryl and my three daughters--Audrey, Emily, and Olivia. Thank you, Cheryl, for standing with me and for being my partner and friend in life and ministry. You are an extraordinary woman who has done me good all our days. Your worth is far above precious gems, and my heart trusts you! (Prov. 31:10-12) To my amazing daughters, you are so deeply loved, and the Divine destiny on your lives is thrilling to behold! May our ceiling truly become your floor as you continue to embody and express the kingdom of God.

The churches I have been privileged to serve and lead have extended me great grace as I have been working out these principles and practices in the laboratory of the local church. We have journeyed and experimented together! Thank you for making room for me as a leader to also be a life-long learner.

Finally, I've so deeply appreciated the many friends, mentors, and spiritual fathers & mothers who have modeled for me, imparted to me, believed in me, and invested in my life. I am a father now because I first became a son, and becoming a son was easier because of so many great people. Over the years I have been privileged to know several world-class leaders, some well-known on earth, all well-known in heaven. My special thanks to the leaders and movements that have modeled for and imparted to me: John Wimber and the leaders of the Vineyard movement, John & Carol Arnott and the leaders of the Catch The Fire movement, Mike Bickle and the leaders of the IHOP movement, Bill Johnson and the leaders of the Bethel movement, and Rolland & Heidi Baker and the leaders of the Iris Global movement.

Preface

Kingdom Churches is a book about how to build churches that are founded on the Person of Jesus Christ while always seeking the kingdom first. It is a different kind of church planting. It is more like church planting as a _byproduct_ rather than as a focus. When the King and His kingdom are the focus, the church happens. When the church is the focus, the King and His kingdom get relegated to second place. Jesus' admonition to seek _first_ the kingdom is central to what it means to build kingdom churches.

My deep desire and prayer is that God will use this book to empower a generation in the West who are seeking the kingdom, who care about the church, who long for revival, and who need handbooks. This book is written both for church leaders and church members to give common expression, understanding, and strategy for the joyful, God-given task of building the kinds of churches that honor the Lord.

With the fear of God and great respect for His people, then, I submit this book to the body of Christ. For all those contending for something beyond what we have now, my heart is joined with yours. Let's build what God is building, because He is building kingdom churches.

Preface To The Second Edition

So much has changed in the world around us since I first wrote _Kingdom Churches_. The kingdoms of this world are quickly becoming the kingdom of our Lord. Our culture is transitioning and reinventing itself at breakneck speed. God continues to bring amazing change and increase to His Church in the West. Most of the principles in the original book remain as true today as when they were first written. There were a few places, though, that deserved some updating. This second edition reflects those updates.

So much has changed in me as well. When I first discovered them, the truths in this book were like shoes that were too big for me, and I have needed time to grow into them more fully. Immediately after writing this book the first time around, I experienced a season of personal testing and growth. It was as though God wanted me to more deeply own and embody what I had written before writing anything further. He has brought greater growth in areas where my theory was way ahead of my practice. I have needed and appreciated the time to 'catch up!' The result is a richer, more meaningful, more heart-felt edition that I think the reader will appreciate.

Finally, my purpose in writing this book has become more clear. I originally wrote _Kingdom Churches_ after a decade-long season of prayer, research, and experimentation. I needed to express some things on paper, and a book seemed like the best, most cathartic vehicle for that. Since that time, I have shared the principles of kingdom churches with individuals and groups of people in many settings, and after much encouragement, I've seen the need to be more strategic and practical in this book. So I've expanded the book by adding new material and new chapters. Soon this book will be accompanied by a workbook and other materials designed to empower kingdom builders. The result, I hope, is a book that will have broader appeal and use for all of us who are engaged in building kingdom churches.

Chapter One
Kingdom REVOLUTION

"...Once more I will shake...the earth...The words 'once more' indicate the removing of what can be shaken...so that what cannot be shaken may remain. Therefore, since we are receiving a kingdom that cannot be shaken, let us be thankful...for our God is a consuming fire." --Heb. 12:26-29

This is the best of times and the worst of times for the Christian church in the Western world. The bad news is increasingly self-evident: much of the church is too often perceived by unbelievers and Christians alike as hypocritical, judgmental, political, cumbersome, antiquated, controlling, and out of touch with reality. About half of all young Christian believers in America are leaving the church by the time they reach thirty. Historical data also suggests that despite fanfare to the contrary, the church in the Western world hasn't seen much real net growth for decades. While revival is igniting the church in so many other parts of the world, believers in the West who care about authentic Christian community are often left scratching their heads as they observe our current church stagnation and decline.

But there is also very, very good news. God is doing something about it. We are in the midst of a major, God-authored shaking, as old ways of thinking and practice are crumbling, and a new move of God is being expressed through a new generation. The strong winds of change are blowing, and it is nothing less than a kingdom revolution authored by God that is changing the way we perceive and 'do' church. We are most blessed and least deserving, but God, being rich in mercy, is sending change our way. New wine requires new wineskins, and God is graciously giving both to His Western church.

This God-authored shaking can be very inconvenient, disconcerting, and even frightening for those who cling to the familiar. While the world has been desperately waiting for the church to be shaken, there are still many frustrated and confused church leaders in the West. God, however, seems absolutely convinced of something we are prone to forget and ignore. It is only in the aftermath of shaking that we can experience anything of real substance. Shaking reveals foundational cracks, shoddy building, hasty methods, hollow promises, and hype. It is God's quality control test, exposing defective construction, so the things built right can remain.

What a great time to be alive! Should Jesus tarry, historians will surely look back at this time as one where the expression of Christianity in the West shifted dramatically from what we've had to something far more Biblical, creative, simple, fiery, and relevant than anything we've seen in our lifetime. Among other things, the Lord is releasing understanding and grace to build new kinds of churches. I call them *kingdom churches*, because they contain characteristics combined in such a wonderfully unique way that the kingdom emerges first, ahead of the church, and the King is honored first as Head over every church in a city or region. The church in North America, Europe, and the Western world is in desperate need of change, and the Lord, in His wisdom and great mercy, in the fullness of time, is bringing that change. Though perhaps we haven't sought Him nor been as hungry for Him as His people in other parts of the world where the need is much more profound and compelling, He is nonetheless answering our weak cry.

> "I revealed myself to those who did not ask for me;
> I was found by those who did not seek me. To a nation that did not call my
> name, I said, 'Here am I, here am I.'" --Isa. 65:1

God is so gracious that He is bringing the change we need, often in spite of ourselves! It is largely the combination of the sovereignty of God and the prayers of others gone before us that has brought us to this place. We are entering into the fruit of others' labors, and we are poised in the West to finally begin to make strides to keep pace with our brothers and sisters in other parts of the world who are living in revival. If you've ever visited places where ongoing revival is happening (and there are many), you know what a miracle it would be for God to do the same in the West. But it is starting to happen. Like the prophet Elijah, we can now see the cloud the size of a man's hand on the horizon. The rain is coming! God Himself is bringing revival and revolution to His Western Bride.

Granted, not everyone is able (or willing) to see this shift of epic proportions. But more and more can--and will. The church in the West has been fast asleep, but she is being awakened. The love of God is awakening the church! Radical change has already begun and is now accelerating! Do you see it?

> "Forget the former things; do not dwell on the past. See, I am doing a new thing! Now it springs up; do you not perceive it?" --Isa. 43:18-19

JESUS THE REVOLUTIONARY

Revolution is defined as "the overthrow of one government and its replacement with another; a sudden or momentous change in a situation." Rev. 11:15 describes this overthrow: *"The kingdom of the world has become the kingdom of our Lord and of his Christ."* We are in the midst of a major power shift. It's not just the world that is coming to Jesus. This revolution is also about *the church* coming back to Jesus and being overtaken by Christ's kingdom.

When Jesus walks into any situation, everything changes. He carries the atmosphere of heaven, and as He 'shows up' in our midst, there is a kingdom conflict and clash. Jesus the revolutionary is invading the Western church! When Jesus looks at us, eyes blazing with fire, revolution begins. Things get turned on their heads.

We read in Luke 22 the story of Jesus praying in the garden of Gethsemane. This garden was located in an olive grove on a hill called the Mount of Olives. In one moment, Jesus is praying fervently while His disciples are snoozing nearby. In the next moment, a huge crowd shows up, armed with clubs and swords. Can you imagine how strange this must have been—a large group of armed vigilantes going after the Prince of Peace who was praying in a garden with sleepy friends? Those vigilantes must have felt very, very threatened.

> "Then Jesus spoke to the leading priests, the captains of the Temple guard, and the elders who had come for him. 'Am I some *dangerous revolutionary*,' he asked, 'that you come with swords and clubs to arrest me?'" --Luke 22:52, NLT

We know the answer to Jesus' question, don't we? Yes! He was, in fact, *a very dangerous revolutionary.* And He is now walking in the midst of another garden—the garden of the Western church. Some parts of the church are like the disciples, sad and asleep. Other parts of the church are quite upset, like the religious priests and elders. They are intent on stopping this nonsense and restoring order so things can continue as they were. But Jesus is a dangerous revolutionary—thank God! And He will not stop until He has brought a kingdom revolution to His Church everywhere. This is tremendously good news for those of us living in

North America, Europe, Australia, New Zealand, and other Western nations.

SIGNS OF REVOLUTION

How do we know it's true? Well, there are several clear, unmistakable evidences that a God-orchestrated change is underway. Signs point to something, and there are clear signs that something big is going on. Here are four:

Holy Dissatisfaction

Great change is always preceded by great dissatisfaction. Dissatisfaction is the vital first step to revolution, and God has spread it throughout the Western church. When revolutionaries need vision for a more desirable future, God begins with raw discontent. Vision is defined as *'a deep dissatisfaction with what is, coupled with a clear picture of what could be.'* Before Nehemiah rallied the people to rebuild the wall, he began by weeping over the broken dreams and rubble all around him. He gathered the people and began with the bad news. God has been rallying us, and part of His rallying cry has been to place holy dissatisfaction in our hearts and minds.

This dissatisfaction has been exponentially increasing. It is no longer the disgruntled wrangling of a few malcontents. What began many years ago as a whisper in the living rooms of a few is now a roar in the mouths of an entire generation unwilling to accept the status quo. We are now in the midst of a massive uprising--a God-orchestrated, holy disquiet meant to produce a deep unwillingness to be satisfied with anything less than the real thing. It is the Lord stirring in His people an unrelenting desire for Himself and His kingdom. People in both the world and the church are standing in solemn protest to the current level and expression of Christianity in much of the church today, especially in the West. It is a holy uprising that demands our attention.

Award-winning journalist Steve Strang, publisher of *Charisma* magazine and founder of Charisma Media, described the issue of discontentment in a recent article entitled "The Real Church Crisis":

> "Do you sense a depression in the body of Christ in America, as if something is badly wrong? We're losing influence within our culture as the anti-Christian sentiment grows, yet you'd never know it in most churches—the smoke, lights, loud music and preaching rolls on as if all is well...Too often people

come to the church, are deeply disappointed and as a result are turned off from the gospel. The church promises solutions but only offers lip service. We've become excellent at giving people a show on Sunday but lousy at showing them how to actually live... I recently spoke with two businessmen friends about why it's hard to find a good church. Both are successful financially and are passionate believers. On the surface, they're what every pastor needs. Yet after being active in a local church, they both became disillusioned with what they saw and how they were treated. As they recounted stories of how pastors felt threatened by their powerful personalities and positions, I felt sorry for my friends (for never experiencing the community they sought) and for the insecure leaders they served. Countless other mature Christians have been so wounded by leadership that they stay home on Sunday and "go to church" by watching Charles Stanley or Jack Hayford. They get a good message, some good music and an opportunity to "tithe" to that ministry. Sometimes this is a transitional period. Too often it's not. But this isn't Christian community. Aren't we supposed to assemble with other believers? Aren't we supposed to bring a hymn or a Scripture or a prophetic word when we meet? In larger churches this need is met in small groups or in various ministries of the church. There are many examples of healthy churches where this happens. But too often it isn't... Until this happens, people—like my businessmen friends—will feel as if they're drifting. They'll never really find their place in the body of Christ. And sooner or later, they will 'vote with their feet' by going somewhere else—or worse still, nowhere."

Within the ranks of American Christianity in particular there has also been a growing sense of discontent. For years, I've seen it among both pastors and people in the church. Many of those in 'full-time ministry' that I know personally or hear from in some other way are expressing a deep, heart-felt desire to see 'the way we do church' radically change. Full-time paid pastors are leaving their posts at local churches in record numbers. While they began in ministry with a confidence that they could make a difference, many are finding the slow, cumbersome process of change in Western church life too difficult to bear. They are 'opting out.' Whether this migration is from the Lord, the enemy, or both, it is nonetheless an indicator of holy discontent and of a church system in radical need of change.

The people, too, who've occupied the pews of churches across the nation have been faithfully attending for years while a great burden and sadness grows in their hearts. They may not know exactly why they feel what they feel, but they know instinctively that the church, while made up of people they love very much, is largely ineffective. Millions of these are also 'opting out' of local churches in silent protest, and they are not 'snapping out of it' as some would like. They refuse shallow comforts and appeals.

> "When I was in distress, I sought the LORD; at night I stretched out untiring hands and my soul refused to be comforted. I remembered you, O God, and I groaned; I mused, and my spirit grew faint. Selah." --Ps. 77:2-3

Over the years I've heard this groaning. I can hear conversations echoing in my brain, words couched in reverence for God and love for the church, but words nonetheless that speak of a deep longing and dissatisfaction. They are summed up in this: "While I am thankful for what we have, we're not even close to where we're meant to be." That doesn't diminish our progress--it only highlights our need. We are hungry for more. This God-birthed, holy dissatisfaction is both a clear sign and a vital first step.

The Prayers Of The Saints

By God's design, this dissatisfaction has led to a huge increase in prayer. Revelation 5:8 tells us that heaven contains golden bowls full of incense, which are the prayers of the saints. The bowls are filling up! Dissatisfaction has given birth to a spiritual groaning that is turning into a massive prayer movement in our day. God's people have always prayed throughout history. But it is a clear sign of change when the church in the West begins to fervently and consistently cry out like never before, interceding for the lost and pursuing Him in intimacy.

> "My house will be called a house of prayer for all the peoples." --Isa. 56:7

This often-quoted verse in Isaiah means much more than renaming the church as a house of prayer. God is giving definition and substance to the church in the future. God Himself prophesied that there will come a day when prayers both from His people and from those trying to find Him will define the nature and activity of His house to such an extent that the only appropriate way to think of and speak about the church will be to characterize it as a 'house of prayer.' We are living in that day!

When Jesus witnessed what had up to then been considered a little harmless profiteering going on in the temple courts, He became more fiery and indignant than perhaps any other time in his ministry. The activity of prayer in His house was so essential, and the invitation for the lost to come to the court of the gentiles to pray was so paramount, that He was zealous to remove anything that hindered this primary preoccupation:

> "Jesus went straight to the Temple and threw out everyone who had set up shop, buying and selling. He kicked over the tables of loan sharks and the stalls of dove merchants. He quoted this text: 'My house was designated a house of prayer; You have made it a hangout for thieves.'" --Mt. 21:12-13, The Message

Notice that God's people have been designated, marked, branded for prayer. Personally, I love houses of prayer, but ultimately, it isn't even so much about a *place* of prayer as it is about a *people* of prayer. After all, the temple was destroyed in 70 A.D. As New Covenant believers, we're *all* called to *devote* ourselves to prayer (Acts 2:42, Rom. 12:12, Col. 4:2). And we are seeing it, finally, in the West. God's people are seeking His face more and more in worship and prayer. This night & day worship and prayer movement is a sign of revolution. Jesus the Great Intercessor is walking in our midst, and God's people are responding with a deep yearning: "The Spirit and the Bride say, 'Come!'" (Rev. 22:17).

Prophetic Objections

As we pray more, we begin to hear more. And as we hear, we proclaim. For some time now, there has been a massive wave of prophetic voices decrying the status quo and calling for change. This is a prophetic revolt against the established thought process and structure within God's church in the Western world.

The need for change is always seen first by those with prophetic insight and keen revelation. During the U.S. 'wagon train' migrations to the West in the nineteenth century, there were scouts who ran ahead so they could spy out, warn, and protect. Prophets are like scouts in the wagon train called the church. As faithful watchmen, they see what is coming, both good and bad, and they alert the church so she can take appropriate action. Sometimes, the appropriate action is repentance.

Prophetic people have been chafing against the status quo (as God intends for them to do) for some years now, and as a result, they've often been labeled as negative and even rebellious. While that is sometimes the case, the key issue here is that by and large, prophets have been seeing and hearing correctly. There is something to prophesy *against*! The way we've been 'doing church' in America and in the West has been largely ineffective and, at times, even unbiblical and injurious. God Himself is objecting *through* His people *to* His people about the epic shift He desires. There is a multitude of prophetic voices, and not just among charismatics, who've been saying the same thing. If you are in touch with what prophetic people have been saying over the past few decades, you know that the message has consistently been: *The church is going to radically change.* Mike Bickle says the Lord told him in 1984 in Cairo, Egypt that God was going to change the nature and expression of Christianity in one generation. I believe we're living in that generation.

Some years ago George Barna, in his book <u>The Second Coming Of The Church</u>, wrote these words: "After nearly two decades of studying Christian churches in America, I'm convinced that...*we desperately need a revolution...*" Barna is right on that point--we need a revolution! And God Himself is bringing it. This exhortation reminds me of what God spoke through the prophet Joel to the people of his day:

> "Blow a trumpet in Zion, consecrate a fast, proclaim a solemn assembly, gather the people, sanctify the congregation, assemble the elders, gather the children and nursing infants. Let the bridegroom come out of his room and the bride out of her bridal chamber. Let the priests, the LORD's ministers, weep between the porch and the altar, and let them say, 'Spare Your people, O LORD, and do not make Your inheritance a reproach, a byword among the nations.'" ~ Joel 2:15-17

To call for change is not dishonoring to the church. I love the church, because the church is the Bride of Christ, and His Bride deserves great honor and respect. In fact, there has been an unhealthy pendulum swing that has occurred in the Western church in this day. Protesting what is wrong has devolved into devaluing and even mocking what is right. The word 'church' has become a dirty word among so many Christians! Millions of *believers* don't want anything to do with church. And yet, the church is exactly what Jesus is building (Mt. 16:18)--globally and locally. When we oppose and devalue what Jesus is building, we oppose and devalue Him.

Having said that, it is also true that we will never experience the revolution God is bringing if we don't open our eyes and recognize the current woeful condition of His Western Bride. It is no denigration of His Bride to see that she has some "spots and wrinkles" on her wedding gown (Eph. 5:27). A friend of mine had a God-given vision where she saw the Bride of Christ in the West. She was malnourished. Her dress was tattered. She was dirty, and needy, and very sad. If we can't see what Jesus sees, we will not be able to make ourselves ready for the wedding feast of the Lamb. There is simply no point in pretending. The landscape of the church is littered with attitudes, mindsets, spirits, and problems we have brought in from the world. Prophets are objecting, and here are some of the spots and wrinkles they're objecting to:

Consumerism. The spirit of consumerism is so pervasive that we can hardly detect it, because it feels right. It is characterized by "You can (and should) make me happy, so pray for me, meet my needs, get me motivated, make me feel special and included. If you don't, I will go someplace else where they can do these things for me." Of course, for a Christian to actually voice these words would sound so unspiritual. Yet this is often how we think and act. Consumerism has bred in us an entitlement mentality. This spirit drives people from place to place, and they are not finding the rest Christ offers. The cultural shift from responsibility to rights that typifies our society today has also permeated the atmosphere of the church. Too many Western believers still unconsciously view the church like a cruise ship, with a large, well-trained staff looking after every need. The church was never intended to be a cruise ship! It was always meant to be more like a fishing boat, with everyone working, everyone helping to catch and clean fish, and everyone enjoying the satisfaction of knowing that they gave their all. In such a crew, there is loyalty and friendship centered around a common mission. Today's Western Christian often sees the church as a Christian cafeteria, where we go to one church for its worship, another church for the message, and so on. While this cafeteria-style Christianity feels right to so many, it will never produce a passionate, close-knit, missional community that changes the world. Churches are not dispensers of religious goods and services, and we are not consumers; churches are specialized revival tribes made up of family-style armies.

Introspection. I believe in recovery, inner healing, and so on. And I'm grateful not only for the healing God has brought to my own life, but also for that which he continues to do in the church. I appreciate and admire those who provide ongoing therapy for parts of the church who are deeply hurting. Yet, the therapy culture in the church has birthed a mindset that says, "I can't really serve the Lord (or really even walk with God) until I feel better." It's certainly true that extreme wounding can temporarily immobilize people. But the other, much bigger problem is that too few of us actually learn how to grow *through* our pain. Instead, people quit serving God because our hurts are bigger than God's call to lay down our lives. A culture of therapy stands in opposition to becoming a missional, outward-focused people who lay down our lives for the many lost people Jesus came to seek and save. The church is a hospital, to be sure. But that hospital is a MASH unit, not a gated retirement center! Jesus declares it clearly when He says, *"For the Son of man did not come to be served, but to serve, and to give His life as a ransom for many."* Freely we have received, and in order to break this inward focus, we must freely give far beyond our feelings. The truth is that as we water others, we will also be refreshed (Prov. 11:25).

Individualism. Individualism can originate from pride ("Don't tell me what to

9

do", and "I can do it myself") or fear ("If I let someone else in, I could get hurt" and "What if they take my place or somehow devalue me?"). Whatever its source, individualism focuses almost exclusively on the individual aspects of Christianity--praying, reading our Bibles, listening to Christian music--while largely missing the fact that Christianity is always and forever centered in a community of faith. The New Testament "you" is like the Spanish "ustedes" or the Southern "y'all." Paul's letters are written mostly to churches and mostly in the plural form. Even the seemingly right emphasis in recent years on gift evaluation has inadvertently helped people to focus on their own destinies, often producing picky servants who only do what their gifts and prophecies indicate. This seems right until you compare the church to a family (which it is), where everyone does chores that may not necessarily fall within their gifting. The heart of the Biblical church in the New Testament is about servanthood in the context of community. We've been called to lay our lives down for many others, longing to be lower still, believing all the while that it is more blessed to give than to receive, and that the greatest person among us will be great by becoming a servant to all.

Spectatorism. Many church historians trace this problem back to 312 A.D., the period of time when Constantine began endorsing Christianity as the official state religion. With that declaration began the great Christian building campaign, and it has never really stopped--at least in the West. In and of themselves, buildings are neither good nor evil. But they can come with a lot of baggage! When Christian churches and cathedrals sprang up throughout the land, a professional clergy developed, with certain people paid to perform church functions and duties for everyone else. As Christians were no longer persecuted, a sense of cultural ease set in. Church became something that you did rather than who you are. Ministry became something professionals did for the rest of the Christians, rather than the church being a living body, a priesthood of all believers. And this spectator mindset has carried on for centuries. The church is often compared to a football game: 65,000 people in desperate need of exercise, and 22 people in desperate need of rest! Spectator Christianity compartmentalizes our lives so church becomes a 2-hour slot rather than a lifestyle. The early church met daily from house to house and in the temple courts. No one was needy, because people laid down their lives for one another in radical ways. Some would even sell their houses and give all the proceeds, just to make sure everyone was taken care of. Church in the West, unfortunately, is often not about a radical army of people connected through vital relationships. Sadly, it is often about a building we meet in and a staff we pay. The inevitable result is religious spectators. Meanwhile, Jesus continues to challenge our idea of what a disciple is. Discipleship is radical, full-time participation with Him.

Cultural Alignment

A final sign I want to mention is cultural alignment. While God has always spoken to His people through His prophets, He is also speaking to the church through the secular 'prophets' of the world. It is intriguing to me that God gives revelation to secular people who are sometimes more responsive to the leading of the Spirit than the church. Secular people with God-given insight often see the future with great clarity--even though their revelation can be incomplete, tainted, and misused. And how do they respond to the revelation God gives them? They immediately trumpet that revelation through the media of movies, books, newspaper and magazine articles, songs, and dramatic arts.

But here's the thing. God intends to reveal parables to the culture only *after* He has already spoken to the church. The church is meant to lead the world in hearing God's voice and shaping culture. When it takes a 'secular' movie for God to speak to the church, you know that we're having a hard time hearing. God knows where He can find His people-- sitting in movie theaters or at home in front of their televisions! So He hopes we will listen there.

> "For God speaks in one way, yet in another, though men may not perceive it."
> --Job 33:14

God is speaking *through* our culture. And He is telling us that the culture is positioned for revival. I believe God Himself has shaped the culture of the Western world to prepare it to receive the gospel. The fields are white for harvest. The people are ready. They're ready for us to become who we were always meant to be. Could it be that God is using the world's culture to unlock passionate Christianity in the church? It's happening. The culture is calling us, and God is speaking through the culture to His church! Here are some examples of how God is aligning the culture to bring about the revolution of the church:

Acceleration. Is it just me, or are things speeding up? The only real constant in today's Western world is change. Everything's moving faster, from transportation to technology to culture itself. The rapid advances we are seeing allow for change to occur more often and more suddenly. And because it is so pervasive, change and speed have become our cultural norm. God is speaking to the church through this cultural phenomenon of rapid, accelerated change. The culture is begging the church to accept change as normal and to become more creative, more spontaneous, and more fresh in its thinking and approach. This acceleration of change has nothing to do with the timeless aspects of the Christian faith or the timeless message of the gospel. Nor is it necessarily to be interpreted as a need to have cooler videos and better graphics on our websites. It is about *breakthrough*. It has to do with a *revival-based thought process.* For example, how long does it take the average Western church to produce a disciple? How about seeing someone go from atheist to missionary—how long? Acceleration is about a profound belief in the raw power of God to produce what our program-based design churches have had difficulty producing. This acceleration is a cultural paradigm shift that is preaching to the church.

Participation. We live in a culture of participation and relationship where people want to experience life with others. God has planted eternity in people's hearts (Eccl. 3:11), which means that people are actually longing for an encounter with God--but not necessarily by themselves. People would really like to see how beautiful Jesus is--and they want us to show them. The rugged individualism that characterized Western countries in the past is over. And when it comes to spirituality, there is a growing desire to walk through spiritual experiences with trusted friends who can also be mentors in spiritual things. I know of Christian leaders today who are so popular that they can fill stadiums, but on an interpersonal level, they are difficult to relate to. Should these ones really be our heroes? God is calling His church to be highly relational and to become a generation of spiritual mentors to people in the world. Relational people may or may not gather crowds, but they do display God's heart for others. This relational call challenges the church on several levels. As it stands now, most people in the world believe that Christians see them as the enemy. This has to change. We cannot win those whom we do not love. Having friends in the world also forces us to take a look at our own authenticity and experience in God. The messenger truly is the message. We can only help people encounter God when we are encountering God. A participatory Western culture is an invitation to the church to get a little messy and to widen our circle of friends.

Reality. Like it or not, we Westerners base more and more of our decisions on our feelings and experiences rather than 'right' answers. While I personally believe that we need an intellectual awakening in the West, we seem to be moving in the opposite direction. People today are throwing overboard anything that bogs down their experiential grasp of reality—even if it's true! This syncrenistic, relativistic approach to truth is disheartening. But there is a silver lining to this cloud. After seeing that rational humanism cannot and will not answer the deepest cries of humanity, our Western world is reaching out for experiences that include the supernatural. In the past, we in the West looked down on those in third-world countries who accepted the supernatural as normative. But things have changed. Today, people in the West recognize and accept the spiritual realm. As the world has gotten smaller and media more global, we've been exposed to enough evil to know that there are spiritual forces at work. While it is entirely appropriate for the church to avoid demonic movies and certain immoral television shows, we must stop seeing this desire for the supernatural as anything other than a move of God on the culture. God has planted eternity in people's hearts (Eccl. 3:11), and people want to encounter God. If the culture ever needed a straight dose of the Holy Ghost, it is right now! People need more than intriguing 'conversation'—they need displays of the raw power of God! This is a huge opportunity for those who can walk in the reality of God's Presence and Power. We owe the world an encounter with God, and people are ready.

These cultural megashifts are highly significant for the church. It is as if God has caused Western culture to pave the way for the gospel. This is not a time for the church to be asleep or to reproduce our familiar forms geared toward predictability and tameness. There are huge implications to how we think about and 'do' church. The church has an amazing opportunity to jettison worldly practices, reinvent itself and 'go Biblical' on the culture. Cultural megashifts are like flashing neon lights inviting the church into a kingdom revolution. The culture is saying, "Here we are, come and get us!" May the Lord give us understanding.

RESPONDING TO REVOLUTION

There is a lot of teaching in the church about how to respond to *revelation*. But what about revo*lution*? How do we respond to this incredible shift God is bringing to the church in the West?

I have a friend who refers to prayer and repentance as 'hitting the deck.' This is our first response to God's shaking and revolution. We need to go low in prayer, humility, and repentance. If there was ever a time to recognize how little we know, it is right now. When we see things as they are, we cannot always picture how they are going to be. But the Master Potter knows. He has the right to reform the clay into a new vessel (cf. Jer. 18). This is what I believe He is doing with His Western church. He is re-forming us into a fresh expression of His heart, and a posture of humility is our first response.

God has been busy bringing about the right conditions for revival to the church in the West. He has birthed within the church a holy dissatisfaction that has led to a global prayer movement. Prophetic voices have been trumpeting the need for change, while the culture has been aligning itself to the purposes of God. Meanwhile, God has been dismantling the church so He can refashion us into a more effective movement.

If you have felt hungry, weak, longing, confused, and yet somehow hopeful, you are not alone. Millions of Christians have been going through a paradigm shift over the past several years, and God has orchestrated it! He is preparing His people and the culture for radical change, and I believe we are going to see both darkness getting darker and the light of God becoming brighter and brighter through His people. Our prayers for the church are about to be answered! This will be the church's finest hour.

PULLED THROUGH A KNOTHOLE

But this paradigm shift can be a grueling process. In my own life, God took me on a decade-long journey that felt like I was being pulled through a knothole. As a successful church planter and senior pastor, my world was shaken the moment I asked a simple, central question: "What is the church?" As I prayed and thought about it, I soon realized how many assumptions I had made about the church. At first, being pulled through a knothole looked like becoming more aware of what I was *against* than what I was *for*...and how much I didn't know! I had more questions than answers, and I had to offload a whole bunch of stuff I thought I knew so that my heart was lighter and freer to respond to His easy and light yoke.

One day several years ago, I went up a hill overlooking our city to pray. I stood at the foot of a large cross on the hillside, and as I stood there in His presence, God spoke to me: 'Go to Akron, plant a church, and do it My way.' When I heard this, I was immediately excited and concerned at the same time. My excitement to go establish a new work in a city I had never been to was mingled with concern that He had told me to do it 'His way.' The response that came out of me in that moment was, "I thought I was doing it Your way?" But He didn't answer me! And His silence forced me to dive deeper into the Scriptures to see again what the Lord said about His Church. I read and re-read every passage in the Bible on the church. I prayed and listened and reflected. I began more than ever to live at a place of much greater dependency and desperation. Things got simpler. All I wanted to do was to hear His voice and obey Him. I just wanted to do what the Father was doing (Jn. 5:19) without being weighed down by what I thought I knew. During the next few years, I found myself continually repenting for relying on my knowledge and training rather than on His kind and wise leadership in my life.

When we planted the church in Akron, Ohio, we ended up doing a few 'unconventional' things that contradicted the church planting training I had received. For example, our growth process didn't fit with our training. We started the church with just our family, but after being in

Akron for about six months and reaching out to many, somehow we had gathered seventy-five people. It should have been exciting, but I felt so tired and drained after every gathering! And then the Lord spoke to me, telling me that I had gathered a whole bunch of people He didn't intend to be with us. He continued by saying that I needed to lovingly and gently help some people 'off the bus.' I remember laughing to myself, thinking that the title of my life right then was 'Honey, I Shrunk The Church!' We did, in fact, say and do some things that helped some people find a better fit at other churches.

Our Sunday gatherings ended up being different, too. I heard the Lord speak to me the words of Martin Luther King, Jr., that 11 am on Sundays was the most segregated hour in America. I got the very clear sense that He didn't like that! And I sensed Him asking us to do something different. So we changed our church service from something predictable to something mobile and risky. At 10 am, we worshipped and prayed for one another for the first hour, getting absolutely filled with God's Presence and power. Then at 11 am, we formed into teams to go to the poorest neighborhoods in Akron. We brought gifts and went door-to-door, loving, praying, sharing Jesus, and becoming friends with the poorest of the poor. Each week, the people of our church, including the children, got out of our cars and walked into the projects, sometimes stepping over condom wrappers and used drug needles in order to bring Jesus. We had stepped out of the box, and we would never be the same.

These experiences and many others helped us 'detox' from some typical American church growth thinking. We experienced a freshness and joy in advancing God's kingdom rather than simply trying to grow our church. Business as usual would never satisfy us, and we knew that we were on a journey into building kingdom churches.

PREPARING FOR REVOLUTION

The journey into revolution is very exciting, but it isn't easy. As we recognize how little we know, and as we see the signs all around us that tell us how much the church in the West needs to change, it is tempting to become discouraged and to throw up our hands in despair. Revolution is a mammoth undertaking! But God knows what He's doing. He is our fearless Leader! He has given us signs along the way, and He never wastes a sign. He puts them there for a reason. Signs point to a destination. We are going somewhere! And He Himself is leading the way.

Even though we may not know exactly where we're going, and even though some of us may be more in touch with what's wrong than what's right, God knows. He sees. He has answers. He has plans in His own heart that are good, designed to give us a future and a hope. And He is calling us into a journey of revolution. As revolutionaries, may we learn to run from the place of rest, leaning on our Beloved all the way!

To prepare for a kingdom church revolution, we must become those who carry the atmosphere of heaven. That's what the next chapter is about.

Chapter Two
Kingdom CULTURE

"One day as Jesus was teaching...the power of the Lord was present for him to heal the sick...and the people all tried to touch Him, because power was coming from Him and healing them all." --Luke 5:17, 6:19

The atmosphere around Jesus was filled with love and charged with power. When Jesus was around, forgiveness flowed, hope filled human hearts, and people began to believe. The impossible became possible. Miracles were invited, expected, and received. In these Scriptures in Luke 5 & 6, we see the longing people had to touch something intangible. Yes, they wanted to touch Jesus, but they were actually also being drawn to something that was beyond contact with human flesh. Power was coming *from* Him, emanating off His being. It was the manifestation of God's compassion through both His actions and His 'atmosphere' that brought transformation.

I have seen the power of atmosphere displayed in dramatic ways. For example, years ago I remember being in Columbus, Ohio, after an altar call at a very large church. I was standing next to a friend, Blaine Cook, as he went down a line of people, praying for each one. Blaine was standing to my left. As he prayed for the person in front of him, I looked to my right, and a woman three people away began to shake, her eyes rolled back in her head, and she began to manifest a demon! I literally watched the power of an anointed atmosphere begin to bring deliverance to a woman while no one touched her. This happened over and over during our prayer time.

Very recently, a couple from our church was looking at a rental unit with a realtor. My friend and his wife are people who are filled with the love of God. They walk in His anointing. As they were looking at the rental unit, the realtor began to quietly weep—for no apparent reason. There was nothing in the conversation or anything abnormal going on in the situation. It was simply the power of God's love dwelling in my friends.

They carried an atmosphere of heaven that began to impact the person around them. Again, I could repeat this story over and over, both in my own life and in the lives of other friends.

Atmosphere is powerful. To build kingdom churches well, we must understand the importance and power of culture, because atmosphere is culture and culture is atmosphere. Kingdom churches are built first and primarily through culture. And it is in the right culture (atmosphere) that everything is transformed.

MISSION FIRST

Let's back up a minute. Before we can properly talk about *culture*, we must first understand our *mission*. Mission is our larger heavenly assignment. It is our purpose as believers in Jesus. We remain on the planet partly because of a heavenly mission, an assignment from God! Biblically and practically speaking, our mission is to bring God glory by transforming lives—personally (our own lives), regionally (where we live), and globally (the nations).

Our mission and our destiny are tied together in Scripture. According to Romans 8:29, we know that every Christian has a destiny:

*"For those whom He foreknew, He also predestined **to become conformed to the image of His Son**, so that He would be the firstborn among many brethren."*

Our destiny, then, is to become like Jesus—in thought, word, and deed. The Father is looking to reproduce the nature of His beautiful Son in humanity. This goal is confirmed in other Scriptures as well:

"My little children, for whom I am in travail until Christ is formed in you." --Gal. 4:29

"God made known His goal: Christ in you, the hope of glory. We proclaim Him... so we may present every man complete in Christ." --Col. 1:27-28

We were originally created in the image of God. Adam and Eve were created in His *likeness*... not a physical likeness, but a likeness of thought, word, and deed. Unfortunately, poor choices led to the entrance of sin into the relationship, and sin mars every image, likeness, and relationship. Now, through Christ, we have been and are being restored to our original image, and we have been given the assignment (i.e., mission) to help others discover and walk in their original design too. Jesus is humanity as God always intended us to be. He demonstrated for all what it looks like to live an abundant life in continual relationship with the Father. Those who receive Christ are now walking down the road of destiny—transformation from the inside out.

With this goal and mission in mind, let's take a look at how kingdom culture helps to accomplish this mission and to build followers of Jesus who bear His image.

CHURCH AS A GREENHOUSE

Ready to put on your thinking cap? We're going metaphorical for a few minutes! One way to think of the local church is as a greenhouse. At our church, we like to say that we are *a greenhouse for revivalists!* Churches can either bog down or accelerate growth in people's lives. When we accelerate growth, we are functioning like a greenhouse.

A greenhouse has three components that each contributes to the growth of the flowers, plants, trees, or whatever is being grown (or in our case, people!). Since our mission is transformation, and since greenhouses help bring about transformation, the metaphor is fitting. The three components are the (1) culture; (2) contexts; and (3) catalysts.

Greenhouse CULTURE. The culture in a greenhouse is the temperature, humidity, sunlight, protection from wind and animals, and so on. The culture in a greenhouse is the environment, the atmosphere, the 'air.' Of course, it is unseen, but it is definitely felt and experienced.

Greenhouse CONTEXTS. The contextual elements of a greenhouse are the visible structures. These may include the planter pots, the tables, the pallets, and the actual poles and plastic or glass sides of the greenhouse itself. These are the seen elements that cause someone to conclude that they are indeed looking at a greenhouse!

Greenhouse CATALYSTS. The catalysts are those things that happen that bring accelerated life. Fertilizer, 'Miracle-Gro', watering, weeding, even human time spent with the plants—these are all events that increase and even accelerate growth. They can be regular or periodic, but they are always catalytic moments.

So let's apply this to kingdom churches.

The *culture* of a church has to do with its **values**. Values are the unseen 'pillars' in any group or organization. They are what we hold dear and what we put emphasis and priority on. They determine what a church feels like. This is why two churches can teach from the same passage of Scripture on the same Sunday morning and have almost identical programs but feel completely different. The vibe is different because a different set of values is being walked out and transmitted in each place.

The *contexts* of a church are its **programs**. The term 'program' has received quite a beating in some church circles, as though anything that smacks of 'program' will surely remove all the life out of the room! But a program is simply an agreed upon time and place for something to occur. It is intentionality. In that sense, a weekly family dinner or a date night is a program. Programs are not bad! Thank God for plans that we can rely on. Thank God for prayer rooms that are open during specific days and times, for healing rooms that minister on a set morning or night. A program is like a container into which we can pour life. The container itself doesn't have the ability to produce life, but it can certainly facilitate life. For that reason, church programs can be very transformational, as long as they also have the right culture.

The *catalysts* of a church are its **events**. Guest speakers, conferences, BBQs, baptisms, special outreaches, retreats, corporate fasts, ministry times, and missions trips are all examples of events within a church setting that have the potential to rapidly advance people's growth, relationships, and breakthrough. Catalysts are essential to keep us fresh and to free us when we get stuck in our routines. They often provide fresh perspective and a needed wake-up call.

These three components are like the three legs on a stool—they are all needed or the stool will not support anything and will fall over. Transformation occurs best when all three of these components are present in a kingdom church. A kingdom church needs culture, contexts, and catalysts.

Too often in church life we under- or overvalue one leg of the stool. Whenever we devalue any of these three components, it is like sawing one leg of the stool shorter than the others. That would make the stool not very useful!

But we all have our preferences, don't we? Some people love events but they don't love routine. So how do these people behave in church life?

They are often flaky in their commitment to programs but eager to do all the fun stuff! Other people love programs. They need routine and regularity, and they can find themselves bothered with events, because catalytic events represent change, and these folks don't really like change! And then there is culture. Culture is probably the least understood aspect of church life (because it is the least visible), and yet it is by far the most important. While culture, contexts, and catalysts all play a vital role in kingdom churches, it is the culture that I believe allows for the most permanent transformation to occur. We'll look at contexts and catalysts in other chapters, but for now, let's go deeper into this issue of culture.

CULTURAL TRANSFORMATION

Remember our mission? We are all about transformation. We want to see God's glory cover the earth as the waters cover the sea! We want to see athiests turned into missionaries! We want to see children grow up to become mighty men and women of God. We want to see our cities transformed and our nation changed. We want to see the crime rate go down and the salvation rate go up! We want to go and make disciples in the nations of the earth, and we want to see the kingdoms of this world transformed and under the leadership of our King.

And culture has a huge role to play in all this. Transformation in kingdom churches occurs largely through culture. And for this cultural transformation to occur, we only need two ingredients. First, we need a *clearly defined set of values*. And second, we need *ways to consistently transmit these values*. Sounds simple, doesn't it?

DEFINING OUR VALUES

Obviously, individuals and churches have unique value systems. I cannot tell you what your values are, nor can you tell anyone else what their values are either. However, as we seek to define our values, we are not left to complete randomness! Depending on your upbringing, you may be able to derive a set of values largely from your parents. But regardless of your natural family, as followers of Christ we have some great tools to develop a value system.

First, we have *Scripture*. The Bible is not merely a book of stories and principles. It is also a catalogue of the values in the heart of God, sometimes clearly spelled out and sometimes inferred so that only the most humble and hungry can find them. But they are there. The Great

Commission (Matthew 28:18-20) and the Great Commandments (Mark 12:28-31) are examples of Scriptures that clearly communicate the values in God's heart. There are many such key texts in Scripture that overtly state God's value system, enabling us to understand and embrace His heart. Two more that come to mind are Isa. 66:1-2 and James 1:27 ~

"Heaven is My throne and earth is my footstool. Where then is the house you will build for Me? ...For My hand made all these things... But to this one I will look, to him who is humble and contrite of spirit, and who trembles at My word."

"Pure and undefiled religion in the sight of our God and Father is this: to visit orphans and widows in their distress, and to keep oneself unstained by the world."

Using just the four texts we've mentioned, we can begin to develop a list of core values that we want to put priority on. These could include (1) discipleship; (2) love; (3) humility; (4) the poor; and (5) purity.

Second, we also have *spiritual heritage*. Hebrews tells us that we are surrounded with a great cloud of witnesses. In Jude 1:3, we are told to "contend earnestly for the faith which has been handed down to the saints." We are part of a long lineage of great saints who have defined, carried, walked out, and shared the values of the Christian faith that we now embrace. Reading about our history is a valuable exercise for several reasons, one of which is to identify values we resonate with. I appreciate some of the values of my spiritual forefathers. For example, I value the priesthood of all believers largely because of Martin Luther.

Third, we have *tribal alignment*. This has to do with whom we are associated with and who is in our 'camp', so to speak. In the acknowledgements of this book I mention several streams within Christendom from which I have benefitted and with which I share affinity. I am currently part of two specific tribes whose core values I deeply identify with: Iris Global and Global Legacy. These two movements within Christendom are like a tuning fork for me. The vibrations I hear and experience in my spirit coming from these two movements strike a chord in my own heart. While neither movement is perfect, I strongly identify with the core values in both.

And finally, we have our *local church*. Whatever church you are part of has a value system, either stated or unstated. That value system is constantly being modeled and imparted. Let me give you an example. At Everyday Church, our highest value is love. We want to express this one heart of love in three directions: upward (toward God), inward (toward one another), and outward (toward our neighbors and the nations). For us, these three expressions of love are founded in the two Great Commandments and the New Commandment Jesus gave us. We are continually trying to model, encourage, and impart this central, core value of love in every relationship and in every gathering. When people come to our Sunday celebration or to one of our microchurches, or even when they meet us for a face-to-face appointment, for example, we make every effort to convey love. We warmly greet them with a smile and a hug. Of course, this isn't all it means to love someone--love is so much deeper than that. But being friendly and affectionate is a good start! When people feel celebrated, they feel loved. We do this because we believe love looks like something. It looks like acceptance, affirmation, and affection. All of us need affection, especially as we get older and as it seems like fewer people are willing to give it. Men, in particular, do not get enough physical affection from other men. If you would have joined us for one of our recent men's retreats, you would have seen a lot of playful hugging, wrestling, and prophetic acts that involved physicality. All of this is done intentionally. It is part of our value for loving one another.

TRANSMITTING VALUES

Hopefully by now we see that values can't simply be listed on a piece of paper, on a website, or in a newcomer's manual at our churches. They must be fleshed out in real life and then released into our churches. But how exactly do we transmit these values? Here are a few ways we can see our values multiplied and spread throughout kingdom churches.

Modeling. When something is important to us, we incorporate it into our lives. And then we become what we value. My friend calls this being 'values carriers.' When it comes to values, much more is caught than taught. So the most important way to transmit values is to model them. Some parents say to their children, "Don't do what I do, do what I say!" But this simply doesn't work. Children are impressionable, and like baby ducks, their little hearts and minds become imprinted by what is modeled by their parents. So it is with us. When we see a value walked out through another person that we love and respect, nothing is more powerful. We find ourselves learning volumes simply by watching those whom we admire. And there is a gravitational pull in the spirit that causes us to become what we behold.

Encouragement. Whatever we encourage gets reproduced. Encouragement is the fuel for reproduction. So when it comes to values, we can and must learn to notice and to praise. Direct encouragement towards those who are walking out values is a great strength, causing them to walk out and to and to *radiate* that value even more, and causing us to notice and appreciate that value we see. Where our treasure is, there our heart is also, and when we treasure a value in another through encouragement, our heart is now invested in that value, and we absorb it even better. When we encourage others, they walk out the value better and so do we.

Testimonies. Years ago, I remember John Arnott teaching that the root word for 'testimony' means to 'do it again.' At Everyday Church, we take time to celebrate 'good news' in our microchurches, and at our weekly celebrations we make room to hear testimonies of what God has been doing. The importance of testimonies is seen clearly at Bethel Church in Redding, California, where testimonies are featured again and again in a variety of ways. My friend Rick Taylor, National Director for the Healing Rooms, displays printed testimonies of healing on the walls of the healing rooms he oversees. Can you imagine walking into a room to receive prayer for healing, and the walls you look at are covered with testimonies of those who have been healed! This idea was modeled by Aimee Semple McPherson at Angelus Temple, where discarded crutches and wheelchairs were mounted on the wall. Whenever we share a testimony of what God has done in the past, we are also asking God to repeat the testimony in the future. God has placed power in the testimony. It defeats the enemy (Rev. 12:11) and becomes a declaration for what God wants to do. Testimonies are one of God's most effective tools to transmit values. When we celebrate the testimony, we encourage others to repeat and imitate that value.

Impartation. This is a tricky one, because some things can be imparted, and some things do not happen through impartation. It is difficult to 'impart' character! That must be fought for and developed through the course of life. However, I believe in the power of impartation. When we lay hands on, we can impart many things. Obviously, gifts can be imparted through the laying on of hands (2 Tim. 1:6). But in a way, values can also be imparted to a degree. For example, if someone wants to value prophecy more, and prophecy is released through the laying on of hands, then it stands to reason that the person receiving the gift will also receive hunger and stirring, which will eventually result in valuing prophecy even more (1 Tim. 4:14). In this way we can 'impart' values.

Prayer. Sometimes, we know what we *want* to value, but we simply aren't there. Perhaps we find that we lack compassion. This classic prayer becomes very relevant: "God, break my heart with the things that break Your heart." When we pray these kinds of prayers, God answers! And He begins a process whereby He shifts our values and priorities. Elisha cried out for a double portion of Elijah's spirit—a difficult request, for sure! And yet, because he asked, God heard and answered. I believe that our God is wanting us to come like little children, recognizing where we lack, and without fear or shame, asking Him to transform us. As we recognize values that we want to carry and express, we bring them to Him in prayer, and His answer begins a process that transforms us.

PRIORITIZING VALUES

After thinking about and working with values for a while, it becomes clear that there are a lot of things that we value! Working with multiple values can become an overwhelming, even confusing process. What do we do with all these values? How do we walk out all these values in a way that demonstrates what we *really* believe? After all, the Bible is filled with the values of God's heart. If we were to take every Biblical value and list it, we might end up with a pretty long list!

The key, of course, is to prioritize. Values must be ranked and prioritized in such a way that it becomes clear what is *really* important to us. When we rank our values, we end up with *priorities*. Priorities are those things that we will truly give ourselves to over time. They bubble up to the surface over and over, because our actions demonstrate that they are important to us. They are not only what we say we value, but these values are what we will give our time, energy, and money to first.

Ranking values is a premiere issue in our day—more than we realize! Most of the social issues that are at the center of hotly contested debates are really priority issues (i.e., the ranking of values). May I give you an extreme, vivid example? I'm going to venture into dangerous territory for just a minute with a very hot, emotional topic for a moment: abortion. In my opinion, the abortion debate inevitably comes down to the ranking of values. To illustrate this point, for just a moment try to ignore the people on the fringes and extremes of this debate, and focus on the large, caring, thoughtful group of people right in the middle of this debate—albeit people on different sides of the issue.

Every thoughtful, caring person I know who would call him/herself pro-life is *also pro-choice*. People who want to save babies also believe in a woman's right to choose those things that affect her own body. It's just that pro-life people believe that the value of a human life, even a so-called 'fetus', is more valuable than a woman's right to terminate a pregnancy and therefore exert control over her own body. And by the same token, every thoughtful, caring person I know who is pro-choice is *also pro-life*. People who want to protect a woman's right to make decisions that affect her body also generally love babies and want to protect them. But here's the real issue: we rank these two seemingly opposing values in different order. And the result is that millions of babies are won or lost, live or die, based on whose priorities win the day (and make the laws). That's the power of priorities.

Jesus gives us a very interesting example of priorities in the parables found in Luke 15. He speaks of a shepherd who clearly values all one hundred of the sheep in His fold--but His priority is on the single one that is lost. The woman values all ten of her gold coins, but her priority is on finding the lost coin. And finally, there is no doubt that the father values both sons, but His priority is to see His prodigal son come home. That's why he stood on the front porch so much. His value was for both his sons, but his priority was for the prodigal son.

This chapter is very instructive if we want to see the difference between values and priorities. There is no doubt that God loves all of humanity. And He really, really loves His kids! He places great, great value on His children. We are the apple of His eye. We are held in the palm of His hand. He loves us beyond description, even singing and dancing over us with great joy (Zeph. 3:17). And yet, it would appear from Luke 15 that perhaps His priority, before the closing of the end of the age, is on the lost members of 'the family'—those in society who don't really know God and who aren't walking in the joy of close relationship with Him.

This is why much of the church in the West is inward and not growing. We have confused the *value* God places on His family (i.e., His kids) with the *priority* He places on the lost members of the human race. If the church had truly understood, embraced, and walked out God's priorities as expressed in Luke 15, we would have evangelized the entire world by now! If we had understood God's priority on the poor, we would have fed and clothed the world by now. And if we would've understood the priority of the kingdom, we would have built churches differently. God places great value on His church, which is the Bride of Christ! But He places first priority on His kingdom (Matt. 6:33).

Values are important. Priorities are almost more important. Priorities define what we will live and die for and how we will spend our time. Articulating values without determining our key priorities leaves us with mere words. Identifying a handful of key priorities is essential for building kingdom churches. And that's what the next chapter is about.

Chapter Three
Kingdom PRIORITIES

"...But seek first the kingdom of God and His righteousness, and all these things will be given to you as well." --Matt. 6:33

I remember a particular leadership meeting I was in many years ago as though it were yesterday. A pastor of a rapidly growing church within our former denomination (and thus an 'expert' on why and how churches grow) was speaking to the leadership of our church on principles of church growth. At that time I was a young leader preparing for full-time, vocational ministry, and I had been studying church growth quite a bit. His talk was interesting and compelling, not unlike other talks I had heard on this subject. He was a nice man with a great personality and a sharp wit. But as I listened to him speak about assimilation plans, sanctuary layout, worship/congregation dynamics, people flow, being culturally relevant, breaking growth barriers, increasing our sensitivity to visitors, and so on, my mind began to drift back to memories of when I first became a Christian...

Shortly after becoming a Christian at 16 years old, my hunger for God's Word was matched by a voracious appetite for missionary biographies. I began reading about the lives of Jim Elliot, Hudson Taylor, David Brainerd, CT Studd, William Carey, and many, many others. I also read stories of intercessors like Rees Howells and John 'Praying' Hyde. These stories filled my heart with fire and deeply shaped my thinking. My burning desire became to take the gospel to the poor. As a teenager, I would run into my prayer closet, which was literally a walk-in clothes closet in my bedroom, and then I would run into the streets. I began by going to the poor in my hometown and openly sharing Christ with others. My long-term desire was to go and see for myself that the gospel would work anywhere, without all the 'props' of the Western world...

Back to the meeting. As I listened to this man speak, I could see that he wanted good things for the churches in our denomination. I wanted to listen with a humble heart and learn from him, because I knew that he was the expert and that I didn't know very much about anything! Still, though, as his talk continued, it became clear that he and I were not on the same page. In my gut, I felt that some of the core motivations of the church growth movement he was advocating were missing the point. I knew there was something more raw and more real that God was after, but I couldn't quite articulate what I was feeling. So during the Q & A time, I raised my hand and asked him a sincere question: "Why can't we do church on dirt floors like they do in Africa? Why do we really need all this stuff? I mean, if the people are truly hungry, and if God really shows up, and if people are getting radically saved and healed, what difference does it make?"

The intent of my question was not to devalue thoughtful planning or sensitivity to culture, but I wanted to get to the essence of what the church is. He smiled at me in a slightly condescending way, tilted his head a little, and replied, "You do it [church] your way and I'll do it my way, and let's see who impacts more people." I didn't ask any more questions that day! His answer, though, only strengthened my growing internal conviction that the motivation of much of the church in the West had drifted from what God originally intended for His people.

Many years later, I found myself in Mozambique, Africa, among a modern-day revival called Iris Global. Blind eyes were opening, the poor were being fed, the dead were being raised, the gospel was being preached with authority, the church was being equipped and sent out, and people were coming to Christ in droves every week. All of this occurred with not nearly enough money, people, planning, or resources. In fact, strategic planners from the West probably could find plenty of shortcomings in this movement. Even so, some of their most powerful ministry has happened through children who have courageously preached in the streets. At times, these little ones have been stoned with rocks while preaching to hostile crowds. Pastors have been martyred for the gospel. But love is winning, and nations are being transformed. Millions are coming to Christ as their Perfect Savior, and thousands of churches are being planted…all without Western props. This is a ministry that is living my teenage dream! My wife and I are no longer part of our previous denomination (which we still love and honor), but we are now privileged to be part of this incredible revival movement. To be among this people, to run with such revivalists, has become one of the greatest joys of our lives.

It never occurred to me to actually check the validity of the statement made by my church growth mentor all those years ago, but as I prepared to write this chapter, I decided to take a quick look at the data. With all of its excellent church growth training, our previous denomination has grown over a period of 35 years to 1,500 churches in 13 countries. The movement we're part of now—the one that has mostly dirt floors--has grown to 10,000 churches in 26 countries in 17 years. Over a million people have come to Christ. At times entire villages have given their lives to Jesus, including many previously unreached people groups. The impact of this lower-still, stop for the one, simple, raw, hungry, laid-down lover movement is explosive and continues to grow.

During my first visit to Mozambique, in a city called Dondo at a pastors' meeting, I remember kneeling with my face in the dirt, weeping uncontrollably, completely wrecked, humbled in the presence of such beautiful, hungry people and hungering after God with them. Later, after returning home from my time in Africa, I also remember one Sunday morning where we were having a celebration in the school gymnasium we rented. It was a powerful time, and at the end, I gave an altar call. Most of the people came up front, responding to the Spirit of God. The fear of the Lord was evident in that meeting, and we were on our faces on the gym floor. But this wasn't just any gym floor. A few months before, there had been a flood, and the wood floor had been removed, leaving only concrete and old glue. Because the new wood floor had not yet been installed, the school itself was neither using nor cleaning the gym, and a significant layer of dirt had accumulated on the floor. So here we were, on our knees and faces before God, on the dirt-laden concrete floor in the Central Coast of California, and it reminded me, ever so slightly, of some of my experiences in Africa. I sensed the pleasure of the Lord as He watched His people humbling themselves and hungering after Him, and I was grateful to see so many otherwise well-groomed, 'cool' California people going after God with abandon, even on a 'dirt' floor! Then I remembered the leadership meeting all those years ago, and I smiled.

All that to say this: God looks at things much differently than we do! There is a recurring rebuke in the Scriptures that is captured in Psalm 50:21, where the Lord says, "These things you have done and I kept silent; *you thought I was altogether like you*. But I will rebuke you..." Isaiah 55 tells us that the ways of God are higher than our ways and His thoughts are higher than ours, in every way. These verses (and others like them) indicate that we need to check our motivation and priorities, because God sees from a superior vantage point, and we are prone to look at things differently than God. Perhaps this concept is best illustrated when Samuel, God's prophet who was always 100% accurate in his prophecies (cf. 1 Sam. 3:19-20), went to the house of Jesse on assignment from God to anoint the next king of Israel. In the midst of examining each of the various brothers to see whom God has selected, Samuel eyed Eliab and thought in his heart that surely this was the guy! Evidently Eliab possessed impressive outward, physical qualities, perhaps even a certain 'air' of dignity, which compelled Samuel to hastily conclude that he was the Lord's choice. But God catches the motivation of Samuel's heart before he was about to utter his very first inaccurate prophecy, and in that moment speaks a powerful word to him and to us:

> *"Do not consider his appearance or his height, for I have rejected him. The LORD does not look at the things man looks at. Man looks at the outward appearance, but the LORD looks at the heart." --1 Sam. 16:7*

If the LORD does not look at the things we look at, then it would be a good idea to find out where He is looking, because we might be looking in the wrong place and at the wrong things! As we think about planting and building His kinds of churches, then we need to lay hold of those things that motivate and attract God, rather than those things that excite us or seem wise to our human understanding. This is a very important distinction. Our priorities will change as we build churches His way rather than our own. We need to look where He's looking. So where is God looking? What makes the difference between lukewarm, irrelevant churches and those missional communities that burn with continual, white-hot revival?

To build kingdom churches, we must embrace the priorities that attract God's eyes and attention. The following five priorities for building kingdom churches are very simple, somewhat controversial, and ultimately not optional.

ONE: WHOLEHEARTED LOVERS

> *"The eyes of the Lord look to and fro throughout the earth, that He might strongly support the one whose heart is completely His." --2 Chron. 16:9*

First and foremost, kingdom churches are filled with people who are preoccupied with the Lord Himself. Without this primary reality, we've stubbed our toe right out of the gate. To be *'completely His'* means that He is our magnificent obsession. The most profound change occurring in the Western church today is the increasing longing to know God, to seek His face and to find Him, to live in His Presence, to experience His love, and to be a people who are deeply in love. In the animated Disney movie *Beauty And The Beast*, Mrs. Potts observes the beast in a particularly moving scene and declares in a lovely English voice, "He's finally learned to love!" The church in the West is falling in love! The world is growing in amazement, the devil is growing in helpless frustration, uptight religious leaders are desperately trying to keep people from being too emotional, while the Lord Himself is experiencing great joy and satisfaction as His Western Bride is being delivered from performance orientation and is finally learning to love by experiencing HIs love and then by falling in love with Jesus! The first priority in kingdom churches is to find and experience God Himself as our great Love. We can and must experience intimacy, communion, and companionship in His Presence as we share His love for righteousness.

In many traditional churches, ministry and mission have been taught and portrayed as disciplined and unromantic; it is obedience to the Great Commission that matters. Prayer is hard work, feelings are irrelevant, and getting the job done is what counts. Many churches and leaders in the West are of the opinion that we don't need spiritual experiences to proclaim the Gospel. After all, they reason, we can't expect intimacy to be normal, nor can we rely on it. Because we live by faith, we can and must learn to function without His manifest Presence and all of the ensuing romance one might expect when the God of the universe draws very near to the human heart.

But people in kingdom churches know a better reality. Enough fire and hardship will convince even the toughest among us that without actually finding God, in fulfillment of Jeremiah 29:13, we cannot do anything of value. We cannot love others with supernatural, world-changing, white-hot, unstoppable love unless we actually experience the love of the Father for us first (Eph. 3:19). As the radiance and exact image of the invisible God, Jesus is a spiritual Lover, our perfect and ultimate companion. He has purchased people from every ethnic group in the world because He longs for loving relationship with us. Our highest value is to know Him in a passionate relationship with a love that is stronger than death (Song 8:6). To change the world, we major first of all not on ministry strategy, church growth, winsome methods, projects or fundraising, but on having the kind of life inside of us that the world needs and craves. This abundant, radical life that Jesus promised is only possible through a deeply personal, intimate, experiential, love relationship with God Himself.

To be clear, we are not talking about some kind of mindless mysticism that is rooted in nothing more than subjective experiences. We are not after experience without content and relationship. We pursue passion because this kind of relationship is offered to us and is rooted in the truth of Scripture. We relate to God with our hearts and our minds both. We engage with Him with our whole being, finding life and joy in meaningful interaction with Him. He's not a means to an end; He's it. And when we find Him, we find and gain everything we could ever want or need. The core motivation and first priority of the church aligns with the Father's original intention for humanity to focus on His Son with tremendous love and affection. He is the Desire of the nations.

And ministry will follow. All fruitfulness flows from intimacy with God. Ministry volunteers and all the rest only make sense in the context of love. I once heard someone say, *"People who are in love outperform people who are not in love two to one."* This is true! I remember as a young man in my twenties courting the young woman who is now my wife. Staying up late, getting up early, and doing extra favors, these were 'effortless' compared to just a few months earlier before I knew her. I was falling in love, and I was 'outperforming' my previous self!

At the end of 1 Corinthians 12, Paul said that the way of love is "a more excellent way." God handpicks people to build kingdom churches. His eyes are searching the earth for wholehearted lovers. He is looking for those who march to the beat of a different drummer, a more excellent way. They are unmoved and unmotivated by many of the things that motivated the church in the latter part of the 20th century, like church size, prestige in the community, being distinct, making a name for themselves, and so on. They are motivated by love.

"For the love of Christ motivates us." --2 Cor. 5:14

This statement by the Apostle Paul had everything to do with an all-out approach to winning lost people fueled by a heart of love. In 1 Cor. 9:22, Paul said it this way: "I have become all things to all men so that by all possible means I might save some." Paul was essentially saying, "Love burns inside me, and I will do pretty much anything to win lost people to my Friend and King, Jesus." For the apostle, form followed function. It wasn't about 'church growth.' It was about a burning passion of love to win people to Jesus! If we're going to see kingdom churches that are different from what we've been producing in the West, we must, in real practice, put God first, not merely as a theological priority, but as a heart-pounding reality. Only when our primary obsession is His Person can we begin to have the right perspective and motivation to carry out the things He desires for us to do.

When the Apostle Paul was knocked off his horse, he asked two questions that hold significance for us: "Who are you, Lord?" and "What do you want me to do?" (cf. Acts 22:8-10). When we ask these two God-ward questions, in their proper order, on a continual basis, as a people in love, then we can build kingdom churches well. Loving God in practice is a prerequisite to building kingdom churches.

Love purifies our motivation by removing false, lesser motives in us and by giving us the energy to lay down our lives just because of love. God so loved the world that He gave. The deeper the love, the more the sacrifice. A people in love are dangerous to the camp of the enemy, because they don't care anymore. They don't care about fame, they're not after titles, they don't really notice whether or not they have more people in their Sunday meeting than the church down the street. Such thoughts don't even register on the radar screen of their hearts. The enemy is deeply afraid of the Bride falling in love with her Bridegroom, because then she is fearless.

> "The LORD is my light and my salvation--whom shall I fear?
> The LORD is the stronghold of my life--of whom shall I be afraid?
> Though an army besiege me, my heart will not fear;
> though war break out against me, even then I will be confident." --Ps. 27:1, 3

Yes, there is a very, very dangerous generation arising! The forces of hell are trembling. This generation will build different kinds of churches, churches that are free from a political spirit, churches that truly rejoice to see others succeed, churches that are in love with their community and bored with small-mindedness and lesser motivations. Kingdom churches are filled with people in love, laid-down lovers living out of God's heart.

TWO: THE GOSPEL OF THE KINGDOM

Another priority for those involved in building kingdom churches is the kingdom of God. The natural byproduct of a people in love with God is that they love people! For centuries people have tried to bring the gospel by preaching alone, but Jesus said He wouldn't return to the earth until the gospel *of the kingdom* was preached (and incarnated) in every nation (Mt. 24:14). To understand the significance of this statement, we need a solid grasp of the definition and centrality of the kingdom of God as well as an understanding of its power.

Defining The Kingdom Of God

To put it simply, kingdom is *rule*. The Greek word is *basileia*, which refers to the realm or base of power by which a king rules. There are two aspects to kingdom. The first is the *right* to rule. In ancient and current societies with a government of monarchy, those kings or queens have a right to rule their realm, which includes all of the physical territory and the content of that territory, including people and possessions. In that sense, God's kingdom is the entire universe, and, as it concerns us, the earth. Psalm 115:3 declares, "Our God is in the heavens, He does whatever He pleases." That is the sovereignty of the King of the universe. Our God has the right to rule anywhere He wishes, because it all belongs to Him. In that sense, his kingdom is everywhere. However, there is a second, more immediate aspect to the kingdom. Kingdom refers not only to God's *right* to rule, but also to the *actual places where God rules*. In other words, wherever God is indeed ruling, there is the kingdom. Where is the will of the king being expressed? That is his kingdom.

For example, imagine a large, sprawling empire ruled by a monarchy. An evil old king used to rule this empire, but he has recently been deposed, and a new, beautiful, good King has come to power. This new king is loved by some of its citizens but hated by others who still have a weird, unnatural loyalty to the previous evil king. While some of the citizens do what the new, good King wishes and desires, there are still pockets of resistance where citizens rebel. In this illustration, we see the two aspects of the kingdom at work.

The King has the sovereign right to rule the entire empire. Thus, the entire empire is his kingdom. But in practical terms, only in those places and people where the will of the king is being expressed is his true kingdom being represented. Those true and loyal subjects of the kingdom, who express the will of the king, might be grieved by the pockets of rebellion and resistance they see around them. They might even want to cry out, "Stop this rebellion! Let the will of the king be done!" This is exactly the kind of prayer Jesus taught the subjects of his kingdom to pray:

"This is how you should pray: "'Our Father in heaven, hallowed be your name, your kingdom come, your will be done on earth as it is in heaven." --Matt. 6:9, 10

In this prayer, the subjects of the kingdom are taught to pray to the King for his rule (i.e., his kingdom) to come to earth. Later, in other passages, we're taught not only to *pray* for the kingdom but to *bring* it.

"...as it is in heaven." --Mt. 6:10

In heaven, both aspects of God's kingdom are perfectly expressed. We know, of course, God has the *right* to rule in heaven. Heaven is his throne (Isa. 66:1). Not only does he have the right to rule in heaven, but He actually does rule heaven. Every being in heaven comes under his rule and reign. There is perfect harmony in heaven, because heaven is populated with angels and saints--those who delight to do the will of their King.

Earth is a different story. On earth, we find some factors that dramatically affect the extent of God's kingdom expressed. First of all, on earth there is another kingdom, an opposing kingdom attempting to be extended by an evil impostor called the devil. And secondly, the people of earth, as in the previous illustration, are not all equally excited about being subject to the rule of the King. It started in the garden of Eden, where the deception of satan (and Adam and Eve's subsequent disobedience to God) allowed the devil to have access to a place of rule not intended for him. God had told Adam and Eve the way the rule of the kingdom worked:

"Then God said, 'Let us make man in our image, in our likeness, and let them rule over the fish of the sea and the birds of the air, over the livestock, over all the earth, and over all the creatures that move along the ground.' So God created man in his own image, in the image of God he created him; male and female he created them. God blessed them and said to them, 'Be fruitful and increase in number; fill the earth and subdue it. Rule over the fish of the sea and the birds of the air and over every living creature that moves on the ground.'" --Gen. 1:27-28

In effect, God said, "I'll rule over you as your King. And as my son and daughter, I've delegated authority to you to rule on earth over the rest of creation." Before the fall of Adam and Eve, satan and his demons existed, but they had no legal right to rule anything or anyone. They had been banished from heaven, where God's perfect rule would not allow them to stay, and satan had no way to expand his power base, his rule, his 'kingdom.' He had first tried to expand it in heaven:

"How you have fallen from heaven, O morning star, son of the dawn! You have been cast down to the earth, you who once laid low the nations! You said in your heart, 'I will ascend to heaven; I will raise my throne above the stars of God; I will sit enthroned on the mount of assembly, on the utmost heights of the sacred mountain. I will ascend above the tops of the clouds; I will make myself like the Most High.' But you are brought down to the grave, to the depths of the pit." --Isaiah 14:12-15

Since satan was banished from residency in heaven, he had no choice but to look for some way to rule on earth. Only one thing in God's creation on earth had been given freedom to choose or not choose God: people. This was his only chance. With cunning strategy, satan tricked Adam and Eve into temporarily looking to him as their king instead of God. The results were catastrophic.

Ever since, we find two kingdoms clashing on earth. The evidence of these clashing kingdoms is somewhat veiled in the Old Testament. We get a brief picture of the clash in the book of Job, where satan is allowed to bring affliction onto one of the subjects of God's kingdom. Only a few other places other than the first two chapters of Job is satan even mentioned by name (cf. 1 Chronicles 21:1 and Zechariah 3:1-2).

In the New Testament, however, we see a very visible kingdom clash happening as soon as Jesus Christ enters the scene. 62 of the 76 times 'satan' or 'devil' appears in the Bible occur as the Son of God begins His ministry on planet earth. In particular, the devil shows up first in the New Testament to tempt Jesus in the wilderness as He was fasting for forty days. This is nothing less than an assault of the enemy against the Kingdom rule of our God. And so it has gone on for thousands of years, this clash of kingdoms.

Because of Jesus' marvelous atoning sacrifice, the victory is already won, of course, and we know how it all ends. But until the second coming of Christ, we have the work of expanding His rule (kingdom) everywhere we go. We are pushing back darkness, the gates of hell cannot prevail, and we are lovingly advancing His kingdom.

The Centrality Of The Kingdom

This is no peripheral message. The kingdom of God is central to our purpose and mission as the people of God. The word "church" is referenced 79 times and only in the New Testament, while the word "kingdom" occurs in both Old and New Testaments nearly 300 times in Scripture. More important than frequency of occurrences, though, is the centrality of the kingdom. Let's look at a few examples of how central the kingdom is in New Testament Christianity:

Jesus modeled the centrality of the kingdom. The kingdom was Jesus' first and continual message (Mk. 1:15; Mat. 4:17). He went throughout Galilee preaching the good news of the kingdom and healing the sick (Mt. 4:23). In the beatitudes, he consoled people with the kingdom (Mt. 5:3-10). Jesus loved to talk about the kingdom, likening it to wise virgins, a wedding banquet, a vineyard, a king settling accounts, a net, a pearl of great price, a treasure in a field, a farmer sowing seed, a mustard seed, and yeast. At one point, Jesus said that He was compelled to preach about the kingdom, because that is why He was sent (Lk. 4:43). Jesus spoke to the crowds about the kingdom of God (Lk. 9:11), going from one town and village to another (Lk. 8:1). After His resurrection and before His ascension, Jesus' final message was to speak for 40 days about the kingdom of God (Acts 1:3).

The early church learned the centrality of the kingdom. Jesus taught his disciples to pray for the kingdom to come (Mt. 6:10). He sent them out with the message of the kingdom (Lk. 9:2). Jesus conferred on his disciples the kingdom (Lk. 22:29) and told them to sacrifice and go to the mission field for the sake of the kingdom of God (Lk. 18:29). Philip preached the good news of the kingdom of God and the name of Jesus Christ (Acts 8:12). Paul taught on the kingdom of God over a three-month period (Acts 19:8) and declared the kingdom of God from morning until evening to lost people (Acts 28:23). He boldly declared the kingdom (Acts 28:31), and Paul said that he and his fellow workers were working for the kingdom of God (Col. 4:11). Paul charged Timothy to fulfill his ministry in light of the kingdom (2 Tim. 4:1).

The church's primary ministry activity is the kingdom! God's kingdom resides within believers by the Holy Spirit (Lk. 17:20-21). The kingdom is not about food, but about righteousness, peace, and joy in the Holy Spirit (Rom. 14:17). We are called into His kingdom and glory (1 Th. 2:12). The Father is pleased to give us the kingdom (Lk. 12:32). The kingdom of God belongs to people with childlikeness (Mt. 18:3; Lk. 18:16). Our inheritance is an unshakeable kingdom of light (Col. 1:12; Heb. 12:28), and we have been made a kingdom of priests (Rev. 1:6; 5:10). We have been given the knowledge of the secrets of the kingdom (Lk. 8:10), and to not understand the message of the kingdom means that the enemy has been at work (Mt. 13:19). We've been given the keys of the kingdom to bind and loose (Mt. 16:19), and deliverance from demons is an evidence of the kingdom (Lk. 11:20). The essence of God's kingdom does not consist of words, but of power (1 Cor. 4:20). Before Christ returns, the gospel of the kingdom will be preached in every nation (Mt. 24:14). We are told to seek first the kingdom of God (Mt. 6:33).

The Power Of The Kingdom

Our King and His kingdom are powerful. To divorce the Gospel from power is to miss the Biblical marriage between the Word of God (which brings illumination) and the works of God (which bring illustration). The Word and works are forever linked in the Gospel of the kingdom. Paul said that the essence and nature of God's kingdom are not primarily words alone but power (1 Cor. 4:20). To try to plant churches or do any kind of ministry without the raw power of God is religious nonsense. In fact, one of the dangers of living in these last days will be people who seem to be godly but who deny the power of God (2 Tim. 3:5). We are warned to avoid such people!

The reality is that we are totally dependent on Him for everything! We need and expect miracles of all kinds to sustain us and to confirm the Gospel in our ministry. When facing great human need with our human frailties, we rapidly reach the limits of our resources, wisdom, and love. At times, we face overwhelming tragedy, poverty, sickness, demonic attacks, and every kind of evil. But with excitement and joy, we aim far beyond what we can imagine doing in our own strength. We run into the darkness looking for bad news because it is the power of God that gives the world hope.

It is Christianity with evidence. When we walk in God's power, we say to the world, "God is here, and God cares!" We don't ever apologize for seeking and valuing power, because without it love is incomplete and ineffectual. We are called to address extreme human need by example as we live free from anxiety, trusting fully in a God who is powerful and who will come through for us in miraculous ways. Our only confidence is Christ and Him crucified, buried, and risen. God doesn't think our faith is deficient because we seek His power. Rather, our God is thrilled to be trusted for miracles, because He is a miraculous God.

Of course, God releases miracles to us as long as He knows that they will not take us further from Him. Love and power belong together—a people in love who also walk in God's power. The marriage of love and power means we do not have to choose. We can look forward to doing even greater works than Jesus (Jn. 14:12), all the while remaining in His love (Jude 1:21).

Kingdom First, Church Second

To build churches with kingdom eyes means that *we build the church with peripheral vision.* Did you know God never asked us to focus on the church? Jesus has always maintained that *He* would build the church! (Mt. 16:18). He asked us to focus on His kingdom by seeking it first (Mt.

6:33). Church was always meant to be a *byproduct* of the kingdom of God. The church is the community of the kingdom, not the kingdom itself. As we give ourselves to the expansion of God's kingdom by loving people, from giving a glass of cold water in Jesus' name to a thirsty child from the neighborhood, to prophesying at the convenience store to a patron, to preaching a sermon, to mowing our neighbors' lawn, to praying for healing for our sick cousin, we are expanding God's kindness (and therefore His rule) wherever we go. Because God is so amazingly beautiful, people are attracted to Him. As a result, they want to hang out with you and others who embody this kingdom. This community of kingdom people is called the church, and pretty soon, the church flourishes, all because we put love and the kingdom first.

THREE: LOWER STILL

A third priority in kingdom churches is lower still. This phrase 'lower still' comes from my friend Heidi Baker. It speaks of the direction of our lives and ministries as well as how we approach the building process. We look for revival among the broken, the humble, and the lowly. When Jesus washed the disciples feet, Scripture says that because Jesus knew that He came from the Father and because He knew that He was going to the Father, He took off His outer garments and washed their feet (Jn. 13:3-4). Love makes us secure, and when we're secure, we are willing to go lower still. This is a huge priority among kingdom people.

As we build kingdom churches, we start at what society considers the bottom. We go to the physically and spiritually poor, the forgotten, the children, and the outcasts. Kingdom churches believe in the 'trickle up' theory of prosperity, which means we begin all ministry 'low and slow.' God's ways are the reverse of the worlds. We waste our time on the uninfluential and the few. We go to the neglected, the forgotten, and the lonely. We stop for just one person and care for just one, spending as much time as God asks with a single person. We will go anywhere, if possible, to minister to the meek and the desperate, the poor in spirit, those who truly understand their need for God. It is not a very grandiose strategy for growth and success, but it is what love looks like.

God chooses the weak and despised things of the world to shame the proud, demonstrating His own strength and wisdom. This frees us from trying to be something that we're not. We're not experts. We haven't learned how to do church and revival. We only know we must humble ourselves under the mighty hand of God (1 Pet. 5:6). We gravitate towards the low things of the world. We are compelled by love rather than worldly success. Competition and comparison don't fit in kingdom churches. We feel no pressure to succeed and excel. Instead, we rejoice in loving people and doing things well by the power of the Spirit.

Redefining Success

Embracing the priority of *lower still* in Western churches means that we will need to redefine success. Many of our churches in the West are deeply immersed in business practices that are self-serving and competitive. The profound lack of honor we see among our churches speaks volumes about where we're at as a culture. Jesus said that the greatest among us would become servant of all. Just think if we applied this Scripture at a church level. Can you imagine churches out-serving one another? Churches not so quick to promote their own name, logo, and branding? Churches that shared resources? Pastors who moved from the fear of sheep stealing to the fear of possessing God's sheep!

Years ago, Steve Sjogren, founder of Vineyard Community Church in Cincinnati, Ohio, coined a phrase called 'Servant Evangelism.' He initiated a weekly 'ServeFest' on Saturday mornings at the church, where people did small things with great love. For example, they would give away free sodas on hot days or feed people's parking meters downtown or scrub toilets at fast-food restaurants. They would leave a church business card explaining that they wanted to show God's love in a practical way. Since that time, many churches have started servant evangelism projects as part of their outreach ministry. But what really caught my attention when I heard Steve speak was this: After doing this a while, Steve and his team decided to start putting *another church's name and contact info* on these cards rather than their own. In other words, they gathered, served, and loved, and it never directly benefitted their own church. They served and benefitted other churches in their city! What an incredible understanding of the kingdom Steve demonstrated. The way up is down. We gain our lives by losing them. He who would be greatest must become servant of all. One of Steve's slogans was 'kindness with no strings attached.' This is what it means to be a kingdom church. To be free from hidden motives is not irresponsible; it is Christlike.

The Problem With Success

I believe in success, and I would always prefer to succeed than fail! God's promise to Joshua and to us is to prosper us and to give us good success in everything (see Josh. 1:1-9). Success is not a problem, but our understanding of success can be problematic.

I mentioned in the previous chapter how God asked me to 'shrink the church.' Evidently, Jesus was also guilty of shrinking the size of His followers at one point. In John 6, after quite an interesting discourse about eating His flesh and drinking His blood, pretty much the entire 'pre-Christian' crowd left. Sadly, some of our definitions of success would have forced us to categorize Jesus as a failure.

Obeying God is sometimes costly. When God spoke to me to shrink our church, it was a difficult word to hear. It ran against everything I had been taught. It would make me look bad, perhaps even causing me to appear as a failure or a flake to those who were aware of my efforts to plant a church. And it was going to cost something financially as well. We were out of money both personally and as a church. I really couldn't 'afford' to obey God! Because God won and my ego lost, there were some very positive outcomes for our family. I found a greater freedom from failure and the need to please people, which made me less driven and much easier to live with! And, we had our first real experience of supernatural provision. That winter, when we ran out of money, we began to seek God in prayer in the secret place. Without asking anybody or putting out a newsletter, we began to receive miraculous provision. We received financial help in the mail—sometimes from people who didn't know us personally and who had to phone a friend of a friend just to get our address! God spoke to people to send us resources. As a family, we had the awesome privilege of watching God supernaturally provide for us. Of course, this wasn't simply a lesson about provision, although we did learn about that! It was a lesson about obedience.

Success Is Obedience

Success in kingdom churches is defined by one word: obedience.

> "To obey is better than sacrifice, and to heed is better than the fat of rams."
> --1 Sam. 15:22

Obedience sometimes works in your favor, and sometimes it just plain costs you. This can be seen in the two very different outcomes in Hebrews 11, aka 'the hall of faith.' We just don't know which part of Hebrews 11 we might find ourselves in—the successful first half, or the sobering second half. All were heroes of the faith who obeyed God, but not all had success in the eyes of man. But obedience is how God defines success in kingdom churches. Over the years I have interacted with hundreds of pastors. It is amazing how many conversations have been redirected around to the topic of church size, number of small groups, etc. It often demonstrates the lack of kingdom thinking in many leaders. Success defined as obedience does not excuse poor quality, laziness, inwardness, nor does it legitimize unwise practices in the name of God's leading. We have worked very hard to be smart in how we've administrated our responsibilities before God and man. We have sought to win the lost, to build infrastructure, and to do things that demonstrate wisdom and produce fruitfulness. But what I am saying is that obedience transcends all these other things, and if we're not careful, we can easily apply wrong standards in a superficial way that devalue the kingdom and inadvertently promote a value of self-preservation in churches.

It seems to me that some pastors really just need to go start businesses! Often pastors have an entrepreneurial bent and a desire to create something that they can be proud of. This is a good thing! They have a strong desire for success, but like blood from a turnip, they are trying to squeeze feelings of success from the church. Everyone can feel this underlying tone, and the people feel that they are being subtly used to help the leaders feel successful. We've gotten so used to it in church culture that we can hardly imagine what it might feel like to have an absence of opportunism in the leadership of the church.

And, of course, it's not simply the leaders. Many people join churches and join ministries in order to gain feelings of success and legitimacy. But the church is not the right place to feed insecurities and the need for outward success. It is a place to come, lay down your life, and die among a house of friends all doing the same thing!

A passage of Scripture that has particular meaning for me is Jn. 12:24-25:

"I tell you the truth, unless a kernel of wheat falls to the ground and dies, it remains only a single seed. But if it dies, it produces many seeds. The man who loves his life will lose it, while the man who hates his life in this world will keep it for eternal life."

This is the Scripture God spoke to me when He called us to move across the country to start another church. At that time, we were pastoring a newer, growing, vibrant church in a beautiful area of California. Life was good. Our church family was close, and the vibe of the church was very positive. The Holy Spirit was moving in power, people were receiving Christ, and the relationships among the people were filled with love and laughter. People in our denomination were beginning to take notice of what was happening in our church, and I was well-positioned for a successful career in ministry! In the middle of it all, God spoke to our hearts and invited us to lay it all down, to give it all away, to move to relative obscurity in a declining, economically challenged city in the Midwest. His call was this: "Come and die!" A wise leader I spoke with put it like this: "God wants to kill you so He can use you."

One ingredient for church growth success is longevity in a single church. I strongly agree with those who advocate staying in one location for a number of years--if that's what you're called to. However, Jesus and Paul would not be part of the "longevity club", because they had other kinds of mandates from God:

> "At daybreak Jesus went out to a solitary place. The people were looking for him and when they came to where he was, they tried to keep him from leaving them. But he said, 'I must preach the good news of the kingdom of God to the other towns also, because that is why I was sent.'" -- Lk. 4:42-43

Paul was a church planting apostle who did his work during a series of three missionary journeys. He often wasn't around long enough at a given church to even appoint elders. Fact is, we're not building a career. Kingdom churches are built by kingdom people who don't own anything in ministry. This is a hard truth. A.W. Tozer, in his book, The Pursuit Of God, calls this "The Blessedness Of Possessing Nothing." This is the call of God to every kingdom church and kingdom leader: an open hand and a loose grip.

FOUR: THE REDEMPTIVE VALUE OF SUFFERING

All of this really points to a fourth priority in kingdom churches. The Christian life involves a significant amount of suffering, and we must understand its value in our lives. Learning to love requires a willingness to suffer for the sake of righteousness. Discipline and testing make saints out of us and produce in us a holiness, without which we will not see His face nor share in His glory. Like Paul, we rejoice in our weaknesses, for when we are weak, then we are strong (2 Cor. 12:9). Under great pressure we learn to rely on God, who raises the dead (2 Cor. 1:9).

Jesus was honored and rewarded for enduring evil opposition without sin. Our reward in heaven will be for the same thing—doing the will of God when it costs us everything. We are called to resist sin, even to the point of shedding blood, if necessary, by considering the example of Jesus (Heb. 12:3). Jesus has been glorified, not because He exerted His Divine power over His enemies, but because He overcame them with His love. His kind of love entails suffering, the willingness to turn the other cheek, to go the second mile, to deny ourselves, to pick up our cross, and to follow Him. Jesus showed us that the only way to be counted worthy involved suffering (Rev. 5:12). There is no shortcut to our heavenly inheritance.

> "Now if we are children, then we are heirs—heirs of God and co-heirs with Christ, if indeed we share in His sufferings in order that we may also share in His glory." --Rom. 8:17

All this talk of suffering may make you cringe. You might even strongly disagree with me. After all, the pop Christian culture of our day is all about you, your success, your destiny, your greatness, your dreams, etc, etc, etc, blah, blah, blah. But check out Rom. 8:17. The promise of inheritance and glory is directly linked to suffering. Don't allow yourself to be deceived and sold a bill of goods born from the Western success-driven culture.

There is a deceptively alluring teaching today that causes us to focus on our destiny more than on the Lamb who was slain and to believe the lie that somehow, because Jesus paid it all, we don't have to suffer. Beloved, we never have to suffer in order to pay for our sin. Jesus really did pay it all! The suffering I'm speaking of does not add anything at all to the finished work of Christ on the cross. But, it is nonetheless part of the Christian life, and God has designed it that way. It is the price of growth, and love, and obedience. Even Jesus learned obedience by the things He suffered (Heb. 5:8). This Scripture is an amazingly perfect antidote to the out-of-balance 'sonship' teaching going on in some circles today. The full text of Hebrews 5:8 actually says, "Although He was a Son, He learned obedience by the things He suffered." Jesus modeled a version of sonship that included suffering as a necessary component for His own development. Which version of sonship do you walk in?

People in kingdom churches see and appreciate the value of suffering as part of the Christian life. If our message preaches well in wealthy Western countries but falls apart in poorer countries, then it is not the message of Scripture. The common people heard Jesus gladly. A little child, even a poor, hungry child, can understand the simple message of the gospel. People in every country in the world suffer and understand suffering. Why, then, do we think we can build churches that somehow sidestep this central element to a mature Christian's life? We are not talking about masochism; we never want to invite suffering for its own sake. But when it comes, may we learn to suffer well and to grow and benefit through it, for the glory of God.

FIVE: EXTRAVAGANT JOY

Although there are many more priorities and values in God's kingdom, I want to finish this chapter with a fifth and final priority that must never be optional for us as we build kingdom churches: extreme joy! The joy of the Lord far outweighs our suffering. In Jesus, it becomes our motivation, our reward, and a powerful spiritual weapon. In His Presence is fullness of joy (Ps. 16:11). Like Paul, our testimony must be that in all our troubles, our joy knows no bounds (2 Cor. 7:4). The joy of the Lord is our strength and energy (Neh. 8:10), without which we die!

The supernatural joy of the Lord has somehow become a very controversial value. Why can it be fine for a follower of Christ to weep before the Lord but not laugh before Him? What kind of mood do we think God is in, anyway? Is He primarily mad, sad, or glad? Because the fruit of the Spirit is joy, I am convinced that our God is filled with continual joy. This is the tenor of His heart. Yes, our God experiences emotions, and at times He is sad and sorrowful over our sin and pain. At other times, He is angry over wickedness, stubbornness and idolatry. But when we think of God at rest, how do we perceive Him? What emanates from His glorious Person? When you stand before Him, do you expect to see a poker face staring back at you, devoid of emotion? Many believers picture God like the statue of Abraham Lincoln in the Lincoln Memorial in Washington, D.C. Somber, staring straight ahead, gripping the arms of his throne, trying to make sense of this crazy planet called earth, trying to keep a lid on his anger. We may need to read again Zephaniah 3:17 in order to see God's posture toward us:

> "The LORD your God is in your midst, a victorious warrior.
> He will exult over you with joy, He will quiet you with His love,
> He will rejoice over you with shouts of joy!"

In reality, we do experience conviction, brokenness, weeping, and sorrow. But it is also true that we turn the valley of Baca (ie, weeping) into a joyful spring of living water (Ps. 84:6). We go from strength to strength because the joy of the Lord is our strength! We pass through the valley of the shadow of death, but we are not left there, because God's kingdom is righteousness, peace, and joy (Rom. 14:17). As we think and live like kingdom people who build kingdom churches, then we will manifest the essence of the kingdom. In His joy, which makes us strong, we are supernaturally capable of true compassion for others, unfettered by our own sorrows.

No revivalist could endure long-term without a river of life, love, and joy coursing through their veins and flowing out of their innermost beings. The joy of God protects us from becoming cynical and downcast about the world and the church. Instead, our eyes are on our perfect Savior, who thrills us as we trust Him to finish what He began in us. Many of those in the church in the West are stuck in angst and anger toward each other, ourselves, and God. But we gain nothing by being negative. We overcome the world through faith, as we cast our cares on Him. Joy, laughter, and a light heart are not disrespectful toward God or irrelevant to the world. Rather, they are evidence of the life of heaven.

When we speak of joy, we are not simply referring to cheap and foolish levity that leaves us empty, but exultation in the truth and reality of our salvation. This kind of joy is a powerful work of the Spirit and an evidence of the kingdom of God among us. Some teach that joy isn't an experience. Nothing could be further from the truth. That's like saying peace isn't actually felt. What is peace if it doesn't affect us at a mental, emotional level? We sometimes hear that happiness is a silly, transitory emotion whereas joy is a deep reality based on truth. But Psalm 68:3 in the NIV seems to say something different: "May the righteous be glad and rejoice before God; may they be happy *and* joyful." The Hebrew word for *happy* is שׂושׂ (sus or sis) which means *to rejoice, exult, and be glad*. The Hebrew word for *joyful* is שִׂמְחָה (simchah from the root samach) which means *exceeding delight, pleasure, with a merry, pleased heart as in a festival*. I guess we could try to remove happiness, light-heartedness, and laughter from the meaning of joy, but I think we'd have a hard time justifying that Biblically.

People who build kingdom churches and who walk in radical joy are like the captives of Israel who were brought back to Zion. This text is a picture of how we are meant to be all the time, not just in special moments of life:

"Our mouths are filled with laughter, our tongues with songs of joy. Then it was said among the nations, 'The Lord has done great things for them.' The Lord has done great things for us, and we are filled with joy... Those who sow in tears will reap with songs of joy. He who goes out weeping, carrying seed to sow, will return with songs of joy, carrying sheaves with him." --Ps. 126:2-6

People who build kingdom churches are wholehearted lovers living in God's Presence who advance God's kingdom in power, loving the last, least and lost and going lower still, suffering and laying our lives down, all the while walking in divine strength as the joy of the Lord courses through our veins. Other chapters in this book delve more into practical strategy. But strategy only works if we are on our faces, steeped in the core values and priorities in God's heart. Let's invite Him to align our hearts with His priorities:

> *Father, I welcome Your loving inspection of my heart to reveal lesser motives and to infuse me with Your priorities. Free me from wrong definitions of success! Fill me with Your heart! Make me a wholehearted lover, a kingdom person of power who moves lower still, unafraid of suffering, and filled with radical joy. In Jesus' name, Amen.*

Chapter Four
Kingdom INTENSITY

"...the kingdom of heaven has endured violent assault, and violent men seize it by force [as a precious prize]—a share in the heavenly kingdom is sought for with most ardent zeal and intense exertion." --Mt. 11:12, Amplified

The curriculum for Bethel's School of Supernatural Ministry defines a revivalist as follows: *"a believer who is **focused** and **passionate, willing to pay any price to live** in **purity** and **power** because they are **loved by God** and **love Him,** whose manifest presence transforms lives and cultures."* There may well be nothing more exciting to the Lord and more frightening to the devil than motivated believers. In Matthew 11:12, Jesus tells us who exactly will carry out this kingdom revolution. It will be those with 'ardent zeal' and 'intense exertion.' Are you one of those focused, passionate believers? If so, you can change the world! Motivation is more than half the battle.

Pete Grieg, one of today's leaders in the global prayer movement, has written beautifully and poetically about kingdom motivation that is always and forever centered in the Person of Jesus. If you haven't read 'The Vision' before, or if it's been a while, you owe it to yourself to read it. Here it is with minimal editing:

"The vision is JESUS – obsessively, dangerously, undeniably Jesus. The vision is an army... FREE from materialism. They laugh at 9-5 little prisons. They could eat caviar on Monday and crusts on Tuesday--they wouldn't even notice. They are mobile like the wind; they belong to the nations. They need no passport. People write their addresses in pencil and wonder at their strange existence. They are free yet... slaves of the hurting and dirty and dying.

What is the vision? The vision is holiness that hurts the eyes. It makes children laugh and adults angry. It gave up the game of minimum integrity long ago to reach for the stars. It scorns the good and strains for the best. It is dangerously pure. Light flickers from every secret motive, every private conversation. It loves people away from their suicide leaps, their Satan games.

This is an army that will lay down its life for the cause. A million times a day its soldiers choose to lose that they might one day win the great 'Well done' of faithful sons and daughters.

Such heroes are as radical on Monday morning as Sunday night. They don't need fame from names. Instead they grin quietly upwards and hear the crowds chanting again and again: "COME ON!" And this is the sound of the underground, the whisper of history in the making, foundations shaking, revolutionaries dreaming once again. Mystery is scheming in whispers, conspiracy is breathing... this is the sound of the underground. And the army is discipl(in)ed. Young people who beat their bodies into submission. Every soldier would take a bullet for his comrade-at-arms. The tattoo on their back boasts "for me to live is Christ and to die is gain." Sacrifice fuels the fire of victory in their upward eyes. Winners. Martyrs. Who can stop them? Can hormones hold them back? Can failure succeed? Can fear scare them or death kill them?

And the generation prays like a dying man with groans beyond talking, with warrior cries, sulphuric tears and with great barrow loads of laughter! Waiting. Watching 24–7–365. Whatever it takes they will give--breaking the rules, shaking mediocrity from its cozy little hide. Laying down their rights and their precious little wrongs, laughing at labels, fasting essentials. Advertisers cannot mold them. Hollywood cannot hold them. Peer-pressure is powerless to shake their resolve at late night parties before the cockerel cries. They are incredibly cool, dangerously attractive inside. On the outside? They hardly care. They wear clothes like costumes to communicate and celebrate but never to hide. Would they surrender their image or their popularity? They would lay down their very lives - swap seats with the man on death row - guilty as hell. A throne for an electric chair. With blood and sweat and many tears, with sleepless nights and fruitless days, they pray as if it all depends on God and live as if it all depends on them.

Their DNA chooses JESUS. (He breathes out, they breathe in.) Their subconscious sings. They had a blood transfusion with Jesus. Their words make demons scream in shopping centers. Don't you hear them coming? Herald the weirdos! Summon the losers and the freaks. Here come the frightened and forgotten with fire in their eyes. They walk tall and trees applaud, skyscrapers bow, mountains are dwarfed by these children of another dimension. Their prayers summon the hounds of heaven and invoke the ancient dream of Eden.

And this vision will be. It will come to pass; it will come easily; it will come soon. How do I know? Because this is the longing of creation itself, the groaning of the Spirit, the very dream of God. My tomorrow is His today. My distant hope is His 3D. And my feeble, whispered, faithless prayer invokes a thunderous, resounding, bone-shaking great 'Amen!' from countless angels, from heroes of the faith, from Christ himself. And he is the original dreamer, the ultimate winner. Guaranteed." --www.24-7prayer.com

That's a good vision! It describes focused, motivated people who are madly in love with Jesus and absolutely free from self-interest and self-focus. And fixing our eyes on Jesus is where it all starts. Jesus is calling a Bride to Himself. He wants His church back! He wants us unmoved by anything or anyone but His very Person.

THE POWER OF INTENSITY

When we are motivated by Jesus and clear about what we're going after, we are free to walk in radical kingdom intensity. Kingdom churches are made up of people who possess an inward quality of divine intensity. This intensity is not related to personality. It has to do with ardent desire birthed from a heart of love. The fruit of intimacy with God is intensity. From God's perspective, intensity is not optional. It is necessary for the kind of people and churches He desires to build.

FIRE

Fire is a Biblical metaphor for kingdom intensity. Since the Pentecostal movement that originated in the early 1900s, there has been a sustained emphasis in much of the church on the doctrine and practice of the baptism of the Holy Spirit. However, we've missed part of the promise. In Luke 3:16, John the Baptist states the full promise: "I baptize you with water. But one more powerful than I will come...He will baptize you with the Holy Spirit *and with fire.*"

This baptism of fire has been largely relegated in our thinking to the idea of suffering and refinement. And it's true that the metaphor of fire in the Scriptures has to do with these things. But the context of John's statement was with reference to power and internal burning. 'Someone more powerful than me is coming,' John said, 'and the result is that people will experience immersion in fire.' Intensity is related to an inward burning released from the God of fire Himself, an inward fire of God dwelling in the human heart. The inward fire that God provides is so powerful that it terrifies sinners and calls to saints as a holy invitation to a spirit of continual burning:

"Sinners in Zion are terrified; trembling has seized the godless. 'Who among us can live with the consuming fire?

50

Who among us can live with continual burning?'" --Isa. 33:14

Hebrews 12 confirms that 'the consuming fire' in Isaiah is God Himself! (Heb. 12:29) There is an invitation to dwell continually with this God of fire. The result will be a continual burning in our own hearts and lives.

The God Of Fire. There are about 450 references to fire in the Scripture, and many of those descriptions have to do with God's nature. When Hebrews 12:29 says that our God is a consuming fire, this is not simply a description of His judgments or refinements, but it is a description of His essence. In nearly every major encounter in the Scriptures where someone saw the Lord, God purposely chose to reveal Himself in a way that involved fire. Moses' first exposure to God was the angel of the Lord that appeared to Moses in the midst of the burning bush (Ex. 3:2). The Israelites saw God's glory, and it looked to them like a consuming fire (Ex. 24:17). In Gideon's encounter with the Lord, fire sprang up from the rock and consumed Gideon's sacrifice (Judges 6:21). At the dedication of the temple, after Solomon had prayed, fire came down from heaven and consumed the sacrifices, and God's glory filled the place (2 Chr. 7:1). When Elijah confronted the false prophets of Baal, he boldly declared, "the God who answers by fire, He is God." (1 Kings 18:24). Later, the fire of the Lord fell and consumed the burnt offering and everything around it (v. 38). When Isaiah saw the Lord, the temple was filled with smoke and the altar of fire was the source of the coal that touched his lips and unlocked his heart (Isa. 6:6). In Ezekiel's introductory vision of the Lord and His dwelling place, fire and brilliant flashes of light were constant. Ezekiel tried to describe the Lord in two categories of "waist up and waist down", but in the end, they were both descriptions of fire!

> "Then I noticed form the appearance of His loins and upward
> something like glowing metal that looked like fire all around within it,
> and from the appearance of His loins and downward I saw something like fire;
> and there was a radiance around Him." --Ez. 1:27

It continues like this throughout Scripture. Daniel's three friends walked with a fourth Man in the midst of fire (Dan. 3:25). The early church received tongues of fire (Acts 2:3). Paul says Jesus will return in "blazing fire with his powerful angels" (2 Th. 1:7). Even in Revelation, John tells us that the Son of Man had eyes like flames of fire and a face that was burning with brilliant light (Rev. 1:14-16). One of the primary manifestations of the God of Heaven is through the reality of burning fire.

It is a universal human reaction to enjoy and embrace the kindnesses and mercies of God. But the common human reaction to this God of fire is illustrated when Moses recounted to the Israelites their own reaction to the fiery God:

> "The LORD spoke to you face to face at the mountain in the midst of the fire, while I was standing between the LORD and you at the time...for *you were afraid because of the fire* and did not go up the mountain." --Deut. 5:4-5

Several years ago, shortly after the renewal began to be poured out in Toronto, Canada, my wife had a two-part vision. In the first part, myriads of people were stretched along the California coastline, lined up on the beach facing the ocean, arms open, smiles on their faces, waiting for a tidal wave to come. It was a wave of refreshing and joy, and all the people were eager to receive it. And then, in part two of the vision, she saw another, larger wave coming. Behind it were intense, fiery lights of amber, blue and other colors that began to shoot up from behind the wave. These lights of fire represented the awesome power and glory of God. In the first wave of refreshing, everyone lined up to receive, but in this second wave, the same people were greatly afraid, and people began to actually run from it. Many wanted the wave of refreshing, but fewer wanted the fire. Our God is a consuming fire, and He will baptize us with the Holy Spirit and with fire. Do we want that second wave?

Fire Is The Issue

Fire has always been a dividing line. For example, when we think about what is wrong with the church and why more people aren't fulfilling their ministry, we are often quick to blame leaders. But it is not primarily the fault of leadership that the priesthood of all believers has been inactive. It is the fear of drawing close to the God of fire that resides in each of our own hearts. We shrink back, just like the Israelites, and we feel much safer allowing a representative to draw close to God while we keep a safe distance from Him.

The story in Exodus 19 dramatically illustrates this point. In Exodus 19, we find God joyously communicating a message to His people through Moses the prophet. The message is about His own love and desire for His people. He explains that the way each person can experience this God of fiery desire is to walk in the role of individual priest before the Lord (Ex. 19:6). The people hear this invitation of love, and their hearts say "yes!" They tell the Lord that they agree to this kind of loving, individual relationship with Him as priests (Ex. 19:8).

After this, the Lord exhorts the people to consecrate themselves and not to act presumptuously by ascending the mountain of the Lord in a careless way. His invitation to relationship is not diminished by His strong call to consecration. In the midst of His instructions, God says, "When you hear the long blast of the ram's horn, then come up the mountain" (19:13). By inviting His people up the mountain with Moses, the Lord literally welcomes each Israelite into the same kind of closeness that previously only Moses had enjoyed with God. Moses himself is confused. He objects to the Lord, saying, "The people cannot come up to Mount Sinai, for You warned us!" (19:23). But God just ignores Moses and tells him to remind the people not to be presumptuous. These restrictions are not meant to keep God's people from relationship, but rather He is testing them in issues of consecration (20:20).

Then one of the most tragic events in the history of Israel occurs. God's people "refuse Him who is speaking." They had clearly heard God's heart of love through Moses and His invitation into direct relationship. They said "yes!" to times of refreshing. But when they encounter the God of fire, He is so overwhelmingly powerful that they opt out of closeness. God expresses Himself with great passion and desire through fire, smoke, divine shaking and the loud sound of a heavenly trumpet. This was their cue to come close and to ascend the mountain of the Lord, each of them! It is an amazing moment in history. Their first reaction is to tremble--an appropriate reaction indeed! But their inappropriate level of fear (v. 20) causes them to misinterpret God's actions. As a result, they subtly reject God and miss out on the direct relationship He had just invited them into and they had just agreed to!

> "All the people perceived the thunder and the lightning flashes and the sound of the trumpet and the mountain smoking; and when the people saw it, they trembled and *stood at a distance*. Then they said to Moses, 'Speak to us yourself and we will listen; but let not God speak to us, or we will die.'"
> --Ex. 20:18-19

The people choose a mediated relationship rather than individual closeness with the living God. After the people's decision to not walk as priests, the Lord no longer invited them up the mountain into closeness. He accepted their decision.

The God Of Fiery Desire

There is something about fire that pleases the Lord. The entire system of sacrificial offerings was based on fire (Lev. 23:25). This issue of fire is more than a metaphor. Fire can represent many things in the Scriptures--purity, refinement, judgment, testing, light, and so on. But central in the metaphor of fire is the expression of fiery desire. I believe fire is precious to God because it speaks of the strength of His desire for us and of the appropriate kind of intense response in our hearts towards Him. Fire means burning, and the love of God burns in His own heart toward us! He desires a people of fire who burn with the same fire that is in His heart.

Though we now live under the New Covenant, this fiery God remains intensely focused on intimate relationship with His people. Jesus gives us a glimpse of the burning in His own heart when He says to His disciples, "I have earnestly and intensely desired to eat this Passover with you" (Luke 22:14, AMP). What an amazingly strong statement over a meal! But this meal, at the culmination of His time of ministry here on earth, represented an intimate, uninterrupted time of relationship with His friends. The same Greek word used here is translated in other places as 'longing', 'yearning', and 'lust.' And the words in the Greek, epithumia and epithumio, are used back to back to indicate the strength of desire in the heart of the Lord Jesus. The KJV has trouble giving proper and culturally acceptable English words to this expression by Jesus, so it gets tongue-tied and says, "With desire I have desired..." We have similar trouble today fully grasping the intensity in the heart of God for us. He is longing with intense desire to be close to us, to have relationship with us, and as His image is formed in us and we become more and more Christlike, we will, without exception, grow in fiery intensity, just like Him.

ZEAL

The appropriate response to a God of fire is zeal. Zeal is a gift from God that creates the kind of intensity needed to become a kingdom people who extend God's kingdom and build kingdom churches. They cannot be built apart from holy zeal.

"The zeal of the LORD will accomplish this." --2 Ki. 19:31

Because zeal comes from God, it is not dependent on a type 'A' personality. It is not hype, nor is it manufactured. This zeal is the inward burning of the Holy Spirit released in the human heart that provides supernatural motivation and intensity. Because zeal is a command, you do not need a certain personality type to walk with Jesus and feel fire on the inside. You may have a personality that is as cool as a cucumber, very phlegmatic in your approach to life. But as you lay back in your emotional Easy-boy recliner, and the Holy Spirit begins to speak to You, it feels like fire on the inside! And you find yourself saying, "Wow. This is the God of fire. He is dealing with me, and I will respond with zeal for Him!" When the disciples spoke with Jesus on the road to Emmaus, they immediately testified of an encounter with fire: "Did not our hearts burn within us?" (Lk. 24:32)

> "Never be lacking in zeal, but keep your spiritual fervor, serving the Lord."
> --Rom. 12:11

Zechariah prophesied that God's purposes are accomplished not by the might or power of man, but rather by the Spirit of God. Jesus called us to an easy burden and a light yoke. This is key. The more we come in contact with the God of fire and fiery desire, the more that divine zeal is released in us. As we experience the love of God, we find that it burns in us and changes everything.

John the Baptist was a "burning and shining light" who carried an internal zeal unlike any other in his generation. But John's zeal was to be the 'norm' among the people of the kingdom! (Mt. 11:11).

Zeal is much more than a personality trait. It is the heart of God growing in us, providing internal fire and motivation beyond our human resources. The Greek word for zeal comes from the root word 'zeo' which means 'to be hot, to boil, to glow, to be fervent.' Jesus expressed this kind of zeal when he turned over the tables of the money changers. Zeal (i.e., ardent desire and jealousy) for the place where the Father dwelt was a complete preoccupation for Jesus (John 2:17). He so loved His Father that His internal fire was commensurate with His love. This is to be the nature of the church, motivated by ardent desire for the Father's dwelling place on earth. To be motivated for lesser things, like growing a church, will easily burn people out. But being motivated by love has a uniquely sustaining dynamic.

Free From Burnout

When we walk with the beautiful Son of God, we walk in the midst of fire, and yet, like the burning bush, we are not consumed. Like Shadrach, Meshach, and Abednego, we find ourselves in the midst of fire with the Son of Man, unbound, unharmed and we don't even smell like smoke (Dan. 3:25- 27).

Many people are afraid to live in the place of zeal, lest they burn out. But this is a misconception. Jeremiah tried to go this route of calming himself down and being reasonable. He tried to deny the internal zeal of God that was his normal motivation.

> "...if I say, 'I will not mention him or speak any more in his name,'
> his word is in my heart like a fire, a fire shut up in my bones.
> I am weary of holding it in; indeed, I cannot.'" --Jer. 20:9

God-authored zeal has divine energy attached to it. People in love don't burn out. Oh, they may tire, and yes, they may need to take some time off to rest. But crash and burn? No. They don't. They can't. The internal fire of love is too strong. You may think this is an idealistic notion, or perhaps, as someone who has burned out before, you may even feel insulted. But we mustn't reduce our theology to make up for where our experience is lacking.

> "Love is as strong as death...it burns like blazing fire, like a mighty flame. Many waters cannot quench love; rivers cannot wash it away." --Song of Songs 8:6-7

The power of love is clear and compelling. It is stronger than death. It burns like a blazing fire, like a mighty flame. Many waters cannot quench it, and rivers cannot wash it away. Can you burn out with such love? No. You cannot. Love never fails. Burnout is not caused by hard work, although working too much can contribute to the conditions that lead to burnout. Burnout is caused by doing things without the internal fuel to do them, doing the wrong things over a period of time without the internal sustaining life and motivation of the love of God, performing for people's approval rather than laboring in love. A people in love don't burn out, because there is a built-in safeguard. People in love with God obey God, and they will not give themselves to activities that are not in God's heart for them to do. When they do, they are close enough to God that He can easily communicate to them, and they will hear a voice behind them, saying, "This is the way; walk in it." Continual rest is available to those who "cease from their own works" (Heb. 4:10). This rest is easily available to a people in love. When you are in love, you have nothing to prove and nothing to fear, so you are not motivated by false things (which leads to burnout).

In John 4, Jesus took the disciples by surprise when he explained to them that he had food they were not aware of. The disciples had gone off to another town, while Jesus remained to converse with the Samaritan woman at the well. Even though his stomach may have been growling before they left, by the time they returned, he had received supernatural sustenance from heaven, so much so that he just told the guys, "Hey, I'm really not hungry, because I was fed by My Father as I was doing His will." In the same way, the love of God 'feeds us' even as we are engaged in the enterprise of His kingdom.

Wake Up

It is not only the job of the enemy to get us to sin, but it is also (and perhaps primarily) the work of the enemy to make us *numb*. If he can succeed in getting the church to not feel and to not care, to be devoid of internal zeal and fiery desire, he has been as successful as if we all entered into deep, dark sin. Why? Because numb people who do not feel anything will fall asleep, and falling asleep spiritually has many dangers associated with it. When Eutychus fell asleep during Paul's talk, he broke his neck and died! How the enemy would like the church to do the same thing. When we're asleep, he has freedom to work:

> "Jesus told them another parable: 'The kingdom of heaven is like a man who sowed good seed in his field. But while everyone was sleeping, his enemy came and sowed weeds among the wheat, and went away.'" --Mt. 13:24-25

> "Be self-controlled and alert. Your enemy the devil prowls around like a roaring lion looking for someone to devour."--1 Pet. 5:8

Spiritual sleep (and sometimes even physical sleep at the wrong times) is a temptation that we are repeatedly warned about. In the garden, when Jesus was praying concerning His appointment with the Cross, He asked His men to stay alert and to pray. Even though they were in a place of great sorrow, and it would normally be understandable to sympathize with them for falling asleep because of their exhaustion, Jesus actually rebukes them and tells them to get up and pray!

"When he rose from prayer and went back to the disciples, he found them asleep, exhausted from sorrow. 'Why are you sleeping?' he asked them. 'Get up and pray so that you will not fall into temptation.'" --Lk. 22:45-46

How often we coddle and comfort our flesh, foolishly thinking that God is pleased with our desire to pamper ourselves. I am no ascetic, and I believe in taking good care of ourselves, in recreating, and in enjoying life. But there is a subtle place where our desire in the West to enjoy life can easily put us to sleep spiritually. When we wonder at times why we've missed some of God's dealings and why our hearts sometimes lack internal fire, perhaps we've been sleeping through very important times and have not known it!

> "No soldier in active service entangles himself in the affairs of everyday life, so that he may please the one who enlisted him as a soldier." --2 Tim. 2:4

Jesus said, "Behold, I come as a thief! Blessed is he who stays awake..." (Rev. 16:15) Jesus strongly warns us stay awake and alert and to not allow ourselves to be sleeping:

> "No one knows about that day or hour, not even the angels in heaven, nor the Son, but only the Father. Be on guard! Be alert! You do not know when that time will come. It's like a man going away: He leaves his house and puts his servants in charge, each with his assigned task, and tells the one at the door to keep watch. Therefore keep watch because you do not know when the owner of the house will come back--whether in the evening, or at midnight, or when the rooster crows, or at dawn. If he comes suddenly, do not let him find you sleeping. What I say to you, I say to everyone: 'Watch!'" --Mk. 13:32-37

'Staying awake' is no small issue in the Scriptures. Paul says plainly in 1 Thess. 5:6, "So then, let us not be like others, who are asleep, but let us be alert and self-controlled." David stirred himself and even spoke to his own soul, "Awake, my soul! Awake, harp and lyre! I will awaken the dawn" (Ps. 27:8). God's people are continually exhorted to wake up and to pay attention!

> "Awake, awake! Rise up, O Jerusalem..." --Isa. 51:17 (cf. 52:1)
> "Wake up, O sleeper, rise from the dead, and Christ will shine on you." --Eph. 5:14

Somebody Needs To Protest

The church in the West must challenge a slumbering spirit in our midst. Like Lazarus, Jesus is saying to us, "Come forth!" Our zeal is precious to God. It is a command to walk continually in holy zeal. Anything less must begin to be met with holy protest.

> "Oh, that You would rend the heavens and that You would come down, that the mountains might quake and flow down at Your presence--as when fire kindles the brushwood and the fire causes the water to boil...that the nations may tremble at Your presence! When You did terrible things which we did not expect, You came down; the mountains quaked at Your presence. For from old no one has heard nor perceived by the ear, nor has the eye seen a God besides You, Who works and shows Himself active on behalf of him who [earnestly] waits for You...And no one calls on Your name & awakens & bestirs himself to take & keep hold of You."--Isa. 64:1-7, AMP

In Isaiah 64, the prophet saw the condition of God's people and the triumph of the adversaries of God, and he cried out for God to tear open the heavens and to release His zealous fire. The cry in Isaiah's heart is commensurate with the fire in God's own heart. He prayed with zeal because He knew a God of zeal. He was dismayed at the people of God for not stirring themselves in a proper way. He knew there was MORE! So he cried out for it with authority. He prayed according to God's will, offering a cry of desire mingled with protest at the lack of fire in God's people.

BREAKTHROUGH

Intensity is more than a good concept meant to accommodate the overly zealous people of the church. Intensity is required. For advancement in the Christian life, and for complete victory over the enemy, the church must walk in kingdom intensity. The church in the West is anemic and yet often unwilling to walk in the level of intensity required for complete victory. Because it is an intangible quality, kingdom intensity is often considered an accessory and not essential. But how essential it is!

I have been in numerous prayer meetings and gatherings where the subject of breakthrough is prayed for and preached. What percentage of believers desire breakthrough in at least one area of their lives? The answer is 100%! Everybody desires breakthrough in one or several areas of intimacy with God, personal growth, relational love, financial blessing, ministry effectiveness, etc. Could it be that intensity, sustained by holy zeal, is a key missing ingredient for breakthrough in the West? Let's look at a few examples of why intensity is needed for breakthrough:

Intensity For Intimacy

Many Christians are aware of the comfort and promise found in Jeremiah 29:11, that God has plans for us to give us a future and a hope. But the verses that follow explain what God hopes will happen when His children understand their future and their hope:

> "Then you will call upon me and come and pray to me, and I will listen to you.
> You will seek me and find me when you seek me with all your heart."
> --Jer. 29:12-13

The promise of finding the God of the universe in this and many other Scriptures is directly linked with wholehearted intensity in seeking and searching for God. Intensity in pursuing the Person of God releases intimacy in the Presence of God. We can literally have as much of the Person of God as we want. The desire in us becomes intensity in our pursuit of Him, which He responds to.

Intensity In God's Word

Some believers wonder why their lives never get past superficial places of obedience. It is a mystery to many how they can have God speak to them so clearly, or how they can see something in the Scriptures that applies to them directly, or how they can make a commitment to close friends in an accountability group, and yet in spite of all these sincere intentions, turn right around and walk directly into sin and disobedience to God.

But at least one of the secrets of obedience has to do with intensity in obeying God's Word. In the first chapter of his epistle, the apostle James compares two types of believers. The primary difference between the two is their intensity:

> "Do not merely listen to the word, and so deceive yourselves. Do what it says. Anyone who listens to the word but does not do what it says is like a man who looks at his face in a mirror and, after looking at himself, goes away and immediately forgets what he looks like. But the man who looks intently into the perfect law that gives freedom, and continues to do this, not forgetting what he has heard, but doing it--he will be blessed in what he does." --Jms. 1:22-25

This word translated "looks intently"--parakupto--is an intentional stopping, leaning in, stooping down, and looking with longing into something. It differentiates the obedient from the casual Christian.

Intensity In Prayer

James 5:16 says that the "earnest prayer of a righteous person has great power and wonderful results" (AMP). The Greek word translated "earnest" is where we get our word "energy." It has to do with effort and intensity! What makes prayer powerful and effective is not necessarily the volume or the length of our prayer. However, you would be hard-pressed to utter prayers of earnest intensity without any energy put into them. This is not the energy of human effort, but it is the working of God in a human heart:

> "To this end I labor, struggling with all his energy,
> which so powerfully works in me." --Col. 1:29

Intensity In Personal Progress

In both of the letters Paul addressed to his spiritual son, Timothy, we see evidences of Timothy struggling with timidity and even intimidation. Perhaps part of his struggle was rooted in Timothy's personality, or perhaps Timothy was a sensitive soul who received some level of wounding from authority figures in his youth. What we do know for sure is that Paul was continually exhorting young Timothy to be bold, confident, strong, unafraid, and intense! Paul linked intensity in Timothy with his progress when he told him:

> *"Take pains with these things; be absorbed in them,*
> *so that your progress will be evident to all." --1 Tim. 4:15*

Intensity For Victory

One of the most stunning passages of Scripture having to do with intensity is found in 2 Kings 13, where the prophet Elisha is about to pronounce a prophetic blessing on Jehoash, the king of Israel. After telling the king that arrows represented the Lord's victory, he told the king to strike the arrows to the ground as a prophetic symbol of Israel's future victory over Aram, their enemy. This was a defining moment, and the king was in the right place at the right time. But he lacked one thing: intensity! He struck the arrows to the ground three times, and even though Elisha didn't specify how many times the king was supposed to strike the ground, it was evident to Elisha (and to the Lord) that the king lacked a certain degree of intensity required for complete victory.

The amount of times the arrows were to be struck to the ground could only be discerned through an intuitive sense and display of intensity. But the king lacked it. As a result, only partial victory was promised.

I am a strong believer in the grace of God. But as believers, we often allow a shallow ethic to creep into our dealings with God. Ever so careful to be people of grace and not a people of works, we sometimes underestimate the need for intensity. While intensity doesn't earn any merit with God, it does unlock partnership with God. Everything has been provided for us through the Cross! We have inherited every spiritual blessing in the heavenly places in Christ, and we have everything we need that pertains to life and godliness! But for complete victory, God requires human effort, born of His Spirit, that is fitting and appropriate to His nature and to the task at hand.

Kingdom intensity is not about a furrowed brow or a serious, no-fun disposition! The joy of the Lord is our strength, and Jesus went with focus and intensity to the Cross because of the joy that was set before Him. Intensity is a wholehearted, leaning forward, adventuresome approach that unlocks fullness. It is about faith-filled focus that accomplishes much! It is living large, but it is more than living large. It is thinking and behaving as though Jesus is worthy of our entire lives and every breath we breathe. More and more, kingdom intensity will characterize the church of the future.

A NEW NORMAL

What is your normal? One of my friends likes to say, "Normal is a setting on the dryer." He means that normal is a relative term. What we normally consider normal on earth may not be normal at all in heaven! We can't look to our contemporaries to define normal for us, because they may not always have a clear grasp on Biblical norms. How true this is when it comes to issues of zeal and fire. We who are part of the church in the West have learned to live with so little, to desire so little, to feel so little, and to have so little internal fire. But it's not normal! There is so much more!

> "Eye has not seen, ear has not heard, nor has it entered into the heart of man how much God has prepared for those who love Him." --1 Cor. 2:9

While speaking to the church in Laodicea in Revelation 3, Jesus explained that for Him, normal is that we would be either completely on fire, in love, holy in our behavior and wholly His in our hearts, or that we would be icy in our affections, distant, self-centered and immoral. It was never normal for Jesus to have a majority of His church be simply moral! Being tepid in our Christianity is quite distasteful to the God of fire.

God is redefining normal--not that it ever changed for Him! He is adjusting the default setting in the heart of the Western church from laissez-faire to fire, from 'balanced' in a wrong way to burning in a right way. Passion for God expressed through wholehearted, extravagant devotion and obedience will become the normal Christian experience of the church in the West.

Revivalists

What we are describing is continuous revival. Kingdom churches are made up of people who are becoming literal walking revival. They are truly ambassadors, sent ones, representatives, of the God of fiery passion on the earth. They can be mocked, ridiculed, even killed, but they cannot be stopped.

When the gospel of the kingdom began to affect Thessalonica, some jealous, threatened, wicked people in the city created a mob scene and cried out in an attempt to stop revival:

> "These men who have turned the world upside down have come here also, and Jason has received them into his house and privately protected them! And they are all ignoring and acting contrary to the decrees of Caesar, [actually] asserting that there is another king, one Jesus!" --Acts 17:6, AMP

This is the normal affect believers who are walking in revival have on a city. Demons are angry, evil people are threatened, religious leaders are jealous, right alongside of people who are being saved, healed, and delivered. In short, nothing can stay the same!

Notice that the proclamation of these revivalists has nothing to do with planting a church or gathering people. It is a kingdom revolution centered around another king, "one Jesus!" This is what is so upsetting to the world and the enemy! The early church never allowed the smoke of programs or church structure to distract them from focusing on exalting the King and on building the kingdom. They were relentlessly "kingdom" in their orientation.

In kingdom churches, revival is our default setting, and the church is made up of revivalists. Therefore, instead of building program-based design (PBD) churches, we build revival-based design (RBD) churches. Revival-based design churches expect things to change. They expect miracles to happen. They expect people to come to Christ. They count on the spontaneous expansion of the church, and they position themselves accordingly. Stronger nets. Simple, flexible wineskins. Rapid reproduction of disciples. The church unleashed to baptize on the spot. A way for spontaneous Bible studies to spring up as needed and in the neighborhoods where people are getting saved. A type of church that is free from bureaucracy and red tape so it can rapidly respond to and agree with all God is doing.

In the West, we have often planned our programs and church structures without any real notion that God could save over 3,000 in a day as He did in Acts 2. Because there is a lack of expectation and a lack of urgency, we have often counted on taking 20-30 years to "raise up" and release an elder. In many of our churches, we sadly create a system of mistrust, where a new person, regardless of their maturity in Christ, is required to sit around for six months while we look them over and figure out if we trust them enough to work in children's ministry or to hand out bulletins.

In the early church, leaders were reproduced much more quickly. Jesus turned young business leaders into powerful apostles in less than four years. Throughout the Scriptures, God seems to entrust individuals with ministry responsibilities far more quickly than we do in the church of the West. Jeremiah the prophet was released somewhere in his teenage years. He wasn't a "junior" prophet, but a Prophet to nations! Josiah was one of the most radical kings in the history of Israel. He became king when he was eight years old! God foresaw this and approved it, prophesying about Josiah by name, so at 16, when Josiah read the law and saw his name mentioned, he became "walking revival" from that point forward. He removed the high places, which no other king had done.

Intensity Is Accessible

What about you? Can you live with kingdom intensity as a student, a mom, a contractor? Yes! Kingdom intensity is available to the person with a seemingly "normal" life.

While you may feel that your external circumstances are unimpressive, God looks upon the heart. Your 'normal' exterior vocation doesn't need to define your 'revivalist' interior life! He sees your extravagant devotion and the strong desire for Him that's inside of you while you sell jewelry or make dinners or attend classes or show up faithfully at your job. Kingdom intensity is for everyone!

> "Whatever your hand finds to do, do it with all your might…heartily,
> as for the Lord rather than for men."--Eccl. 9:10; Col. 3:23

Intensity Is Sustainable

This is *sustainable* intensity, burning by the Spirit of God in the human spirit, regardless of circumstances, geography or any other factor that may have limited our thinking in the past. I have seen great people go to great ministry and missions schools, only to come home, become disillusioned, and actually fall away from the Lord. But this is not how intensity is mean to be—in fits and starts.

It is possible, of course, in our zeal to run to have missteps and to stumble. I am encouraged both by examples in Scripture (like King David) and Scriptural encouragements (like Isaiah 40) that God works with those of us who stumble! I have stumbled more than a few times—haven't you? And yet, here are the kinds of promises we find:

> "The steps of a man are established by the LORD, and He delights in His way. When he falls, he will not be hurled headlong, because the LORD is the One who holds his hand. Though youths grow weary & tired, and vigorous young men stumble badly, yet, those who wait on the Lord will renew their strength! They will mount up with wings like eagles, they will run & not grow weary, they will walk & not faint." ~ Ps. 37:23-24, Isa. 40:30-31

What a relief! There is room for us in our weaknesses even as we learn to walk in sustained intensity. The secret, of course, is learning to be sustained by the love of God. People rooted in God's love can live with kingdom intensity in an ongoing way. It works. One of my favorite verses in the Bible is 1 Chronicles 16:10--

> "Let the hearts of those who seek the Lord be glad."

This verse has meant so much to me as I am growing into an intense lover of God and an ardent pursuer of His kingdom. There is joy in the seeking and joy in the finding. It is not simply those who attain a new level in God or those who have radical, memorable experiences (although we want these things!) who have joy. Great joy is available on the journey! As we pursue Him, we find joy along the way. This is a strong comfort and encouragement to all of us. It guards us from elitism and hyperspirituality. We are glad in the seeking!

Like children, we find pleasure in the "hide and seek" reality of God. We are not put off by our pursuit of Him. We are not intense in a sad way. Rather than being miserable, we are joyful in our childlike pursuit of God! We find Him compelling, and we pursue Him and His kingdom with childlike wonder and abandonment.

Comparison is a trap, and appearances can be deceiving! Who was more intense in the Scriptures: Peter, who loudly proclaimed he wouldn't deny the Lord (and then did anyway), or Anna, who spent her time in secret, praying and fasting night and day in the temple (cf Lk. 2:36)? Who is more intense, the preacher shouting powerful prose, or the dad, weeping quietly over his sleeping children, asking God to cover and protect them? Kingdom intensity is sustainable, because it works in real life, with real people, who are focused on Jesus in simple devotion to Him.

Running To Win

In order to build kingdom churches with Biblical intensity, our pace of thinking and activity as a corporate people will need to change. Revivalists are people who run! Their pace is more vigorous than what we're used to in the West, and in order to build kingdom churches together, our default pace will need to change!

There are several ways to relate to God in terms of our activity. The Bible speaks of certain postures we can and should have before God, either expressed in our physical conduct or metaphorically in our spiritual walk with Him.

Lying Down. In Psalm 23:2, David describes one desirable posture before God: "He makes me lie d o w n in green pastures." Laying or lying down speaks of a posture of dependency, rest, refueling, death to self, and surrender to God as living sacrifices. It is good for individuals and churches to lie down before the Lord. Over the past decade or so, many churches have discovered the posture of lying down for the sake of renewal, refreshing, and rest in the Father's love.

Bowing Down/Kneeling. David also models a posture of bowing down and kneeling in Psalm 95:6 when he says, "Come let us bow down in worship; let us kneel before the LORD our Maker." This posture represents a heart of humility and reverent worship before Almighty God. The saints of old understood the importance of kneeling and bowing low, and God is helping the church in the West embrace a widespread kneeling and bowing low before Him. This is good!

Sitting. The first two chapters of Ephesians, which describe our position in Christ, tell us that Jesus is seated at the right hand of the Father (1:20), and that we are seated with Him in the heavenly realms (2:6). Sitting has to do with sonship and strength of position. It is a position of honor and privilege given to us by the Father. In the place of sitting, we can enjoy relationship with God as His heirs. We are sitting at His table, feasting on His provision for us, and we are sitting in heaven, enjoying His perspective. How the church needs to sit with God!

Standing. Standing is our posture of strength, endurance, and victory. Standing speaks of stability. It is our unwillingness to be moved by circumstances, difficulties, and even demonic attack. Ephesians 6 tells us to take our stand against the devil's schemes, so that when difficult times come, we may be able to stand our ground, and after we have done everything, we find ourselves still standing. We are commanded to stand firm while wearing the full armor of God.

Walking. Galatians 5 tells every believer to walk in the Spirit. We are told to avoid walking in the pathway of wicked people (Ps. 1), but instead to walk with like-minded people (Amos 3:3). Walking is a metaphor for flow and continuity of life. It speaks of our maturity and the consistency of our lifestyle as expressed in our actions. We walk in the light and love of God while following in the footsteps of Jesus Christ (1 Jn. 1:7; 2 Jn. 1:6; 1 Jn.2:6).

Running. If we take the time to lie down with the Lord, to bow low and kneel before Him, to stand up and fight, to walk with God and our brothers and sisters, then it is only appropriate that we would finally get to RUN! It is time for the church in the West to run. In fact, it is the promise of God that as we engage in these other postures, we will run...and not grow weary! (cf. Isa. 40:29-31) Running has to do with acceleration, multiplication, and miracles. It is the kind of life that cannot be fully explained. It is a holy urgency and a joyful aggressiveness that removes self-consciousness and faulty inhibitions. When Mary found out that Jesus had risen from the grave, she ran to tell the disciples, and when Peter and John heard, they ran back to the tomb! Running is part of the Christian experience, and it is a vital expression of kingdom intensity. Churches in the West are going to learn how to run together!

At one point, our local church started a Running Club. Because we live near the beach, a group of us met several afternoons each week to run together. The running club was for exercise, but more importantly, it was a metaphor for what God was doing with us spiritually. We were learning how to run together. What we found is that everyone runs at a different pace. Some are not in the right condition to run, so they walk all or part of the way. But no one is criticized for where they're at. Instead, we all encourage each other. We prayed and then started together at the same time. Those who finished first would wait for the rest and cheer them on as the crossed the finish line.

In kingdom churches, it is not good enough if the pastor and staff get to fulfill their destiny while everyone else watches and applauds. It is time for *every* believer in every church in the West to reach their full potential and to fulfill their destiny in Christ. We are living in a divine season of acceleration, and we are learning how to run together. There is joy in running, but there is more joy in running together. Kingdom churches are designed so everyone can run. For that to happen, we must learn how to become a kingdom of priests. That is the subject of our next chapter.

Chapter Five
Kingdom PRIESTS

"He has made us to be a kingdom, priests to His God and Father" --Rev. 1:6

There is a dream in the hearts of many people in the Western church. It is a dream of communities of faith where the playing field has been leveled and where everyone gets to play. It is the yearning to dwell in a company of believers where mutual honor and respect is the norm, where everyone truly rejoices to see others reach their full potential in Christ, where everyone's voice counts and is heard, where 'one another' ministry outweighs and outshines ministry by leaders, and where there is a refreshing absence of jealousy, politics, hierarchical dominance, and control. The Biblical and historical phrase for this is *the priesthood of all believers.*

Many have carried on an internal debate, not quite sure how in the world this beautiful dynamic could ever happen in the kinds of churches we've been part of, while knowing unequivocally that it absolutely *must* happen. There is a hope against hope that we could all become part of something so refreshingly Biblical as a true, New Testament, modern-day priesthood of believers.

But the truly stunning reality is that *it is happening.* As I watch the move of God in our day, I am thrilled beyond description by the conviction that out of all the generations that have gone before us, we are a generation that is going to live out the revelation of this priesthood! This generation will have the privilege of walking in something that many previous generations have longed for but have never really experienced. We are becoming what we were made to be all along: kingdom priests.

THE PROMISE OF PRIESTHOOD

The hope that every believer could walk with and serve God on equal footing with every other believer and have no mediator but Christ didn't originate with our generation. Even Martin Luther, great reformationist that he was, didn't invent this reality, though it was part of his historic posting and protest of 95 theses nailed to the door of the Castle Church in Wittenberg on October 31, 1517.

The promise of a functional priesthood of every believer goes farther back. It is mentioned several times in the New Testament, but it originated thousands of years before the time of Christ, way back in the book of Exodus. Think about that for a minute. God has been waiting for a long, long time—over 3,000 years--to see all of His people on earth live like priests at the same time! We are entering into an historic, *kairos* era of history.

Old Testament Priests

In one of the more tender passages in the Old Testament, God speaks of this longing in His own heart:

> "Then Moses went up to God, and the LORD called to him from the mountain and said, 'This is what you are to say to the house of Jacob and what you are to tell the people of Israel: "You yourselves have seen what I did to Egypt, and how I carried you on eagles' wings and brought you to myself. Now if you obey me fully and keep my covenant, then out of all the nations you will be my treasured possession. Although the whole earth is mine, you will be for me *a kingdom of priests* and a holy nation." These are the words you are to speak to the Israelites.'"" --Ex. 19:3-6

We only know God as He reveals Himself, and this exchange is one of those places in Scripture where there is an intimate revelation into God's heart and thought process. The great I AM initiates a conversation where He reveals vulnerability in His own heart by vocalizing what He deeply desires. He describes the strength of love He has for His people by narrating His version of their recent history coming out of Egypt. God discloses that it wasn't simply the great and powerful Almighty God dramatically delivering a people out of a pagan nation so that someday these stories would be recounted in church classes all across the world. Instead, He remembers it as a time when He personally carried His people "on eagles' wings"--not to a desert, nor even to a promised land, but to Himself.

While the subject of this chapter on priesthood is not primarily the profound love of God, we could pitch our tents here for quite some time and worship before a God like this. He is worthy of our praise. O blessed be His name! His love endures forever. We are His treasured possession! *Thank You, most beautiful God, for loving us the way that You do.*

After speaking tenderly to His people, the LORD then offers a profound invitation in vv. 5-6. 'Even though the whole earth is mine,' He says, 'and I have everything under my control and Lordship, I will gladly disperse priestly hearts and roles among all my people so every single one of you can partner with me in ministry' (my paraphrase). God is saying, in effect, that the Aaronic priesthood system He is about to set up is really only a very limited picture of what His heart desires for all His people. While a few would be designated to serve in an official, paid, full-time capacity in the tabernacle, God's real desire is that *all* of His people would love and serve Him as priests, regardless of their vocational role in society.

> "you will be for me a kingdom of priests..."

Within this Old Covenant context, specific priestly activities belonged to the priests and Levites. Priests were male descendants of Aaron, who was a Levite (see Num. 3:10), and Levites were other male members of the tribe of Levi. The primary duties of the priesthood took place in the tabernacle and later in the temple. Priests looked after the vessels used during special ceremonies and performed the offerings and sacrifices. The Levites assisted the priests and served the congregation in the temple. They sang the psalms, carried out administrative functions, such as keeping the temple courts clean and helping to prepare certain sacrifices and offerings, and they also had a teaching function.

What was meant to occur in every believer's home occurred in a larger and more ceremonial way in the temple, and what occurred in the temple was a spiritual picture of the kinds of activities God had reserved for all of His people, a kingdom of priests.

New Testament Priests

The priesthood was always about the kingdom, even under the Old Covenant. Priesthood has never been about the church. *This is a very important distinction.* God's intention is that these priests would be authorized through His *kingdom* rather than through a papal system of human government. God Himself initiated and credentialized priests of the kingdom, and collectively, a kingdom of priests.

When we come to the New Testament, we see that under the New Covenant, our interactions with the temple and thus the ceremonial law of the Old Covenant ceased from operation and relevance. Nevertheless, God persists in sharing His dream with His people again under the New

Covenant, first through Peter and then through John. These Scriptures are worth taking a moment to read and even meditate upon:

> "As you come to him, the living Stone--rejected by men but chosen by God and precious to him--you also, like living stones, are being built into a spiritual house **to be a holy priesthood**, offering spiritual sacrifices acceptable to God through Jesus Christ. For...you are a chosen people, **a royal priesthood**, a holy nation, a people belonging to God, that you may declare the praises of him who called you out of darkness into his wonderful light. Once you were not a people, but now you are the people of God; once you had not received mercy; now you *have* received mercy." --1 Pet. 2:4-10

> "[Jesus] loves us & has freed us from our sins by his blood; He has made us to be **a kingdom and priests** to serve his God & Father..." --Rev. 1:5-6

> "Then I saw a Lamb, looking as if it had been slain, standing in the center of the throne, encircled by the four living creatures and the elders...And they sang a new song: "You are worthy to take the scroll and to open its seals, because you were slain, and with your blood you purchased men for God from every tribe and language and people and nation. **You have made them to be a kingdom and priests** to serve our God, and they will reign on the earth." --Rev. 5:6-10

> "Blessed and holy are those who have part in the first resurrection. The second death has no power over them, but **they will be priests of God and of Christ and will reign with him** for a thousand years." --Rev. 20:6

Peter says twice in a few verses that collectively we are a priesthood, both holy (uniquely set apart) and royal (privileged with access and authority). Our very identity as the people of God is synonymous with our role as a priesthood. The Apostle John elaborates by describing the priesthood as part of what Christ purchased for us on the cross. Notice that in the passages in Revelation, we have already been made into priests and we will also be priests in the era of the millennium.

In other words, our role as priests is *significant* and *permanent*. With the physical temple now long gone, these Scriptures urge us under the New Covenant to understand our privilege and responsibility before God and man.

Prioritizing Our Priestly Duties

Our ministry as priests under the New Covenant is comprised of two basic realities: *ministering to the Person of God*, and *serving God by ministering to people*. This is our two-fold priestly function today. One of the tragedies of any believer or church, whether the church in Ephesus then or much of the church in the West today, is when we lose the art of ministering to the Person of God:

"Yet I hold this against you: You have forsaken your first love." --Rev. 2:4

The church in Ephesus was excellent at serving God, but they had neglected their primary priestly role of ministry to the Person of God. Ministry to God was a significant part of the role of the priests in the Old Testament, and it was modeled again for us in the New Testament by the early church in Acts 13:2 ~

"While they were ministering to the Lord and fasting, the Holy Spirit said..."

As the early church focused on the Person of God, their first priestly ministry, God released apostolic strategy for their second priestly ministry of serving, in this case the sending of church planters.

Many years ago I received an exhortative word of prophecy from James Ryle touching on this very point. Among other things, this wonderfully accurate prophet said to me, "Never let your zeal for serving Him get ahead of your prayer for seeking Him." This was an exhortation from the Lord to me so I would remember my priestly ministries and give them the proper priority in my heart and life.

Several years later, it happened again. I was in a pastors' meeting in Toronto, Canada, sitting on the back row with Heidi Baker. As the speaker began discussing modern strategies to engage seekers in renewal churches, I felt incredibly grieved. It wasn't that the speaker was communicating things that weren't true; it was simply that I felt the entire meeting wasn't under the leadership of the Holy Spirit. Heidi became grieved too. Then, for some reason, I fell down, out of my chair and onto the floor, and I began weeping. And Heidi put her hand on my back and began to pray. She then said to me words I've never forgotten: "I don't mind strategy as long as we're on our faces when we get it."

As we seek to build kingdom churches, our priestly functions must be in proper order—the first commandment must take first place, and the second commandment must be second.

TENSION BETWEEN INDIVIDUAL & COLLECTIVE CHRISTIANITY

While it is true that each believer is a priest, it is also true that God intends for us to be built together as a collective priesthood. These two truths, the individual and collective expressions of Christianity, exist side by side in the Scriptures, creating a 'both/and' kingdom tension. Let's look at what is at stake.

The Powerful Dynamic Of Individual Christianity

One of the primary reasons for the dramatic increase in holy dissatisfaction we wrote about in the first chapter is that for too long, the leadership of local churches has been underemphasizing the powerful dynamic of individual Christianity. We who are leaders in the church have been guilty of disempowering the individual believer. Believers throughout much of church history deserve a huge apology by leaders. In its most innocuous form, there has been a surprising lack of Biblical understanding. However, we also need to acknowledge the elephant in the middle of the room. Church leadership has often used its positional authority to control believers who have expressed a desire for more individual freedom within the church. Because we haven't known what to do with individuals who are strong in their expression and who have a high view of their individual authority in Christ, we have *over-preached* collective Christianity. We have continually emphasized the dimensions of Christianity that have to do with family, togetherness, belonging, and membership. Please don't misunderstand. These truths are vital, and I believe in their validity. But when they are presented out of balance, they can do great damage. And let's face it: they have been presented out of balance.

It is time to emphasize the individual realities of Christianity that will liberate a generation of believers to be and do the very things we've tried to accomplish through church programs. Pastors, don't be afraid. The people you serve will appreciate you so much more if you will honor their individuality instead of being threatened by it. The people of God are starving to be affirmed for who they are and where they're at as individuals, regardless of their level of participation in church programs. They want to be affirmed as *kingdom* priests, not church priests.

Part of the role of a kingdom church is to communicate high value for individual Christianity and to affirm the validity of contributions to the kingdom made by the people of God in whatever stage or sphere of life they find themselves. I am not simply saying that people need to be encouraged to "be the church" in the marketplace, although that is true. Nor am I primarily saying that we must release people to serve in any ministry in the church that matches their gifting, although, again, that is probably a good thing to say to people. Actually, the things I am talking about have nothing to do with the programmatic side of church. There are truths in the New Testament that need to be meditated on before we immediately try to qualify them. Every believer has both the privilege and responsibility to stand before God as a priest without qualification. Here are a few truths that illustrate this fact:

We Are Complete In Christ. As an individual believer, without any input or help from anyone else in or out of the church, I am absolutely, 100% complete in Jesus Christ, because fullness and completeness have been given to me as a gift (Col. 2:9-10). I have already received everything I need to be successful in life and to be godly by His divine power (2 Pet. 1:3), which works mightily in me (Col. 1:29). Amazingly, I have been given every single spiritual blessing that exists from my Father, in the Person of Jesus Christ (Eph. 1:3). All of this should be obvious, of course, because Jesus died for me, but I am doubly assured that with Christ, I am freely given all things (Rom. 8:32). If, in a difficult moment, I forget how complete I am in Christ, all I have to do is remember how much my Father is for me, and He will make all grace abound towards me so that in all things, at all times, having all that I need, I will abound (2 Cor. 9:8). If there is any doubt about what I do or do not have, Paul says plainly that all things are mine (1 Cor. 3:21).

God Is Our Clergy. God is our Senior Pastor! Clergy as mediation is entirely unbiblical, because there is only One mediator, the man Christ Jesus (1 Tim. 2:5). God, in fact, is our Clergy, because we go to Him to confess our sins (1 Jn. 1:9), and even when we go to people to seek prayer, it is to 'one another', not just to a pastor (Jms. 5:16). The Father is our Source (1 Cor. 8:6), and when we look to people as our Source, we commit great sin (Jer. 2:13). God is our covering (Ps. 91:4) and His hand of blessing covers us in everything (Isa. 51:16). We already know the truth, because we have an anointing from God that is more important than any human teaching (1 Jn. 2:20, 27). If we lack any understanding, the Holy Spirit is our Teacher and Counselor and He will teach us all things (Jn. 14:26), not in words taught by human wisdom but in words taught by the Spirit (1 Cor. 2:14). Not only does Jesus provide us with the most wonderful counsel (Isa. 9:6), but Jesus Himself is our great Intercessor (Heb. 7:25), along with the Holy Spirit, who prays for us in our weakness (Rom. 8:26). In the Father, Son, and Holy Spirit, we have the best pastoral team there is! (2 Cor. 13:14).

Ministry Belongs To Every Believer. Because we are a kingdom of priests (Rev. 1:5), we have inherited a ministry straight from heaven (2 Cor. 5:18). We are all commissioned as ambassadors (2 Cor. 5:20) and authorized by Jesus Himself to make disciples (Mt. 28:19), which includes the activities of baptism, teaching, and modeling the Christian life (Mt. 28:19- 20; 2 Tim. 2:2). We have each received a unique ministry destiny (Eph. 2:10) and unique gifts to administer God's grace (1 Pet. 4:10). We must obey God rather than men (Acts

5:29) because we will each be held individually accountable to God at judgment for our ministry effectiveness (1 Cor. 3:13). Therefore, we must be motivated by God Himself (2 Cor. 5:14) to fulfill our ministries that we have received from God Himself (Col. 4:17), because we are responsible to God to discharge all the duties of our ministry (2 Tim. 4:5). The responsibility of our actions in life and ministry falls on each individual believer (Gal. 6:4-5), as do our entrustments and individual rewards from God (Mt. 13:23; 25:15-28).

Now, when you read these truths, some questions may pop in your mind, like: "Then why do we need the church?" And, "Why do we need pastors?" That, my friend, is a healthy response to undiluted truth! It can startle us. It is the response Paul anticipated in Romans 5 when he spoke so freely about the grace of God that he anticipated the question: "Well, if grace is this good and free, why don't we just sin so grace will abound even more?" (Rom. 6:1). Grace is that amazing, and the priesthood of every believer is that amazing. The fact is, we must honor individual Christianity far more than we have been doing.

The Vital Necessity Of Collective Christianity

The other truth that brings dynamic kingdom tension to the first is the vital necessity of collective Christianity. Regarding this issue of collective Christianity, there is a powerful Biblical warning that needs to be trumpeted at this time, even as we're trumpeting the revolution into the priesthood of all believers and the strength of individual Christianity. With much freedom comes much responsibility. As more and more of the church is embracing holy dissatisfaction, there is a subtle deception occurring right alongside it. In 2 Thess. 2:7, Paul warns us about the mystery, or secret power, of lawlessness. The Greek word for lawlessness is "anomia", which means illegality. In other words, as the day draws near for Christ to return, there will be an increase in wicked, illegal operations in the world and in the church. In the church, there will be many who will no longer put up with sound, healthy doctrine (2 Tim. 4:3-4) even as it is preached and administrated through those with God-given authority (2 Tim. 4:1-2). These things will be occurring secretly or mysteriously in people's hearts and in murmurings. They will be difficult to detect, because they will not be talked about in the open but rather subtly administered through seemingly spiritual people! This is the definition of "musterion", or mystery. Even as we herald priests as individuals, we must also trumpet the priesthood as a group. Here are a few important realities regarding our collective expression of Christianity:

We Are Called To Real Christian Relationships. Our Christianity has to look like something *relationally*. The many *'one another'* Scriptures in the New Testament (some have counted 59 such commands!) clearly speak of the need for real Christian relationship, not simply to the larger body of Christ, but among a local community:

- Love one another (Jn 13:34-35; 15:1-17; Rm 13:8; 1 Th 4:9; 1 Jn 3:11,23; 4:7-12)
- Increase your love and make it overflow for one another (1 Th. 3:12)
- Love one another deeply from the heart (1 Pet. 3:8; 4:8)
- Be devoted to one another in brotherly love (Rm. 12:10)
- Greet each other with a holy kiss (Rm. 16:16; 1Co. 16:20; 2Co. 13:12; 1 Pet. 5:14)
- Accept one another as Christ has accepted you (Rm. 15:7)
- Be at peace with each other (Mk. 9:50)
- Live in harmony with one another (Rm. 12:16; 1 Pet. 3:8)
- Be patient and bear with one another in love (Eph. 4:2; Col. 3:13)
- Be kind and compassionate to one another (Eph. 4:32)
- Forgive each other whatever grievances you may have (Eph. 4:32; Col. 3:13)
- Honor one another above yourselves (Rm. 12:10)
- Wash each other's feet (Jn. 13:14)
- Offer hospitality to one another without grumbling (1 Pet. 4:9)
- Clothe yourselves with humility toward one another (1 Pet. 5:5)
- In humility consider others better than yourselves (Phil. 2:13)
- Wait for each other [when you come together to eat] (1 Cor. 11:33)
- Have equal concern for each other (1 Cor. 12:25)
- Carry each other's burdens (Gal. 6:2)
- Confess your sins to one another (Jms. 5:16)
- Pray for each other (Jms. 5:16)
- Submit to one another out of reverence for Christ (Eph. 5:21)
- Serve one another in love (Gal. 5:13)
- Use the gift(s) you've received to serve others (1 Pet. 4:10)
- Teach and instruct one another (Rom. 15:14; Col. 3:16)
- Encourage each other, daily (1 Th. 4:18; 5:11; Heb. 3:13; 10:25)
- Build each other up (1 Th. 5:11)
- Speak to one another in psalms, hymns, and spiritual songs (Eph. 5:19)
- Spur one another to love and good deeds (Heb. 10:24)

How can we fulfill these *'one another'* Scriptures if we're not in meaningful relationship with other believers in a local setting? It's not possible. We grow best in relationships, because it is in relationships that our character is formed. When I was a child, I had a poster on the wall of my bedroom with a photo of a rushing stream. The caption read: "Talent is produced in solitude, character in the stream of life." Indeed, we need the mutual support and ministry of Christian relationships, and these relationships provide a context for us to learn to love. Love is our goal and aim in everything we're doing, and love happens in the context of relationships.

We Are Called To Dwell Together. More than simply fulfilling 'one another' Scriptures, we are called as Christians to actually dwell together in unity (Ps. 133). We are called living stones (1 Pet. 2:5), meant to be fitted together into a spiritual house, a collective dwelling place of God in the Spirit (Eph. 2:22; Rev. 21:3). The early church modeled life together to such an extent that they were completely unified in their hearts and minds (Acts 4:32), and because they knew each others' lives and shared material possessions, there was no one needy among them (Acts 4:34). Part of dwelling together means that we gather regularly (Heb. 10:25) just as the early church practiced (Acts 2:46; 5:12) for relationship and ministry (Acts 5:42). Each of us is called to bring our spiritual offering to the gathered assembly and to worship God together (1 Cor. 14:26). Every believer is designed by God to be part of something bigger than ourselves.

We Are Called To Minister With Other Believers. While it is entirely true that each of us has been given a ministry by God, and while it is true that we must each be responsible before God to fulfill our ministry, it is also true that we are called to join other Christians in service to God. Jesus modeled team ministry when he sent his disciples out two by two (Lk. 10:1). Moses learned the power of shared responsibility and team ministry from his father-in-law, Jethro (Ex. 18:13-26). Scripture teaches the power of working together by telling us that two are better than one (Eccl. 4:9-12) and that multiplication occurs when we work together. "Five of you will chase a hundred, and a hundred of you will chase ten thousand..." (Lev. 26:8). Paul clearly teaches us that we cannot walk in the completeness we are destined for unless we have all parts of the body functioning together (1 Cor. 12:12-27) and working together in the joints (i.e., places of coming together) of the body (Eph. 4:11- 16). Ministry with other believers is part and parcel of what it means to be the church.

These two truths, individual and collective Christianity, when honored and not diluted, create a powerful kingdom tension. What are we to do with this tension? Clearly, the Scriptures teach both realities, and yet the struggle we've had over the years is how to reconcile the two dynamics in the local church setting. As we come together in collective Christianity, how can we honor the individual? And, as individual believers, how can we come together in a way that results in healthy, Biblical expressions of church life? This kingdom tension is perhaps the premiere issue facing churches at this time. How does it actually work? Over the past few decades, we have seen various ways that local churches have dealt with this dynamic kingdom tension.

FIVE KINDS OF CHURCHES

The priesthood of all believers is ultimately just a concept until we begin to look at how it works (or doesn't work) in the real setting of a body of believers. To move from concept to practice, let's take a look at the five most common ways that individual and collective Christianity relate and interact in the context of a local church. Keep in mind that these assessments are not addressing all aspects of what is good or not so good in each type of church. We are simply addressing the issue of how the individual and the collective dimensions of Christianity interact with each other in the context of a local church. In other words, how does an individual believer relate to the local church? Each of these five kinds of churches stand alone in their explanation, but as you read these descriptions, you may find that you or someone you know has actually progressed through each of these kinds of churches in sequence!

ONE: The Institutional Church

The institutional church is best characterized by its ongoing *focus on the church*. In other words, the goal of the church is the church. Now, every Christian church would claim that their focus is Jesus. We concede that in every Christian church the focus is Jesus! But what we're talking about specifically is how the local church relates to the individual. In the institutional church, the church 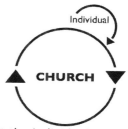 is first and the individual is second. This means that the individual exists to serve the church, and the individual's validation comes through their participation in the church. Who are the most important people in the institutional church? Those who are most engaged in the church's ministries and programs.

The good news about this kind of local church is that many people who are part of institutional churches feel that they are part of something bigger than themselves. In the institutional church, people learn how to set aside their personal wishes for the greater good of the church, and since all of us need to learn to serve, the institutional church is a great environment to learn how to serve.

The difficulty with the institutional church is that people feel they are valued in the context of how they serve the institution. They begin to feel used, and over time, this can turn into resentment. After some years in the institutional church, many good, godly Christian people become either hurt, offended, or burned out, and they leave. They often don't feel that their individuality is valued. Christians are leaving the institutional church by droves.

TWO: The Invitational Church

In the invitational church, the *focus is on growth.* The goal of the church is to reach out and gather people into the church. Therefore, the church is designed as a consumer-oriented place that takes special care to make sure the red carpet is rolled out for visitors and guests. A highly trained staff puts forth great effort to 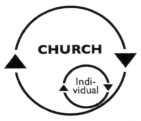 ensure the very best experience for everyone who comes to the church, with special attention paid to visitors. Invitational churches are often successful at growth because this is a large part of their goal and focus.

There are many wonderful aspects of the invitational church. I believe God sovereignly birthed the church growth and seeker movements to help the institutional church get beyond itself and start caring about the millions of people trying to find God who were unable to fit into the institutional church. I deeply appreciate and value invitational churches, because they have come up with a way to re-create a modern day "Court Of The Gentiles" aspect of the temple, a place where God-seekers can come and find God. They have unselfishly set aside their desire for church to be about themselves, and they have designed church services for lost people and seekers. What a refreshing change when invitational churches hit the scene! They have really harvested many people for Jesus and helped thousands of churches become outward-focused. This is a good thing!

The difficulty with the invitational church is that the individual is essentially irrelevant. What I mean is, when most people walk into an invitational church, it really doesn't matter whether or not they show up. Why is this true? Because the invitational church has, by default, set the bar very low to make sure that whosoever will may come. However, the inadvertent message is that the individual is not really needed. Little is asked or required of people, and it is very clear that if they aren't part of the overall goal to facilitate growth, their gifts may not be needed. To prove the point: where do many of the people who have left institutional churches go? They often sit in the back of invitational churches where they can go unnoticed and where they can have very little asked of them. The invitational church is a great place to recover from the institutional church.

Some go on and become involved in meaningful ways. But often over time, two negative things happen to believers who have been in invitational churches. One, they become sedentary, consumer-oriented Christians. Those who joined the institutional church and who wanted to make a difference have all but lost their initial fire. Often they no longer burn with zeal for God and His purposes. Instead, they unwittingly adopt the culture of the invitational church into their Christianity, and they, too, lower the bar to the point where, for all intents and purposes, they are now just showing up at a weekend service. Or two, they begin to feel the need for a more personal, relational church, and they move on to something more personal and meaningful to them.

THREE: The Interpersonal Church

The interpersonal church is a refreshing change for many who spent years in the institutional and invitational church environments. The interpersonal church is best characterized by its *focus on the warmth and belonging of each individual.* Interpersonal churches tend to be smaller in size, most often meeting in homes or other  more intimate settings. Common names for interpersonal churches are 'house church' and 'simple church.' The interpersonal church is a refreshing alternative to both the institutional church and the invitational church. Of the three, it is the type of church that best demonstrates value for the individual. People who join interpersonal churches feel validated for who they are, and because the goal is the warmth and belonging of each individual, there is an atmosphere of acceptance. We've needed the influence of the interpersonal church to move us away from the CEO mentality of many churches. The interpersonal church is leading the way in creating environments of grace and acceptance.

Interpersonal churches tend to be filled with people who've left other church environments after feeling unsatisfied and underappreciated. Often they also chafe against structure in general. As a result, these churches also tend to lower the bar, but in a different way. There is often more participation but in a very low-key, relaxed manner so as not to scare off or stress out people who are burned out on most aspects of familiar church life. Structure is simple and demands are few.

The great strength of the interpersonal church is also its weakness. It is often, by necessity, inward. If it becomes too outward or too large too quickly, the very warmth and belonging that made it special is lost, and the feelings of institutionalism rapidly increase, bringing uncomfortability for those who signed up for its smallness, simplicity, and closeness. Further, interpersonal churches have difficulty embracing individuals with strong gifting or authority from God. They are, by nature, very egalitarian. A world-class worship leader is often told in these kinds of churches that his gift of worship is no more or less important than the worship offered by everyone else in the group. What does the interpersonal church do when a young Billy Graham shows up? He must go outside the church to preach, because the little group would be dominated by his legitimate gift from God. And, once Billy starts having impact, he will bring so many people with all kinds of personalities and expectations that he will mess up the environment! Many of these kinds of churches have great difficulty knowing what to do with someone who has a gift meant for a larger environment. Interpersonal churches can sometimes 'dumb down' the environment to such a basic level that people begin to feel unchallenged and never really called out into their unique destiny. If the interpersonal church ends up being a part of something bigger than itself, it thrives. But by itself, it remains incomplete and can leave mature, gifted saints feeling unsatisfied. People who want to express their gift more or be more outward often leave to find another expression of their Christian faith.

FOUR: The Individual Church

The very latest trend in church life is the individual church. The individual church is *focused on freedom* and obtains it to its maximum degree. Some of those who opt out of other types of churches do so because they are looking for the ultimate expression of their individual Christianity. Individuals (and sometimes families) who consider themselves the church all by  themselves know what it is like to have no rules. And this is not entirely a bad thing.

There are some good reasons why the individual church is flourishing at this time in history. Many people are getting in touch with the fact that they are priests before the Lord and they are choosing to validate their individual Christianity by removing themselves from structures that often constrict or at least fail to affirm their individual Christian expression. They are weary of systems that put too much emphasis on leadership, submission, etc., and they are exploring another way to experience God.

Those who have opted out of all forms of organized church life are a voice for change, and we would do well to listen to the Lord in the midst of this trend. The departure of individual believers from organized church must at least be sympathized with and understood.

Of course, there is a down side. Individuals who do not participate in a community of believers are missing a huge part of the way Christianity was meant to be experienced. In their desire to walk in freedom as an individual, they are violating Scriptural principles and commands to dwell in community with and submission to other believers. Eventually, if they stay away from a community of faith, their own expression of faith will become lopsided, and they will be susceptible to the mystery of lawlessness. This temptation is not new. Hebrews 10:25 tells us not to forsake believers' gatherings, "as is the habit of some." At this point in some people's church journey, believers who have been unsatisfied in institutional, invitational, interpersonal, and individual church expressions often don't believe there are any other options. But there is a fifth kind of church that God is quickly raising up.

FIVE: The Interdependent Church

As we begin looking at the interdependent church, let me affirm again that each of the previous four kinds of church are providing at least some benefit. Although they each have faults and deficiencies, they are still serving the Lord and His people in some way, and many of them will be around for years to come.

Whenever God adds something new to His work on the earth, His previous works still stand on their own merit. As long as there is mutual appreciation and understanding, all of these kinds of churches can get along and enjoy the contribution each one makes to the kingdom.

Having said that, my favorite kind of church, from both a Biblical and practical standpoint as it relates to the kingdom tension between individual and collective Christianity, is the interdependent church. The interdependent church *focuses on kingdom partnerships.* It is a relationally-based, network style structure rather than a hierarchy. It is a kingdom society of like-minded, like-hearted people all moving together. It has similarities to each of the other four kinds of churches, but the contrasts are significant. Let's take a quick look at each one.

Like the *institutional church*, everyone in the interdependent church is involved in something bigger than themselves, but unlike the institutional church, there is no institution. It is a partnership of priests who have joined together as like-minded believers going after the same vision and modeling the same values. There is no "church" to build, because the people are the church. Each member in an interdependent church is living for Christ as a lifestyle. Gatherings simply celebrate this fact and support one another in the process.

Like the *invitational church*, the interdependent church is an outward, missional church where everyone is meant to reach lost people. But unlike the invitational church, the default setting for outreach is not a "come ye" focus on numerous "services" as the primary net, but instead on a "go ye" mobilized army infiltrating society. Because each person is vital to the success of the whole, the interdependent church ultimately cannot move forward with just a great staff. The interdependent church is a flexible wineskin that changes as each new person is added, because each person brings a new set of gifts and contributions. Ministries in the interdependent church are largely determined by who shows up and their respective gifts and callings from God, more than by the declarations of a senior leader or board.

Like the *interpersonal church*, each person in the interdependent church is highly valued and appreciated. And like the interpersonal church, the interdependent church has no agenda for individuals, other than to help see each individual reach his or her full potential in Christ. But the interdependent church differs in that it is captivated by huge vision. Because of its commitment to fullness, the interdependent church could never be satisfied with an inward orientation. It is too missional for that. The interdependent church is vitally linked to other churches and ministries in the city/region. The interdependent church makes room for both smaller expressions of church life (i.e., cells, house churches, etc.) and larger gatherings (celebrations, multi-church gatherings, healing rooms, houses of prayer, conferences). Neither is seen as inferior, because both are Biblical, and both contexts reach the lost and help people fulfill their destinies in Christ.

And like the *individual church*, each person in the interdependent church is encouraged to fulfill his or her destiny in an environment of freedom. But unlike the individual church, the interdependent church honors the collective Biblical mandate to dwell together and to submit to one another out of reverence for Christ. It is impossible to be an independent lone ranger in an interdependent church.

The interdependent church means that each person is vital. The atmosphere is filled with mutual honor and respect. The church is unleashed without walls or religious control to hold it back. The environment is 'yes' instead of 'no' and faith rather than fear. The paradigm of interdependence may at first glance appear unrealistic or even anarchistic to some, but it is quite the opposite. Proverbs 29:18 tells us that it is the absence of vision, not control, that causes people to act in unrestrained ways. A holy vision for a kingdom of priests functioning together in mutual honor, mutual submission, and interdependency is the God-given dream inside the hearts of God's people! Given the opportunity to honor that dream, the church will model kingdom living in a fresh way, and we will all be pleasantly surprised with the outcome.

CHURCH WITHOUT WALLS

The goal here is the church unleashed, the church without walls, flowing in grace, giving room for one another, serving and laying down our lives individually and together, each person fulfilling his or her unique, God-given destiny while partnering with others to do the same by creating win-win relationships.

The Mobilized Priesthood

Each person who is part of the interdependent church is living as a priest before God in his or her world while also dwelling in unity with the rest of the church. As priests before God, our first ministry is to Him, both to worship Him and to enjoy Him. As John Piper says, "God is most glorified in us when we are most satisfied in Him." We receive directly from God all that we need pertaining to life and godliness. We consecrate ourselves to Him in a holy life, and then we press in for more of His Person, His Presence, His Power, His Provision, and His Peace in our lives! This is how the priests were to bless the people in Numbers 6:24-26, and this is how we are to receive blessing from God--directly. He wants to bless us directly through the mediation of Christ. Individuals are directed to God as their Source, and we drink deeply from His throne and from His heart.

Then, we function as priests in our world. This includes our home, our work environment, and everywhere we go. Each of us becomes "walking revival" wherever we are, a literal mobile church, an open heaven, carriers of the glory of God to the streets. We are the priests, each one of us, of Joel 2, weeping and contending for souls between the porch (representative of God seekers) and the altar (representative of intimacy). We are priests of intimacy unto fruitfulness. In kingdom churches, this identity must be affirmed over and over until people get it and live it.

Finally, we then also function as priests in the contexts of Christian friendships that we call "church." The church is about life-giving relationships that come together in gatherings. When we gather, we don't primarily assemble in the style of the synagogue: to learn, to receive, to evaluate, and to contemplate. Rather, we assemble in the style of the temple: to worship, to pray, to encounter God, and to bring our offering. We come as living stones, fitted together in the house of God as a collective dwelling place.

Priestly Order

Even though we've meant well, I believe that for years we've been miscommunicating wrong priorities in the church. As I was being trained in church environments to pastor, I was taught that you could essentially map out a view of the church in concentric circles. The outermost circle represented the people who weren't a part of the church but were coming your way--the seekers. The next circle represented the people of the church

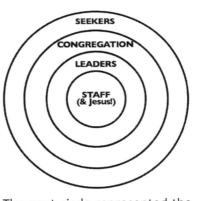

who were members--the congregation. The next circle represented the people who were serving and leading in the church--leadership. The final circle represented the inner circle of the pastoral staff. Over the years I have seen variations, but this is a commonly held view of the church.

Now, there are a couple of unintentional but nevertheless important miscommunications in this diagram and perhaps in the thinking behind it. First, it implies that in order to get closer to Jesus, you have to become more committed to the church, because the most spiritual people are in the center. Second, it views the life of the individual in relationship to the church and therefore creates an artificial mediation process and unintended institutionalism.

I do not believe the Biblical goal of the church is to move people toward the center of these kinds of circles, because I believe the New Testament would diagram things completely differently. Here is what I think is a more Biblically accurate diagram.

I want to point out a few important truths about this diagram. First, only Jesus is in the center. No pastor, staff, or church should ever be there. Second, you and I as individuals are closest to Jesus. This honors individual Christianity without mediation and communicates both the privilege and responsibility of each believer to seek the Lord for all we need. Third, your world is next, which honors you as a priest bringing revival to your world. It speaks of the ministry that you have in your *oikos* (sphere of influence) without any red tape or church bureaucracy. And finally, the church is outside of it all, with the spokes representing your connection to the church. These spokes represent ministry to you and your family to strengthen and equip you as a priest, and they represent your partnership in servanthood ministry in team with others that becomes a context for you to equip and empower those in your God-given ministry sphere.

Kingdom Lifestyles

A kingdom church is a society of individuals who are expressing their Christianity through their lifestyles. This means that it is theoretically possible to be an amazing church without a single 'program' or ministry. Of course, that sounds very counterintuitive. After all, most churches are scrambling to have the best youth/singles/children's ministries in town. But it is possible. As God's people continue to be validated as priests and as 'kingdomizers' in whatever sphere of influence they find themselves, then the ministry of the church will return to the hands of the people. Again, this isn't anarchy. This is empowerment, ownership, and responsibility.

Part of the revolt against the organized church that is happening today is because people are intuitively objecting to the lack of honor toward kingdom lifestyles. Believers are feeling too pressed by the church as an organization and not honored enough for living lives where people are being influenced for Christ in the other 'mountains' of culture—arts, entertainment, politics, education, family, and so on. When we begin to view the church as a society of spiritual entrepreneurs, we will then design things within the church differently.

Our local church is called 'Everyday Church.' We named the church *Everyday* to clearly communicate our value for kingdom lifestyles of love. This is our first and greatest strategy! As God's people are validated, equipped and empowered within their circles of influence, they will bring God's kingdom in naturally supernatural ways.

Several years ago, I remember hearing Bill Johnson at Bethel Church in Redding, CA talk about the church's 'mall outreach.' Some members of Bethel Church, largely students from their school of ministry, would go to the local mall and ask the Lord to reveal to them people who needed ministry. Words of knowledge, healing, prophecy, deliverance, and salvation were becoming commonplace through this eclectic group of individuals and friends. So, when visitors would visit Bethel Church, they would ask, "So, how can I connect with the mall outreach?" Bill chuckled as he recalled that they didn't actually have a mall outreach. It was simply people living kingdom lifestyles of love and power. This is a sign of true kingdom churches—the people outpace the programs! We have had a similar dynamic at Everyday Church, where many of our young people have begun ministering as a lifestyle in ways that have far exceeded any program we could have come up with.

Making Changes

God brings about repentance by changing our minds. Once we see things from his perspective, we can easily change our behavior, because we believe in the changes we are making. We are learning to see the church and ourselves differently, and from that place of a paradigm shift, we can begin to see how these things translate into shifts in our activities within the church. We are learning to become the church without walls or ceiling!

Repentance means that our mind catches up with what God is already doing in our hearts. We agree with Him by changing directions and by allowing Him to realign our thought patterns so we are consistent and not in turmoil.

We are priests, beloved. And identity always precedes work. When we see ourselves as a royal priesthood, we will be ready to roll up our sleeves and build kingdom churches. We become the people, the army, of God's kingdom, building what He is building, blessing what He is blessing. Hallelujah!

Chapter Six
Kingdom BUILDERS

"...I will build My church, and the gates of hell will not prevail against it!"
--Matt. 16:18

It is possible to embrace God's priority of His kingdom but still miss the commitment in His own heart to the building process. To be part of the company who help bring about a kingdom church revolution, our hearts must not only align with the priorities in God's heart; we must become those who *build* what God is building.

Like all groups of society, the Western Christian community goes through phases, seasons, and pendulum swings. The longer you are a citizen of the kingdom, the more clearly you can see these trends. Having been a follower of Jesus now for decades has afforded me the benefit of perspective. This is especially true if you travel and talk to enough people. And one of the patterns I've noticed over the years is a knee-jerk reaction against the local church, often followed by a return to the local church.

Let me give you some examples (details have been changed):

> I have a friend whom I've known for years and years. When I first met him, he proudly talked about his exodus from what he perceived to be the 'institutional' church. He bragged about the 'leaderless' community he was part of, where leadership in his current community was shared and egalitarian, and where no one would ever be a CEO. Three or four men shared the leadership roles in the group. He would never again have anything to do with a typical church that met weekly in a building and had a senior pastor. Fast forward five years: the leadership team blew up and several people got hurt. Fast forward another five years: this guy is the senior pastor of that same community/church, meeting weekly in a building. More and more, he and his church look very much like all the other churches and pastors around town. He has become what he vowed never to become.

> Another guy I knew longed to build unity among the churches. His passion

was to start a ministry that would gather local churches together and be the outside catalyst for churches. He most certainly didn't want to be a pastor, be on staff, or be in any way associated with the local church. He somehow felt he had graduated from the local church, which to him was ineffective and without merit. His appeal to people who had been hurt or disillusioned was that he understood; he, too, had 'left' the church. As he tried to build his ministry, he was only ever able to gather 10-15 people. And, of course, none of those people he gathered wanted to do anything that resembled the work of the local church, so they never really did anything in his new ministry either. He was stuck reaping what he had sown for years, with an ineffective, unmotivated work force in his ministry. So what did he do? He tried to become a pastor and start a church! But by then, his credibility was shot, and no one really wanted to follow him. He ended up losing his marriage along the way. Last I heard he was still trying to gather people and become a church leader of a congregation.

Several people I've known over the years who referred to themselves as 'prophetic' loved to visit various churches as the Spirit would lead, blow the shofar, pull people aside and prophesy to them about the need to be 'outside the camp', and generally be the self-appointed salt and light of the larger body of Christ without ever committing anywhere in particular. They didn't believe in submission, and they didn't play well with others. Most of these folks have had major deficits in the areas of social skills and conflict resolution. In extreme cases, there was chemical and/or mental imbalance. But challenging these folks was simply not allowed, because they were convinced everything they did was led by the Spirit. Anything questioned or challenged was always responded to with, "God told me/God said/The Spirit led me..." And of course, those kinds of statements are conversation stoppers! After all, who wants to argue with God? Over the years, I watched them show up at any event that wasn't a local church. Often their expressions were hollow and their smiles forced. Their decisions to isolate were wearing them down. And then, after more years, I noticed something very strange. Many of them started joining local churches and getting plugged in! And get this: many ended up in more *conservative* churches than the ones they originally left.

I know colleagues who spent many years traveling and speaking and ministering in conferences and even in churches. In the early years of their ministry, their talks were often seasoned with witty, sarcastic comments about the how 'dead' the church was. The crowds loved it! They told stories about where the real action was—outside the walls of the church. They urged people to pretty much do anything for Jesus except be committed to a local church. As the years passed, I watched these same people get tired of purely itinerant ministry. The longing in their hearts for relationship and community became so strong that they eventually reduced their itinerant speaking schedule and joined a local community. Many of these colleagues ended up starting churches or joining the staff of a local church.

These are a few examples among thousands. The stories themselves could fill another volume—some funny, some tragic. But what do they have in common? I hope you're seeing a pattern. There is a gravitational pull towards building the local church! So this begs the question: If Jesus is bringing revolution to the church because the local church is so messed up and in such desperate need of change, why are so many people nevertheless being drawn [back] to the local church?

UNDERSTANDING THE MINISTRY OF JESUS

One of my heroes that I refer to often in this book is the late John Wimber. I remember him describing ministry something like this:

> "People talk about their ministry as though it is the title of a business. I don't understand that. The only ministry I'm aware of in the New Testament is *the ministry of Jesus*. I don't have a ministry. I have the privilege of entering into *His* ministry, of continuing *His* ministry through the power of the Holy Spirit. I am like change in His pocket—He can spend me any way He wants."

In other words, if we're going to understand the church, or itinerant ministry, or anything else we do in the kingdom, we need to start by understanding the ministry of Jesus. Because it's all about Him.

Jesus' ministry was like a two-sided coin. On the one side was the **blessing** ministry of Jesus. When I say 'blessing' ministry, I'm referring to that part of His ministry that could be done anytime, anywhere. It was not dependent on a building, a staff, a budget, or other people.

He announced His blessing ministry in Luke 4:18-19, where He stood in the temple and read from the scroll of Isaiah 61:1-3~

> "The Spirit of the Sovereign LORD is upon me, and He has anointed Me to preach good news to the poor, to bind up the brokenhearted, to proclaim release to the captives, and recovery of sight to the blind, to set free those who are oppressed, to proclaim the favorable year of the LORD."

This is the blessing ministry of Jesus. He didn't do it in order to build a church or a ministry. It was simply His mission and His manifesto. It was a lifestyle of love.

> "You know Jesus of Nazareth, how God anointed Him with the Holy Spirit and with power, and how **He went about doing good** and healing all who were oppressed by the devil, for God was with Him." --Acts 10:38

You could say that Jesus' *itinerant* ministry is best described here in Acts

10:38. He *'went about'* doing good. Itinerant ministry often has immediate and tangible results to show for it through the impact of the moment. It is a *'going about'* ministry of doing good. It is also a sowing ministry, a serving ministry, and a blessing ministry. There is often not as much ownership or legacy in itinerant, blessing ministry. In fact, this kind of ministry does not lend itself to longevity in relationships in a specific location. It often requires a person to sort of 'keep moving.' This was the case with Jesus in Luke 4:42-44:

> "When the day came, Jesus left and went to a secluded place; and the crowds were searching for Him, and came to Him and tried to keep Him from going away from them. But He said to them, 'I must preach the kingdom of God to the other cities also, for I was sent for this purpose.' So He kept on preaching in the synagogues of Judea.'"

On the other side of the coin was the **building** ministry of Jesus. We already know from Matthew 16:18 that Jesus is committed to building His church. So what did this look like for Jesus?

> "And He went up on the mountain and summoned those whom He Himself wanted, and they came to Him. And He appointed twelve, so that they would be with Him and that he could send them out to preach, and to have authority to cast out demons." --Mark 3:13-15

Jesus began this part of His ministry by building twelve men. He invested in them for three and a half years. He did life and ministry with them. He hung out with them, spent time in ministry settings, debriefed in 'leadership meetings', and equipped them to change the world. These were Jesus' leaders-in-training. He was very committed to them. In His High Priestly prayer recorded in John 17, Jesus is careful to report back to the Father about the results and status of His disciples, while also praying urgently for them. Listen to His heart of care and protection for His men that He was committed to:

> "I glorified You on the earth, having accomplished the work which You have given Me to do... I have manifested Your name **to the men whom You gave Me** out of the world; they were Yours and **You gave them to Me**... Now they have come to know that everything You have ben me is from You; for *the words which You gave me I have given to them*; and they received them... <u>I ask on their behalf</u>; I do not ask on behalf of the world, but of those whom You have given Me; for they are Yours... Holy Father, *keep them* in Your name... While I was with them, **I kept them in Your name... I guarded them**... I do not ask You to take them out of the world, but to keep them from the evil one... *Sanctify them* in the truth... As you sent Me into the world, *I also have sent them* into the world." --John 17:4-18

This was pretty much the opposite of itinerant ministry. Jesus felt very accountable to the Father to reproduce Himself in these men, who would then do the same with others (cf. Mt. 28:18-20, 2 Tim. 2:2). He was committed to these same people, over a long period of time, in a specific geographic location, desiring specific results from His training, with increased responsibilities for those in His care. In other words, if Jesus' *blessing ministry* resembled the activities of an itinerant 'kingdom' ministry, then Jesus' *building ministry* very much resembled the activities of the local church.

THE PENDULUM SWINGS AGAIN

So with this understanding about the dual blessing and building ministry of Jesus as a backdrop, let's look again at this issue of why there is such a return to the local church.

There are seasons in our lives where God emphasizes one truth over the other. However, even though there are definite seasons, when we look back on our lives from an overall perspective, I believe that what remains behind us ought to be both blessing and building. Like a boat on a lake, we are leaving a 'wake.' And that wake needs to be like Jesus—a legacy of both blessing and building.

Prophetically speaking, I believe God Himself has emphasized the *blessing* ministry of Jesus for several decades. He has been mobilizing the church to get her beyond the four walls and into the marketplace, and to do accomplish this, He has been getting His people focused on the kingdom more than the church. I personally believe this mobilizing and blessing emphasis from the Lord began with the Jesus movement, and it is still going on today. It is the Lord focusing His people on the kingdom. I remember when I first became a Christian many years ago, very few believers were talking much about God's kingdom. Language tended to center more around the church. But today, much of the church is aware of the priority of bringing and expanding the kingdom of God.

However, I also believe that we are now on the other side of the pendulum swing. For many years there has been a reaction to the ineffectiveness of the Western church as discussed in chapter 1. Like a huge pendulum swing, the need for revolution and reform in Western Christianity has caused a mass exodus from the local church and proper focus on the kingdom in the streets and in the marketplace. That exodus is still happening, of course.

God has been trying to expand the focus of the church to seek first and to embrace His kingdom, which of course is good and right. However, in the minds of many believers in the West, where instant results are highly prized, where the church has been commonly held in distain, and where the stories of itinerant people tend to 'wow' the conference crowd, there has been a migration away from 'church' ministry and towards what is commonly referred to as 'kingdom' ministry. I've observed countless believers in North America express that they are now, finally, involved in 'kingdom' ministry, as though ministry in and through their local church doesn't count as advancing God's kingdom. This fundamental misunderstanding about kingdom ministry has created a pendulum swing. Somewhere along the way, many 'kingdom-minded' believers became blessers who forgot to also become builders.

And yet, in spite of this overemphasis, the pendulum has now begun to swing in the other direction. There is now an emphasis on becoming builders like Jesus. There is a call back to the local church—even with all her flaws! It is the Lord preparing builders for His end-time harvest.

If Jesus is our model in ministry, which He is, then that means every believer has been called to be both a *blesser* and a *builder*. There ought to be aspects of our lives and ministries that very much look like the *blessing* ministry of Jesus, where we bring the kingdom of God, pure and simple. And there ought to be aspects of our lives and ministries that very much look like the *building* ministry of Jesus, where we are actively making disciples and investing in specific people's lives in a specific geography over time, consistently.

I believe that what is happening in this hour is that God's people are being drawn to the local church, because revival is coming! The nets are being prepared for a great haul of fish. The wineskins are being oiled and softened and prepared to contain what God is pouring out and about to pour out. There is a loud trumpet call for apostolic alignment, where believers are sensing the need to be properly aligned and submitted for what's ahead.

And I also believe God Himself is calling in the harvesters and the builders. As His Church, we've had plenty of time to complain and throw rocks and describe in great detail what is wrong with the church. Now it is time to put our money where our mouth is and to begin to build what is *right*. It is time for answers and solutions, not simply questions and problems. And so the pendulum swings again, moving us from a primary focus on blessing to a fresh re-focus on building—but hopefully with a kingdom heart and perspective.

We have all inherited the building ministry of Jesus Christ. And He is building His Church! The return to the local church is a move of God that reflects the maturity of the Western Bride. We're getting over ourselves and coming home. All we need is a little faith!

FAITH FOR WHAT GOD IS BUILDING

The kind of heart posture required for those who are called to build kingdom churches is faith. Conversely, one of the greatest enemies of the church in the West right now is overfamiliarity. Many have adopted a *'been there, done that, bought the T-shirt'* kind of attitude when it comes to radical change in the church. When Jesus emerged on the scene, the sentiment of those around Him was, "Can any good thing come out of Nazareth?" We have a similar problem in the Western church. We have access via the Internet to the most amazing worship and messages on earth. We've heard so many great stories about what God is doing in other countries, and with the incredible increase in travel, many of us have seen it with our own eyes. The great hunger, desperation, and need we see in second- and third-world countries seem to pave the way for the move of God in those places, whereas here in the West, our need is dulled, our hunger is less, and things seem to kind of chug along mostly unchanged.

As a result, weariness settles deep into our bones, and that weariness and overfamiliarity can easily turn into doubt and cynicism. So, we must zealously guard ourselves against unbelief. The Scriptures clearly warn us not to develop a cynical attitude towards the prophetic message God is sending to His people:

> "Do not put out the Spirit's fire; do not treat prophecies with contempt."
> --1 Thess. 5:19-20

This was the mistake made by the strong, self-assured military officer that served as an assistant to the king of Israel in the time of Elisha the prophet. During a time of severe famine, Elisha prophesied that suddenly, in one day, the famine would not only be over, but food would be so amazingly abundant that its price would be very inexpensive (2 Kings 7:1). This required such a phenomenal miracle that the officer said to Elisha, "Look, even if the LORD should open the floodgates of the heavens, how could this happen?" Even though it seemed far-fetched, the officer didn't properly esteem what God was saying. The results were tragic:

> "You will see it with your own eyes," answered Elisha,
> "but you will not eat any of it!" --2 Kings 7:2

God understands our propensity towards unbelief, especially when it comes to dead things coming alive, or dry things being drenched, or scattered things coming together. For Him, it is not a problem, but for us, we can hardly conceive of it. God came to one of His most faithful prophets, Ezekiel, who was continually privileged with great revelation, and He showed Ezekiel a large valley full of dry bones, after which God asked him a question: "Son of man, can these bones live?" Today, God is asking us a similar question: "Western church, do you believe that I can bring revolution in your generation?"

Over the doorway of this revolution is the word 'faith', a doorway we must pass through in order to be part of this change. The Bible says that without faith, it is impossible to please God, and yet, Jesus throws us a curve ball when He asks the question: "When the Son of Man returns, will He find faith on the earth?" (Lk. 18:8)

Faith is needed in transition, and the church has been in transition. This transition is vital, but it is also painful. Just at the end of pregnancy and just before the joy of birth is 'transition.' Transition is when you have watched and waited for so long to see the church come into a place of maturity and fullness, and then when it starts to happen, you experience even more pain. Transition is when your hope has been deferred so that you have become heart sick, and when you hear vision announced and prophesied, your mind knows that you agree but your heart is unable to feel excitement. Transition is when you have paid a great price in the secret womb of intercession to see something birthed, only to have strange people yelling, "Push!" in your face.

Every time I have been waterskiing, faith has been required, because there is a place between when you say "Hit it!" to when you're standing up and enjoying skiing where the water is spraying in your face and you can't see, and somehow you have to remember what works--which is counterintuitive. This is especially true with 'slow' water ski boats! The longer it takes for the boat to pull you up, the harder it is to stand up. Faith is required to water ski, to deliver a baby, and to move from where we've been to where we're going as the church. And the boat has been slow! But God is in the business of filling us afresh with new faith for the journey we are on. Have faith in God! He will surely have His way on the earth. The church will be unified, and the church will be one in heart and mind, because Jesus' prayers are always answered, and He prayed for unity! The church will not always be about the glory of man, because "the Lord alone will be exalted in that day." The church will experience the glory of God, because "the glory of the latter house will be greater than the former", and because God has promised through Habakkuk that "the glory of the Lord will cover the earth as the waters cover the sea!" The dream in your heart for His church will happen. God gave it, and He intends to see it come to pass. Rest in His ability.

VALUING THE BUILDING PROCESS

I love the kingdom, and I love the church. I love to see heaven come to earth as the kingdom crashes into our reality and the lost are saved, the sick are healed, the blind see, the deaf hear, the poor are fed, and love looks like something. And I also love to see communities of the kingdom spring up so the kingdom can continue to be expressed through spiritual families in particular geographies.

Jesus seems to feel the same way. He told us to seek the kingdom (Mt. 6:33) while also promising to build His church (Mt. 16:18). The church and the kingdom belong together. Whenever we try to build the church without seeking first the kingdom, we get into serious trouble, and the result is inferior churches with ambitious leaders and ingrown people. Conversely, when we seek the kingdom without caring about the church, we dishonor what Jesus is building, and we run the risk of becoming arrogant and cynical toward His precious church.

God is building kingdom churches! The process of building kingdom churches is first and best described by Jesus in Matthew 16:18, where He reveals the secrets of the building process:

> "Upon this rock I will build My church;
> the gates of hell will not prevail against it."

Here our Lord Jesus establishes several key building principles by assuring us of His role and involvement in building His church:

- The church is built on the solid foundation of a revelation of the Person of Christ--"Upon this rock"
- He is taking both credit and responsibility for the building process--"I will build"

- He assures us that it really will happen, that He is absolutely committed to His Church--"I *will* build"
- He reminds us that it is a process that takes time and requires steps--"I will *build*"
- He is clear with us about ownership, that we are stewards of what really belongs to Him--"*My* church"
- He instills great confidence in our hearts--"the gates of hell will not prevail against it"

Because these promises are so powerful, we could easily miss or dismiss our part. From what Jesus has said, it seems like He's got it covered! The foundation of the Person and promises of the Lord Jesus Christ in Matthew 16:18 are so powerful and comprehensive, we could easily wonder if there is anything we can do, really, to build the church.

CALLED TO BE BUILDERS

That's why in 1 Corinthians 3:9-15, God uses the Apostle Paul to write striking and sobering words about the work of building churches that complement so well what Jesus has already said:

> "For we are God's fellow workers; you are God's field, God's building. By the grace God has given me, I laid a foundation as an expert builder, and someone else is building on it. But each one should be careful how he builds. For no one can lay any foundation other than the one already laid, which is Jesus Christ. If any man builds on this foundation using gold, silver, costly stones, wood, hay or straw, his work will be shown for what it is, because the Day will bring it to light. It will be revealed with fire, and the fire will test the quality of each man's work. If what he has built survives, he will receive his reward. If it is burned up, he will suffer loss; he himself will be saved, but only as one escaping through the flames."

Paul's first key insight is that *human involvement is essential* in the building process. We have a vital role in the building process as God's 'fellow workers', or 'co-laborers.' We have been given the privilege of working in partnership with Almighty God to build His church! This is an awesome privilege and invitation extended to us.

But Paul takes it to another level when he calls himself "an expert builder." The Greek words here are 'phronimos', which means thoughtful, wise, and intelligent, and 'architekton', from which we derive our word, 'architect.' It means chief constructor, master builder, or in today's terms, general contractor. While all of us are called to be 'co-laborers' with God, there are some uniquely called and gifted by God as architects, developers, and general contractors in the Spirit, to whom God gives wisdom and skill to build. Paul was one of those people. Perhaps you are one, too! And certainly, all of us are called to build what God is building.

Paul also explains what we are building, that we who build churches are building people. The Greek word for "building" is oikodome, which means 'an architecturally designed structure where people dwell.' We are building a spiritual structure designed by God called the church, which is made up of people, not a physical building. We are building people who fit together in such a way that they comprise a dwelling place in the Spirit—a corporate structure where God dwells in our midst.

Finally, Paul discusses for us the materials used in building. Jesus Christ is always and forever the foundation of every local church and of the global Church. Those who build churches must build in such a way that the foundation is Jesus, through and through. To build on anything else-- personality, hype, good interpersonal skills, marketing, etc.--is not even conceivable to Paul. He simply says, "No other foundation can be laid, because Jesus is already the foundation." He goes on to say that it is possible to have the right foundation and still build with the shoddy materials of wood, hay, and stubble. This ought to be a sober warning to all of us involved in the building process. We are exhorted and invited to build well--with quality materials that will stand the test of fire. I believe that the materials Paul is talking about here--gold, silver, precious stones--are the materials of the kingdom.

The Lord wants us to learn how to build churches that are founded on the Person of Jesus Christ while always seeking the kingdom first. It is a different kind of church planting. It is more like church planting as a byproduct rather than as a focus. When the King and His kingdom are the focus, the church happens. When the church is the focus, the King and His kingdom get relegated to second place. Jesus' admonition to seek first the kingdom is central to what it means to build kingdom churches.

Of course, kingdom churches are being built all over the earth right now in every nation—naturally, organically, and gracefully. It seems that in the West we struggle a bit more with this simple concept of building kingdom churches. But here is a key: We don't have to know all the answers to make the decision to become a builder. Many have abandoned their building role, opting to be only a blesser, because building has been confusing and disheartening. Beloved, we must together help accelerate the radical transition the Western Bride is going through! She must see with new eyes--the eyes of her Beloved. God is raising up voices, friends of the Bridegroom, for such a time as this, to help His Bride in the West awaken, see, bless, and build.

FROM THE CAVE TO THE CASTLE

God has given me a unique, ongoing burden for the kinds of people I mentioned at the beginning of this chapter. I call them cave-dwellers. This is not a negative or derogatory term. It is a term of respect. I happen to love the prophets, the rebels, and the iconoclasts. I understand and sympathize with those who have opted out of the organized church and who are waiting in the shadows, wondering if it will ever be safe to come out of the cave again. I long to see those stuck in caves restored to their proper place in the castle.

David was the rightful king of Israel, but His installation as king was delayed for quite some time by a coup involving his son Absalom and a bunch of Absalom's friends. David ended up having to run for his life, humiliating himself in the process and landing in a cave, hiding, sulking, and waiting. Fortunately for David, there were some men—some very mighty men—who were also in David's shoes. In fact, not only were they displaced like David, but they had some additional issues:

> "Everyone who was in distress, and everyone who was in debt, and everyone who was discontented gathered to him [ie, David]; and he became captain over them. Now there were about four hundred men with him."
> --1 Sam. 22:2

These mighty men had great potential! They were destined for greatness. But they were not walking in their destiny. They were living far short of their potential. It was not God's plan to have them live in the cave forever. The cave was a temporary home for those destined for the castle. A people of royalty were occupying the dark, damp cave of Adullam. These were people designed for the light and joy and freedom and space of the castle. They were called to be mighty champions *and* to live like royalty at the same time! To be living in the 'institution' of the castle didn't make them any less mighty! It just made them more favored and blessed while being mighty!

This is God's heart for the millions of believers who made the exodus out of the local church. The Father is calling His people back home. It is safe to come home. It is time to come home. Your gifts, your wisdom, your experience, and your heart are needed and wanted. While you've been away, God has been messing with His church, aligning, tweaking, rebuking, humbling, and preparing her. The Church (collective) is ready for the church (individual) to come home. It's time for a homecoming party for the scattered parts of the church!

And as the whole church comes home, we will be ready to really build something together.

BUILDING LIKE A CHEF

So, then, how do we build? And what do we build? One of the most common and compelling questions for those of us on the journey of discovery into a new kind of church is, "So, what's it going to look like?" If God is really bringing great change to His church in the West, how will things be different? This is a fair question—and a vital one. Revelation is progressive, and because it always begins with prophetic groaning, for years we've mostly had dissatisfaction and questions. But knowing that something is wrong is only the beginning. At some point, someone has to begin forging the path that goes beyond endlessly articulating the problem. We need *solutions*! It really is time for some answers.

As I've prayed about solutions over the past several years, I have repeatedly heard the Lord speak to my heart a very profound truth: "It's about a recipe."

For those of you with cable or satellite TV, perhaps you've noticed the increasing number of food shows on television these days. Most of these food shows ask chefs to take familiar ingredients and prepare them in fresh ways to create a completely different tasting dish. Beloved, I believe God is prophesying to the church through secular media once again—in this case, food shows! And He is saying, "Church, it's time for a new recipe."

A recipe is defined as 'a set of directions with a list of ingredients for making or preparing something' and 'a means to a desired end.' As God began speaking to me about a recipe, I understood Him to mean that all of the ingredients for building kingdom churches are already in the earth. A recipe combines familiar ingredients. A chef takes those ingredients and puts them together in fresh ways so as to create a brand new dish that tastes delicious. And I believe God is asking us and inviting us to combine His kingdom ingredients in different amounts and in different ways to create a fresh expression of church life in the West that is delicious to this generation.

This is the job of a new generation of church planters and builders, along with all of God's people. We've all been called to build kingdom churches with a fresh, new recipe that combines Scriptural ingredients in new amounts and in new ways so as to create a new expression of church. Some folks are under the false notion that in order to have a fresh expression of community, God is trying to get us to discard ingredients, such as leadership, gatherings, financial giving, worship leaders, and so on. But as we will see in other chapters, these ingredients are Biblical. God is not trying to get us to *discard* Biblical ingredients, but He does want to *change the ratios* of certain ingredients so everything tastes better! Rather than two cups of leadership, for example, what if we had just two tablespoons? How would that change the taste of a dish?

God is releasing understanding and strategy for new kinds of churches. At first glance, these kingdom churches will look mostly familiar to the casual observer, because there will be familiar ingredients of prayer, gatherings, leadership, outreach, worship, and so on. But the underlying 'cooking' philosophy, the amount of the ingredients, how they're combined, and what is done with them will surely be different. This book is an attempt to articulate some of these ingredients and how to apportion them in a fresh way.

PREPARING OUR HEARTS TO BUILD

In order to become a builder, it is vital to receive a fresh download of motivation from God Himself. We need to be motivated by God to build, lest we become disillusioned or weary in the process. Our motives matter, because motivation matters.

Scripture makes it clear that our motives are examined and tested by the Lord. Godly motivation is at the core of building kingdom churches and all other ministry. People with wrong motives can't build right churches-- no matter how successful they may look on the outside. In gathering materials for Solomon to build the temple, David spoke aloud about his motivation and the process by which God examines us:

> "I know, my God, that you test the heart and are pleased with integrity."
> --1 Chronicles 29:17

We cannot get free of false motivations by focusing on them. We can only become free as we have a greater motivation that pales lesser ones. Jesus explained this principle in John 5:44:

> "How can you believe, when you receive glory from one another and you do not seek the glory that is from the one and only God?" (NASB)

A continual pursuit of the glory of God must become our chief motivation and goal in life. And where is the glory of God found? Is it at the next conference we hope to attend? Will we find the glory at the next worship night, or with that special guest speaker? 2 Corinthians 4:6 tells us the answer. The glory of God is found **in the face of Jesus Christ**. As we look at Him, as we gaze upon Him, we will find our motivation purified and increasing. It's all about Jesus! He is our goal, our motivation, and our desire.

REMOVING EVERY HINDRANCE

When we find ourselves lacking motivation, often there are hindrances blocking our hearts and keeping us from soaring with godly fire. It is no coincidence that John the Baptist was referred to by Jesus as a 'burning and shining light' who had a primary ministry of removing hindrances. When we get rid of false idols, we allow our hearts to come into alignment again with the very heart of God.

In Ezekiel 16, the prophet confronts the people with three dominant sins:

> "Now this was the sin of your sister Sodom: She and her daughters were arrogant, overfed, and unconcerned; they did not help the poor and needy."
> --Ezekiel 16:49

Because the people of Sodom lacked true kingdom motivation, they became arrogant, overfed, and unconcerned. Tragically, this is the state we find much of the church in today. Thank God that there is an antidote for this three-part poison. If you are lacking in motivation, you came to the right chapter.

The antidote for arrogance is *humility*, for being overfed is *hunger*, and for being unconcerned is *holiness*. There is a doorway standing open in heaven (Rev. 4:1), but it is small and low, entered on our knees. On the other side of this doorway is revival, revolution, unspeakable joy, and glory. All the resources of heaven are on the other side of this doorway. But the only people that will fit through this doorway are the ones who are marked by these three traits--humility, hunger, and holiness. These are the riches of revival.

Humility. There is an invitation to humility happening in the church in the West. For years, we've thought of ourselves more highly than we ought. While other parts of the world have been experiencing great revival, God has bypassed much of the church in the West in order to reveal to us where we're really at and to provoke us to jealousy. Humility attracts God's presence and releases God's promises in our lives. Francis Frangipane says that humility is the armor of heaven. It is the dividing line between faith and presumption. It keeps us safe from the many difficulties associated with arrogance and pride. Humility is much more profound than honesty about our problems or looking at the ground when we speak. It's about dependency and childlike trust, and it doesn't contain a whiff of self-righteousness or defensiveness. Jesus declared Himself to be humble of heart (Mt. 11:28-30). This is where God is taking the church, because humility is absolutely essential in order to walk in the kind of power and authority God desires to release in His church.

"God resists the proud but gives grace to the humble." --James 4:6

Hunger. There is also an invitation to hunger happening in the church. Desire for God's Person, His Presence, His provision and His power are growing in this hour. Did you know that hunger in our culture is actually a miracle? It's one thing to be hungry when you're in the middle of the desert and you don't own anything but the clothes on your back. You don't know where you're going, where your next meal is coming from, and you're like a dependent child. This can create hunger! People who live in countries where food and basic necessities are in short supply are prone to understand their need for God! But much of the West is a land of abundance. Where I live, in the Central Coast of California, with beautiful weather, vineyards, orchards, ranches, farms, retirement accounts, nice vehicles, nice church buildings, tidy sermons, sweet worship, great sound systems, good friends, great soccer teams for our kids, fun vacations, coffee shops and convenience stores just for us...where does hunger fit with that? *Sustained hunger is a miracle here in the West.* But God is granting it as a gift to those who will embrace hunger and all that it means.

"Blessed are those who hunger and thirst for righteousness,
for they shall be filled." --Mt. 5:8

Holiness. There is a gracious invitation to holiness in the church in the West. This is good news for every sincere believer who has felt stuck in patterns of sinful impurity. God is extending great grace for the Bride is to "make herself ready" for the wedding feast of the Lamb. Holiness is a choice made by each believer, empowered by God's grace. Psalm 29:2 says, "Worship the LORD in the beauty of holiness." It is as we engage this beautiful God that we find issues of holiness easier to walk out. Millions of believers are now rediscovering or discovering for the first time the majestic beauty of the Lord Jesus Christ and the deep love of the Father. The result is great freedom from sinful patterns that previously bound them. The definition of holiness is "being pure in heart and life, set apart for God's purpose." Holiness means becoming more like Jesus and being wholly given to God as His very own possession. As we rest in His ability to bring about holiness in our lives, we experience the victory that was already purchased for us long ago.

"I, the Lord, am holy, and I make you holy." --Lev. 21:8 (NLT)

In the following chapters, we will review more strategic elements of building kingdom churches, but none of it makes any sense if our hearts don't own kingdom motivation. God is raising up a people with the right heart and the right motivation. His eyes are looking throughout the earth for those wholehearted, kingdom people filled with humility, hunger, and holiness. My prayer is that you and I will cultivate kingdom motivation through a life of prayer filled with intimacy with God. Let's be a generation postured before the throne of God so that He can have access to our hearts and change us from glory to glory.

MAKE ROOM FOR THE BUILDERS!

The Holy Spirit is recruiting a new generation of builders! The winds of change are blowing. And in order for something new to live, often something old needs to give. As God is changing the church, we cannot remain smug and comfortable and also be filled with the adventure of the journey. Whether we're in the church or out, we cannot hide in the cave or cling to the railings of our pews so tightly and also have revolution. Something is going to have to go for new life to come. My vote is that we lay down our preconceived notions of church life and allow the Holy Spirit to come and breathe fresh wind in our sails.

I love what Paul says in 1 Cor. 1:18-20, expressed so well in *The Message* paraphrase:

"The Message that points to Christ on the Cross seems like sheer silliness to those hell-bent on destruction, but for those on the way of salvation it makes

perfect sense. This is the way God works, and most powerfully as it turns out. It's written, 'I'll turn conventional wisdom on its head, and I'll expose so-called experts as crackpots.' So where can you find someone truly wise, truly educated, truly intelligent in this day and age? Hasn't God exposed it all as pretentious nonsense?"

Jesus is turning our conventional wisdom and understanding about His church on its head. Much of the way we've been doing church is finally being exposed as pretentious nonsense. It *is* going to change. Little children will lead us. The last will be first. Every mountain will be brought low, and every valley raised up. Ego will be banished. Anointing will increase. Simplicity and gladness of heart will rule our gatherings. God's heart for His church, the strategic ways of God in relation to the church, the way Jesus builds His church, it will all be revealed to us, and it will make perfect sense if we'll just let go of the advice of so-called experts and humbly seek Him for a fresh expression of missional community. It is time for fresh, new dialogues among hungry believers in the West that result in building kingdom churches.

We need to hear from heaven. And in order to do that, we need to make room for change. And we need to become kingdom builders. Are you ready?

Father, thank You for bringing change to Your people! We ask You to raise up kingdom churches throughout the West. Would you grant revelation to see and grace to embrace this shift that you are bringing about? We trust You to lead us and to shape us into the people You want us to be and to transform us into effective kingdom builders. In Jesus' name, Amen.

Chapter Seven
Kingdom LEADERSHIP

"Then I heard a loud voice in heaven say: 'Now have come the salvation
and the power and the *kingdom* of our God, and the *authority* of his Christ...'"
--Rev. 1:6

Because kingdom churches are filled with powerful people, the need for
and purpose of government, authority, and leadership can be a bit
unclear. Kingdom churches thrive in environments of freedom, so issues
of control often associated with church leadership can be challenging to
reconcile with a liberated kingdom people.

For us to function as kingdom priests who work together as builders, it is
essential that we understand and walk in God's authority in human
relationships. The two are linked. The kingdom of God is advanced
through the authority of Christ. Jesus referenced this principle of
kingdom authority in the Great Commission:

"All authority in heaven and on earth has been given to me.
Therefore go and make disciples of all nations..."
--Mt. 28:18-19

The kingdom activities mentioned in the Great Commission of going to
the nations, making disciples, baptizing, and teaching are directly linked
to the complete authority of Jesus extended to us. As kingdom priests,
we have been authorized and credentialed by God to advance His
kingdom. But walking in God's authority *as individuals* is one thing.
Learning how to walk in God's authority *together* means that we need to
take a fresh look at *authority*, *government*, and *leadership* in kingdom
churches. So let's take a look at each of these.

TYPES OF AUTHORITY

There are three types of authority revealed in the Scriptures that all play a part in the building process. They are: *spiritual* authority, *relational* authority, and *delegated* authority. Each of these kinds of authority serves a unique purpose and must be functioning in any local church. When exercised rightly and used in proper proportion, they unlock the church to move forward and to function in kingdom rhythm.

Spiritual Authority

As believers, we have authority. This is sometimes called 'positional' authority. Because we belong to Christ, seated with Christ in heavenly places, and indwelt by the Holy Spirit, we carry God-given internal, resident authority. Before coming to Christ, we were people without identity and place (1 Pet. 2:10). Now, having been adopted into God's family as His own dear children (1 Jn. 3:1), we have become royalty! (1 Pet. 2:9). As His children, we are His heirs (Rom. 8:17) who carry a unique place of privilege and position. Whatever we need to do, He provides the power and wisdom we need to get it done (1 Cor. 1:24). Wherever we need to go, He goes with us, because we are His representatives (2 Cor. 5:20). When we invoke the Name of Jesus in prayer according to God's will, results happen! Our prayers are answered as though Jesus prayed, and the enemy is defeated (Jn. 14:14; Rev. 12:11).

The significant authority God gives each believer is our primary type of authority and ought to be the type of authority in the church that is most encouraged and exercised. This authority is equally accessible by every Christian. It is what we need in order to obey Scripture. As every believer in the church understands and walks in this authority, there is great joy and freedom in the body and great effectiveness in ministry.

In years past, ministry schools focused their training on the *task* to be done—ie, training evangelists to win the lost, training prophets to prophesy, etc. Today, it is encouraging to see that some of the most successful training schools being raised up in our generation are those that spend much of their early training time helping believers understand their identity and authority as sons and daughters. No wonder such schools are growing. It is another sign that God is building kingdom people with a new understanding of their authority as priests.

While every believer walks equally in the bestowed, *positional* authority gained through our relationship with the Person of Christ, some believers carry more significant *spiritual* authority than others. All of God's authority is ultimately spiritual, but spiritual authority comes from believers' intimacy with God, their level of obedience, and the resulting grace released by God. This authority might also be called *anointing*. It is not dependent on a position in the church, because it comes straight from heaven. It gives force and credibility to those who walk in it. We notice it, for example, when we gravitate to certain people when asking for prayer. We know that they walk in something that will strengthen our heart. We know that their prayers will be answered. We know that they have significant spiritual authority. They really walk in the authority of the believer by living lives of intimacy with God and obedience to the Holy Spirit that releases the anointing of spiritual authority.

When Jesus spoke, the crowds marveled at His spiritual authority that they could tangibly feel accompanying His words (Matt. 7:28-29). It had nothing to do with his position as a spiritual teacher or rabbi in Israel, because there were many religious leaders teaching the people. Jesus stood out because a tangible authority went out with His words. When Peter and John stood boldly before the priests and the Sadducees and proclaimed the gospel, the religious leaders "took note" that these men had been with Jesus (Acts 4:13). The Greek word for "took note" is *epiginosko*, a compound word meaning to really know through experience. It was tangibly evident that these men carried an authority the religious leaders could not refute. Paul the apostle repeatedly claimed he had received spiritual authority directly from the Lord (2 Cor. 13:10; 1 Tim. 4:2). This heaven-sent authority was related to Paul's ministry function and not simply his role as a believer who was part of God's family. It was not released through elders or any other church leadership. Rather, it is released through *intimacy* and *obedience*.

Relational Authority
Relational authority is the grace and permission we give to each other to speak into our lives. It is founded on trust and respect. We speak of 'history' with someone, and we know they have a proven track record that makes us feel safe. This relational authority is developed over time as we serve and care for each other. Someone famously said, "People don't care how much you know until they know how much you care." When I know that you care about me, I can more freely share my heart and invite you to speak into my life.

Relational authority is appealed to and granted because of *relational love*. Even though Paul was an apostle with great authority himself, we see at times that he appealed simply to the relational love he shared with others:

"We have spoken freely to you, Corinthians, and opened wide our hearts also.
We are not withholding our affection from you,
but you are withholding yours from us. As a fair exchange--
I speak as to my children--open wide your hearts also." --2 Cor. 6:11-13

Delegated Authority
Authority given by God to individuals through a human chain-of-command is called delegated authority. Scripture states that all delegated authority originates with God, regardless of whether or not people use delegated authority in a right way. In Rom. 13:1 and 1 Pet. 2:13, this delegated authority is called 'governing' or 'institutional' authority, because it relates to government, law enforcement, and the court system. To rebel against this delegated authority is to rebel against God (Rom. 13:2). We are called to submit to such authority for the Lord's sake (1 Pet. 2:13).

Delegated authority is also given in the church. This is the point of church leadership, elders, etc. There are differing opinions on who should have authority in the church and how much, but one thing is certain: delegated, structural authority has been grossly over-emphasized in the church, and the authority of the believer, spiritual authority, and relational authority have all been underemphasized and underappreciated.

AUTHORITY IN PROPORTION

So how does all this relate to kingdom churches? Well, let's think about a financial illustration. When discussing investments, many financial advisors use a pyramid to illustrate wise investing. They encourage investors to wisely distribute their investments by putting the largest sums of money in the most secure investments, represented by the largest portion of a triangle at the base. Slightly more risky investments, with a potentially higher yield, are represented by a smaller portion of the pyramid in a narrower, middle section of the triangle. And the smallest, top area of the triangle represents the riskiest but potentially most rewarding investments.

Authority in the church works much the same way, as illustrated in the following triangles. Fig. A represents the way we are meant to think about authority. The large foundation and base is the spiritual authority of the believer. This levels the playing field, deemphasizes position and title, keeps our Christianity based in faith rather than subjectivity, and makes the promises of God equally accessible to every believer. It is the endorsement of our credibility by the Holy Spirit, who puts authority on our words and deeds through Christ. He 'backs up our act.' Just above that in the same part of the triangle is relational authority that is cultivated horizontally in relationship with people. And finally, like those riskier but potentially rewarding investments, delegated authority in the church has a small, powerful role to play. Delegated authority released well can help the heart of individual believers to soar and reach their full potential in Christ. But handled poorly through overemphasis, delegated authority can cause difficulty and injury.

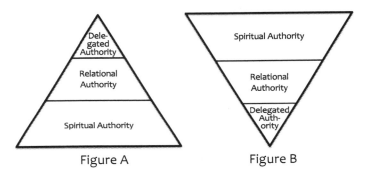

Figure A   Figure B

This is the problem with the upside down triangle in Fig. B. It attempts to make delegated authority the foundation of the church. Delegated authority is a necessary ingredient but a poor foundation. Fig. B illustrates how the church has typically handled authority. In many churches, we have continually preached submission to delegated authority in the church, while failing to really honor the authority of the believer and recognize spiritual authority in people who may not have a particular position in the church. This has made the church unstable, teetering on human authority rather on than the foundation of God's authority flowing through every believer.

The subject of delegated authority has become a sensitive issue for many in the West. A large percentage of Western believers have stories to tell of how they have been dominated or abused by church leadership. Of course, many church leaders have their own stories about how they have been undermined, manipulated, or verbally assaulted by church members who have been flaky, unkind, or divisive! The bottom line is that delegated authority has become a dividing line in the church, largely due to its disproportionate use. Unfortunately, the net result is that even the word 'authority' as it relates to human beings now carries negative connotations for many in the church. A growing number of Christians believe authority is bad. Sadly, many believers have come to "despise authority" (2 Pet. 2:10), even though authority is given by God to humanity as a gift for our good (Rom. 12:8; 13:1-2).

I once received a gentle rebuke from a godly saint who told me that, because of hurts in my past, I perceived authority as bad. This man urged me to repent. As I thought about his comment to me, I realized that in my past I had observed church leaders who had mishandled God's authority. Somewhere along the line I made the unspoken, internal decision that because I didn't want to abuse authority the way I had seen it done, I would avoid using delegated authority. In my mind, it only injured people. I had judged and condemned something that God gave to the church as a gift. Many Western Christians have also made this same unfortunate judgment.

Understanding how authority works in kingdom churches is key to building the kinds of churches that empower rather than disable. Adjusting the proportions of how authority is used in the church will strengthen the members of individual churches while helping leaders think about ways to empower people that don't resort to control.

TYPES OF GOVERNMENT

Government is another one of those hot potatoes! Like the word 'authority' in churches, church government has few avid supporters and a growing number of detractors. Typical definitions of the word really don't help, either. In general, government is (1) *a group of people who have the power to make and enforce laws*; or (2) *a type of political system*; or (3) *the management or control of something*. Power...politics...control. None of those choices sound like the kind of dynamic that ought to be operating in a vibrant kingdom body of believers!

It would be much easier to simply not deal with church government. In fact, as we've already discussed, a growing number of believers are opting out of any organized church experience. In doing so, they are answering the governmental question. For them, there is none! But part of the role of the church is to govern, and government is a gift to the church.

"If a man's gift is...leadership, let him govern diligently." --Rom. 12:6, 8

113

The Greek word here is 'proistemi', which means to stand before (in rank), to preside, maintain, be over, to rule. This implies significant authority. The word for diligently is 'with speed; eagerly; earnestly.' According to the New Testament, the role of governmental leadership is not mere facilitation or just being one of the brothers. It involves focused, earnest, diligent leadership. Church leaders are given specific charges, such as directing the affairs of the church (1 Tim. 5:17). The spirit and manner in which this government is expressed is key. In spite of potential misuse, godly government is God's gift to the church. Let's take a moment to look at the different types of government: *God's government, self-government, brotherly government,* and *fatherly government.*

God's Government

All government starts and ends with God. Isaiah 9:6 makes this abundantly clear:

> "...the government will be on *his* shoulders." --Isa. 9:6

God is able and willing to govern His people. And even when there is human government, we must learn to see 'the God behind the man.' God is governing in His power, through people and sometimes in spite of people. The heart of God's people must always be for the direct government of God in our lives. Sons and daughters understand this. Romans 8 tells us that those who are led by the Spirit are sons. As we think about government in kingdom churches, we must always start with the idea that God can and will govern His people.

> "All the elders of Israel gathered together and came to Samuel at Ramah. They said to him, '...now appoint a king to lead us, such as all the other nations have.' But when they said, 'Give us a king to lead us,' this displeased Samuel; so he prayed to the LORD. And the LORD told him: 'Listen to all that the people are saying to you; it is not you they have rejected, but they have rejected me as their king.'" --1 Samuel 8:4-7

Many people mistakenly think that this text proves that God doesn't want human government. But there is a bigger issue going on. It was the rejection of His Person that grieved God's heart. God had previously appointed judges in the land, and He was fine with this expression of human government alongside His own. People who live under God's government can also live within the government of the land (cf. Rom.

13:1ff). It is when our hearts long to replace God's direct government with human government that God is grieved.

God shares His desire for direct government in Psalm 32:

> "I will instruct you and teach you in the way you should go; I will counsel you and watch over you. Do not be like the horse or the mule, which have no understanding but must be controlled by bit and bridle or they will not come to you." --Ps. 32:8-9

Clearly, a mediated relationship of control is not God's heart or first choice for His people. Only through a lack of understanding does the church chomp down on a bit and a bridle. We are designed for His gentle voice to lead us, not external controls. Circumstances, extra incentives of the Holy Spirit, and additional input from church leaders beyond what should normally be needed can all become God-allowed bits and bridles in our lives.

God is building a people who, in the midst of proper human administration, keep their eyes fixed squarely on Jesus Christ. They know who their King is, and they are therefore able, for the Lord's sake, to submit themselves to every God-given form of government among men (1 Pet. 2:13). As we focus on the kingdom, we will see the church with peripheral vision, and as we focus on Jesus, we will see church leaders with peripheral vision as well. This is not disrespectful but appropriate and right.

Church leaders must repent for not recognizing God's government working *through* them and sometimes *in spite of* them. The plantation mentality operating in many churches in the West dictates that everything must pass beneath the head leader and/or board. Healthy people who do not have a need to control anyone make the best leaders. Their egos do not demand the church to focus on them. They continually point people to God and refuse to be a King in anyone else's life. Decision-making is done on their knees, in the fear of God.

In the book of Judges, Abimilech had a desire for leadership that was unhealthy, manipulative, and dangerous. He not only sought to be a kingly leader, but he also rose up against the legitimate, established authority and killed 70 of his brothers out of competitive insecurity. But there were 71 brothers, and the youngest brother, Jotham, hid from his older half-brother Abimelech to avoid being slaughtered. Later, Jotham stood before all the people and told a parable to the citizens of Shechem and Beth Millo to illustrate the difference between good leaders and ambitious ones. In Jotham's parable recorded in Judges 9, he likened people to trees and healthy leaders to olive trees, fig trees, and grapevines--all fruitful in their own right. But those leaders who are insecure, ambitious, controlling, and willing to have others bow before them he likened to a thornbush:

> "One day the trees went out to anoint a king for themselves. They said to the olive tree, 'Be our king.' But the olive tree answered, 'Should I give up my oil, by which both gods and men are honored, to hold sway over the trees?' Next, the trees said to the fig tree, 'Come and be our king.' But the fig tree replied, 'Should I give up my fruit, so good and sweet, to hold sway over the trees?' Then the trees said to the vine, 'Come and be our king.' But the vine answered, 'Should I give up my wine, which cheers both gods and men, to hold sway over the trees?' Finally all the trees said to the thornbush, 'Come and be our king.' The thornbush said to the trees, 'If you really want to anoint me king over you, come and take refuge in my shade; but if not, then let fire come out of the thornbush and consume the cedars of Lebanon!'" --Judges 9:8-15

Healthy leaders have no desire to "hold sway" over others, but ambitious leaders create dependency on themselves ("come take refuge in my shade"). In kingdom churches, God is truly in charge as the only King and Jesus really is the Head of the Church. Kingdom leaders are unwilling to become kings in anyone else's lives. Without a trace of false humility, they point people to Jesus.

God gives authority to people in the church to bring government and leadership, all the while expecting them to have the right heart posture of humility that would never usurp the place in people's lives reserved for God alone. This is a stewardship and an entrustment given to leaders to walk in the government of God without becoming a king over people. Jesus said that we should let people see our good works in such a way that they would glorify our Father in heaven. It's not that our good works are unseen. People will see leaders, but they will see Jesus beyond them. Leaders lead, but they lead veiled behind the government of God.

John the Baptist understood this dynamic when he called himself "a friend of the bridegroom." He wasn't personally married to the bride or trying to get anything from her. He was an ally of the authentic Bridegroom and always acted in a manner that pointed people to Jesus.

At one point, John even said, "He must become greater and greater, and I must become less and less" (John 3:30). This is the heart posture that allows God's government to flow in and through human vessels freely and without agenda or control.

Self-Government

The first human realm of functional authority within God's government is self-government. Self-government means that every Christian is regulated by the Holy Spirit through the fruit of self-control (Gal. 5:23). This is a restoration of the direct, unmediated relationship God enjoyed with Adam and Eve in the garden before the fall. It is available to God's sons and daughters who are indwelt by the Holy Spirit and who follow His inclinations.

When Paul was concerned about whether or not he would be able to walk in integrity before God and man, he didn't first go to his pastor for counsel. Nor did he go to his small group and confess his sins, relying on his small group leader to tell him what to do. While both of these are fine to do at the right time, we are addressing the priority of self-government over other forms of human government in the church. Paul took personal responsibility to self-govern His life:

> "...I do not fight like a man beating the air. No, I beat my body and make it my slave so that after I have preached to others, I myself will not be disqualified for the prize." --1 Cor. 9:26-27

For years, Western culture has been developing a culture of victimization and blame-shifting. In short, this allows believers to bypass self-government and instead blame the church for our own lack of governing. Many have created a codependent relationship with church leadership. By contrast, the Apostle Paul tapped into the internal power of God through the Holy Spirit and placed His flesh in subjection to the Holy Spirit inside of him. Because we live under the New Covenant and the Holy Spirit dwells within every believer, we have every resource in heaven we need to walk in self- government. It is not the church's job to govern individuals in these ways. This is the privilege and responsibility of each individual believer. We are called to become self-feeders in God's Word, to be individuals of prayer and the presence of God, to initiate our fellowship and follow-up needs, and to minister with His authority. We have the power of God to govern and control ourselves in the Holy Spirit!

Brotherly Government

When I was being trained in church growth principles, the local church was essentially likened to a fish tank. Those leaders with large, beautiful 250-gallon fish tanks would gather a bunch of local pastors with 10- and 20-gallon fish tanks. There, we would learn how to break the 20-gallon "growth" barrier. We would find out that in order to break the 20-gallon growth barrier, we needed to have a better filtration system, more interesting rocks, some fish that would serve full-time to clean and care for the tank, and so on. Like thousands of other pastors in North America, I was under the assumption that my goal was to get a bigger and bigger fish tank. What I didn't realize at that time was that whether the fish tank was 20 gallons or 250 gallons, it was still just a fish tank, with glass walls and a glass ceiling. We've heard of the glass ceiling in business. Most churches are not aware of the glass ceiling (and glass walls) that exist in their thinking, structure, attitudes, and views towards the members of the church. Members of churches can never experience the freedom of the kingdom when they're in a fish tank.

Then I came to realize that the context of the church was never meant to be in a fish tank at all. It was meant to be in an ocean! In the ocean, there are endless possibilities and many significant dangers. But there are no walls and no glass ceilings. There is freedom to swim and play and explore! Discovery is returned to the fish, and the joy of 'fish without walls' is experienced!

How you handle yourself isn't quite so important when you're in the fish tank. Everything is governed for you. You can be rebellious and swim over in the corner if you want, but ultimately, the fish tank manager will make sure you get your food and the tank is cleaned. But how different it is in the ocean! There, choosing to be independent could cost you your life! Survival and well-being are often found in schools. Fish voluntarily swim together out of instinct because they know it is the best way for them to survive and to thrive (and it's more fun!).

This is why brotherly government, or voluntary mutual submission, is a superior form of government to top-down forms of control. The wineskin of the past provided safety and predictability, but with limited experience, surprise, and discovery. Kingdom churches are full of endless possibilities because the people are in the ocean, not a tank. They understand and gladly yield to mutual submission and relational accountability. It is vital for the health of the church, and it originates from the place of love, respect, and care for one another.

"They are defying all of Caesar's decrees, saying that
there is another king, *one* called Jesus." --Acts 17:7

Church government has often been about submission to a leader, a board, and/or a staff who were responsible for you. In kingdom churches, we submit to one another out of reverence for Christ. Leaders in kingdom churches are approachable and correctable along with everyone else. While we give honor to whom honor is due, and we lavish love on one another because of Christ, we don't treat anyone like a king...except Jesus.

Fatherly Government

With God's government, self-government, and brotherly government in place, we can now turn our attention to spiritual fathers and mothers. The church is a family, and dad and mom lead the family. I love what my friends and mentors Kris Vallotton and Paul Manwaring teach in this regard. If the church gathers around doctrine, it divides over disagreement. But if the church gathers around fathers, a family can handle disagreements and still stay strong together. God is building kingdom churches around fathers and families.

People come to churches with all kinds of authority issues. For them, church has meant hoops to jump through and men to cower before. There has been an emphasis on structure, authority, submission, and titles, which lends itself toward the fear of man, a man-pleasing spirit, favoritism, jealousy, and all kinds of accompanying evil and problems. Unfortunately, the church often hasn't driven out the orphan spirit but strengthened it.

Wherever church government is mingled with ambition, we find leaders who value members primarily for how they contribute to the church's vision. But when true spiritual fathers (and mothers) lead spiritual families, we see a culture of celebration, where my victory is your victory, and your success is my success.

When true spiritual fathers lead churches, the orphan spirit is driven out, and people actually begin to think and act like sons and daughters. There is safety, laughter, exploration, forgiveness, and freedom to try and fail. This is really the heart of the apostolic reformation that has been taking place in the church in recent years. Psalm 68:6 tells us that God sets the individual into family. And families have government—relational government.

LEADERSHIP LESSONS FOR THE LOCAL CHURCH

With these principles of authority and government in mind, we turn now to the practical aspects of church leadership. What does all this mean for the local church? How does leadership work in kingdom churches? Who is meant to lead kingdom churches? And what does that look like on a practical level?

Volumes and volumes have been written about church leadership. There is excellent material available on how to be a great leader, written by those in the world and in the church. My goal in this chapter isn't to duplicate those efforts. This section has more to do with a birds-eye view of what the New Testament says about church leadership and then looking at how that perspective can help us build kingdom churches.

The New Testament presents two categories of church leadership: those with authority to *oversee*, and those with authority to *equip*, as shown in the following chart:

Authority To OVERSEE	Scriptural Support	Authority To EQUIP	Scriptural Support
Apostles	1 Cor. 12:28-30	Apostles Prophets Evangelists Pastors Teachers	Eph. 4:11-12
Elders	Acts 20:28; 1 Tim. 3:1-2, 5:17; 1 Pet. 5:1-3		
Leaders	1 Cor. 12:28-30; Heb. 13:17; Acts 6:1-7; 1 Tim. 3:8-15		

Leaders Who Oversee

A survey of the New Testament will bear out the fact that all Scriptural references to church rule have to do with the three leadership categories of apostles, elders, and leaders. In fact, all three of these groups of overseers are listed in Acts 15 (cf. v. 1, 2, 4, 6, 22-23). Note that Judas and Silas are leaders who also happen to be prophets. Their prophetic gift did not automatically qualify them as leaders. Leaders are more like *generalists* who are gifted by God to oversee all aspects of a particular area of ministry.

Apostles. Apostles are sent by God with unique authority to establish churches, to set in place the foundational elements of a given church, to appoint elders, to exercise discipline, to impart gifts, and, depending on the arrangement of the local church, to exercise apostolic oversight over a church or group of churches in a geography or network. Usually for at least part of their ministry, apostles establish churches and then move on, but it is also Biblical and appropriate as the Lord directs for apostles to remain as primary leaders in a local or city church, such as James in the Jerusalem church.

Elders. Elders have authority to watch over and shepherd the flock, to teach, to model the Christian life, and to exercise rule in the form of counsel, correction, and even direction of the overall body. Elders always function in a plurality and are the primary governing body in a local church.

Leaders. Leaders are those who exercise oversight of and provide direction for ministry arenas and tasks. Apostles and elders are also leaders, but not all leaders are apostles and elders, as there are other kinds of leaders. 'Leaders' is an all-purpose term to describe all who have delegated authority to oversee ministries.

Leaders Who Equip

Ephesians 4:11 identifies five equipping roles in the church: apostles, prophets, evangelists, pastors, and teachers. While there are many gifts listed in 1 Corinthians 12, Romans 12, 1 Peter 4 and so on, the gifts listed in Ephesians 4 describe five functional roles for equippers in the body of Christ. These five kinds of gifts have authority to equip and build up the church and are to be recognized and honored as having such authority. This set of ministry functions, often referred to as the 'five-fold', comprise a specific equipping arena both in local churches and also in the larger body of Christ. Equippers are more like *specialists* gifted by God to train, model, and impart.

Gift Mix. While these distinctions of governing and equipping are important for developing a Biblical paradigm for kingdom leadership, the reality is that most of God's people have been given more than one gift or talent. The example given above is about Judas and Silas. Someone who is a prophet may or may not have also been given the gift of leadership. In Acts 15, Judas and Silas were referenced first as leaders

(15:22) and then later as prophets (15:32). Here we see *gift mixes*, where people operate in multiple roles based on their gifts.

DEFINING APOSTOLIC LEADERSHIP

At various times in church history, God has breathed on truths in the Scriptures in a pronounced way. His ability to highlight what has always been there causes us to rediscover important revelation that we had previously not understood properly. Jesus came to earth in what Paul terms "the fullness of time" (Gal. 4:4). In similar fashion, God is releasing in the Western church a fresh revelation of New Testament roles during this time before the return of Christ. In particular, there is currently increased revelation and understanding on the subject of apostolic leadership.

As we discuss apostolic leadership, we are looking for the Biblical truths that are applicable today and not solely reserved for the Lamb's twelve (Rev. 21:14). These specially selected men had unique authority and a unique call that cannot be duplicated. However, there are apostles today with a small 'a', and God desires to release encouragement to His entire church to become apostolic in its nature and expression. The word itself, 'apostle,' simply means sent one. God desires all believers to be apostolic or missional in our orientation, because according to Matthew 28:18-20, we have all been sent! Because apostolic leadership is essential to build kingdom churches, it is very helpful to understand and embrace the role of apostles today and the nature of apostolic ministry.

More and more is being revealed and written about apostolic leadership, because God is allowing us to understand all leadership through apostolic lenses. For numerous reasons, I believe it is essential that we come into a place of real understanding about what it means to be apostolic and how this matters in the churches that we build. To that end, I want to bring definition to apostolic leadership by boiling things down to just a few categories. Here are three defining aspects of apostolic leadership: (1) the *evidence* of apostolic ministry; (2) the *activity* of apostolic ministry; and (3) the *heart* of apostolic ministry.

The Evidence Of Apostolic Ministry

When we're wondering what is truly apostolic and what is simply a word on a business card, we must see clear evidence or proofs of apostolic ministry. The activity and heart of apostolic ministry, which we will look at in a moment, are also evidences in a broad sense. But there ought to be three particular evidences accompanying ministry today that is apostolic or claims to be. Jesus commends those who understand His requirements for apostleship and then judge accurately by those standards (Rev. 2:2). Some teach that there are dozens of different kinds of apostles and prophets. This teaching has a tendency to greatly broaden and unnecessarily complicate the terms and their definitions. I don't know if the Scriptures support these complex definitions or not. Personally, I believe God defines His terms in simple, clear, and understandable ways. When it comes to the evidence of apostolic ministry, I believe all three of the following evidences must be present in order for us to be accurate when we call someone an apostle.

New Believers. Paul wrote to the church in Rome that he was given grace to be an apostle "to call people from among all the Gentiles to the obedience that comes from faith" (Rom. 1:5). In 1 Corinthians 9:2, Paul reinforces this evidence when he says, "Even though I may not be an apostle to others, surely I am to you! For you are the seal (i.e., stamp of authenticity) of my apostleship in the Lord."

Again, Paul told the Thessalonian believers that they were his "joy" and his "crown." The evidence, joy, and reward of apostolic ministry is changed lives and, in particular, new believers brought into the kingdom of God. Anyone who is truly apostolic will have changed lives in his or her wake, including new believers.

New Churches. Apostles lay foundations and set things in order. They are not fond of building on another man's foundation but are wired to start things--in particular, churches--by bringing the gospel to new areas (Rom. 15:20). Apostles aren't building just any ministry. They are planting and building churches (1 Cor. 3:8-11). After laying apostolic foundations, they insure elders are appointed and churches are properly cared for (Titus 1:5).

Signs & Wonders. Again, Paul is very plain about a third evidence of apostleship in 2 Corinthians 12:12-- "The things that mark an apostle--signs, wonders, and miracles--were done among you with great perseverance." These are evidenced in Paul's ministry as he brought the gospel (Rom. 15:19). Modern-day apostles regularly move in the supernatural as an evidential sign of their God-given apostolic ministry and authority from God.

A person can plant and pastor a church without being an apostle. People can win others to Christ and they are not necessarily apostolic. And a gift of healing or miracles does not make someone an apostle. But where the combination of these three evidences exist, the likelihood of apostleship increases. In addition to these three evidences, apostles engage in key activities as well.

The Activity Of Apostolic Ministry

Acts 6:1-7 is a very instructive passage for understanding what the activity of apostolic ministry is about. In the midst of a church management crisis, it becomes clear that a team is needed to oversee the food ministry. Without any misgivings or false guilt, the apostles do not come under the pressure to provide pastoral care or administration. Instead, they articulate the job description as they passed on this responsibility to another group of servant-leaders while they remained true to their primary activities:

> "It would not be right for us to neglect the ministry of the word of God in order to wait tables. Brothers, choose seven men from among you who are known to be full of the Spirit and wisdom. We will turn this responsibility over to them and will give our attention to prayer and the ministry of the Word" (Acts 6:2-4).

Apostolic activity centers around two primary activities: (1) being with God in private and public prayer and intercession, and (2) the ministry of preaching and teaching God's Word both for the purpose of evangelizing the lost and for equipping the saints. Apostolic leaders are drawn to the realm of prayer and the ministry of God's Word, whether in small or large settings, one-on-one and in crowds, among the lost and among the church.

The Heart Of Apostolic Ministry

The evidences and activities of apostolic ministry must be in place for someone to be an apostle, but at the core of all of it is the apostolic heart. This is really the most transferable aspect of apostolic ministry for all of us.

My favorite description of the heart of apostolic leadership is found in 1 Corinthians 4 where Paul describes the nature, character, and heart of true apostolic ministry. Paul articulates four vital aspects of the heart of apostolic ministry that characterized his own life and ministry and that I believe are meant to characterize all apostolic ministry and really every kingdom church today.

Servants of Christ (4:1). The heart of apostolic ministry is servanthood. Apostles are not trying to take over--although others might perceive them that way! They realize they have been given great authority from God, but they are constantly using that authority to build people up and to make others great (2 Cor. 13:10). Paul vigorously defended his 'right' to be an apostle so that others might receive his ministry to their own benefit. He fought hard with churches to 'prove' his authority, all so he could turn around and lay down his life on their behalf.

As a young believer I was excited to learn that God had placed a large call on my life and significant authority in my hands. Then I read Jesus' words in Luke 22:24-27 about how the greatest must become a servant. With fresh resolve, I figured that I would pay the price and go through a season where I really learned how to serve. This would then release me and qualify me to come into my true calling as a leader with great authority. So I worked as an usher, sweeping floors and setting up chairs. I worked in other varied ministry positions, mostly in a "servant" versus leadership capacity. Over time, I began to move into positions of authority and leadership, until finally I was released and commissioned to become a senior pastor at my very own church! I was so excited. At the beginning of this time, as I entered into "full-time" paid ministry, a very reliable prophet spoke to my wife and I, explaining that God wanted to take us from where we were to a place where we became servants of all. He essentially prophesied the Luke 22 passage over my life. With even more resolve, I figured God wanted to take me through another phase where I learned about servanthood even more. Greatness and destiny would soon follow.

I don't remember exactly when it occurred, but not too long after becoming a recognized leader I had an epiphany. Suddenly, I realized that servanthood wasn't a phase that we pass through to get where we're going. It is the destination. God wants to help all of us become "great!" In order to do that and to reach our full potential of ministry, we must become servants, not as a phase we go through, but as a permanent place of residence! Servanthood isn't a means to greatness. Servanthood *is* greatness. This is meant to be true for all believers. And certainly, servanthood is at the heart of all true apostolic ministry.

Stewards of a mystery (4:1-8). Paul's entire orientation was that God had given him the greatest treasure, the Person of Christ, who dwelt in the earthen jar of his body. This mystery of Christ in us as our entire hope of glory was something that Paul was thrilled to release to others. He saw himself as a steward, someone who had been entrusted with truth and reality of incredible value that he was glad to give away to the people in his God-given sphere.

When apostles come to others, they do not come to take. They come to give. They know that they are full of a mystery, and as good stewards, it is their responsibility before God to give this mystery of Christ away. As carriers of God's glory and as servants, they are constantly trying to help others come into their destiny. They see themselves not as anointed masters but as childlike messengers, bringing fresh bread from heaven and dispensing it among the people. Apostles are those who have been entrusted by God to unfold the mystery of Christ to the people in their spheres. It is required of a steward that he be found faithful, and apostles are faithful to "preach Christ crucified" (1 Cor. 1:23). In order to keep their message pure, apostles keep the focus on the Person of Jesus. Again, Paul said, "For I resolved to know nothing while I was with you except Jesus Christ and him crucified" (1 Cor. 2:2).

Spectacles of men (4:9-13). Apostolic ministry has a stigma of misunderstanding attached to it. People whom Paul loved and laid his life down for were constantly misunderstanding Paul's motives and devaluing his authority. For example, Paul spent significant time his letters to the Corinthians trying to lovingly convince them that he was the real deal and that they needed to listen to him! He summarizes this dilemma in 1 Cor. 4:10 when he says: "We are fools for Christ, but you are so wise in Christ! You are honored, we are dishonored!"

I used to work in the building industry--in particular in foundations and framing. I know personally that foundation work is not glamorous. It is dirty, hard work that doesn't draw the wows of people like, say, the work of the interior decorator does. Apostolic ministry is about making sure foundations are right and things are set in order. It is, in many ways, the 'grunt work' of the building process! But it is also extremely important. God is raising up apostolic leaders who are secure enough to be hidden, who are rooted in the love of God so much that they are OK with the fact that many don't understand or recognize the place they occupy in the Spirit or the price they pay by standing in the gap for others.

Because God has given apostles great authority, he requires a very high degree of death! Every believer is called to lay down his life and follow Christ, but where there is great authority, there is great responsibility. Paul told the church of his close association with death when he said this: "I die every day--I mean that, brothers--just as surely as I glory over you in Christ Jesus our Lord." --1 Cor. 15:31

John Wimber used to say, "Never trust a leader without a limp." This was a reference to Jacob, who wrestled with the angel and found his hip put out of socket for the rest of his life. It also refers to the need to qualify leaders based on their brokenness before God and their humility before men. It is impossible to truly be 'apostolic' without truly being dead! God entrusts great authority to dead people--those who have died to their own aspirations and have become voluntary bond slaves dedicated to building the kingdom of God and not their own ministry. Others may have anointing that makes them look apostolic, but death to self is a major requirement for and mark of true apostolic ministry.

Spiritual fathers (4:14-21). We live in a fatherless, latchkey generation, and the concept of someone acting as a spiritual mentor to us, or of us acting in that role with others, is hard to grasp for many. Most of the protestant church has steered clear of the concept of spiritual fathers and mothers. The abuses that came out of the 'shepherding movement' have caused the church to overreact and avoid the issue of healthy mentoring in the church altogether. Even our own trust issues come up when we think of trusting a spiritual father, or much less of asking someone to trust us to help them in their lives. We have much to overcome!

In his book <u>The Father Heart Of God</u>, Floyd McClung agrees:

"So many people are orphaned, not just from their physical parents, but from any kind of healthy spiritual or emotional heritage. The church is filled with spiritual orphans. Either...they have not been nurtured in their faith, or...they have not become a part of a spiritual family...They need a spiritual father or mother who can help them grow in the Lord. Others need to be 're-parented'...if proper parenting was missing during a person's developmental years...he or she needs someone to provide an example. Being a father or mother in the Lord is not limited to those who are pastors or spiritual leaders. There is also a very crucial need for other spiritually mature, caring people to act as 'fathers' and 'mothers' to other believers. By their very presence, they minister to those around them because of their maturity and depth in God. We need to turn loose these 'moms and dads' in the church to be who they are."

Paul boldly declared himself to be a spiritual father both to individuals, as in the case of Timothy and Titus, and also to entire churches, such as the churches in Corinth and in Thessalonica (1 Tim. 1:2; Titus 1:4; 1 Cor. 4:17; 1 Th. 2:11).

This apostolic mandate of spiritual fathering and mothering is an essential part of kingdom leadership and a defining characteristic of the apostolic heart. Again, there are many who display powerful anointing and do great ministry. But until we are willing to lay down our lives and invest in other people, rolling up our sleeves and being vulnerable emotionally to the point where people can trust us as spiritual parents, we will never move from anointed to apostolic. The ministry of apostle is about investment in people--not from a distance, but with those we relate to personally. We'll look at this more in the next chapter.

Chapter Eight
Kingdom MEMBERSHIP

"God places the lonely in families." --Psalm 68:6

The kingdom of God is *relational*. This is one of the most important revelations we could ever receive. And the relational nature of God's kingdom is based on the relational nature of God Himself.

God, of course, is One. And yet, He is also three-in-one—the Trinity. The very nature of God is community and relationship through unity. He is One God who has manifested Himself in three distinct Persons—Father, Son, Spirit. He dwells in *perfect* community. And the great mystery that the angels are forever trying to comprehend is why God would place such extremely high value on relationship with fallen human beings when He already enjoys perfect community in and of Himself. Why all the fuss about relationship with such weak, fallible people? At first glance, it hardly seems worth it. But God's design and desire for humanity is to take each one of us and bring us into the community of the Trinity. He longs to place us into the center of His heart and into the center of His Trinitarian nature, so that we will fully and forever experience the deep fulfillment of living in perfect community. He wants to share His love with us. It is in this environment that our hearts are healed, our identity transformed, our worth secure, and our purpose clear.

I met Ian McCormack in 1995. He spoke at our church. And I had the opportunity to speak personally with him. I'll never forget riding down Highway 101 in my 1960 Ford F-100 Pickup with Ian as the literal, tangible Presence of Jesus filled the truck cab. I nearly couldn't drive. You see, years before, Ian had died and gone to heaven for about 20 minutes. And in that experience, as he moved through the proverbial tunnel, he said that waves of love emanated from God's throne and came into the tunnel. And as those waves moved toward him, they began to heal his heart. He began down that tunnel as a shell of a man, broken and empty, but by the time he was finally standing in front of God's throne, he had been made whole by love. God had brought Ian into the community of the Trinity. He had entered into heaven, the place where God dwells, and he was drinking in this most beautiful of all relationships with the Living God! And all these years later, in my truck, as we rumbled down the highway, to be with Ian was to be with Jesus. At least that's how it felt to me. It was powerful!

When we get to heaven, we will experience the eternal bliss of perfect community with God and others. Until we get to heaven, however, God's plan for community and relationship is meant to take place on the earth—through His Church. Yes, that's right! God's perfect plan, the plan for the manifestation of His beautiful family heart, is meant to be displayed by us, His imperfect, in-process, 'under construction' kids! We are called to display His glorious, perfect love through spiritual family.

And it is indeed a glorious, perfect love. Jesus prayed and declared that we are moving towards a level of relational unity together that is only enjoyed between the members of the Trinity. Listen to Jesus describe in John 17 the level of relationship and community that we are going to enjoy:

> "I am praying... for all who will ever believe in Me... that they will all be one, just as you and I are one—as you are in me, Father, and I am in you... I have given them the glory... so they may be one as we are one... May they experience such perfect unity that the world will know that you sent me and that you love them as much as you love me." --John 17:20-23, NLT

This is a staggering invitation, declaration, and prayer by Jesus! We are invited and called into a radically high level of relational closeness! At some point, we will be as close to one another as the Father is to Jesus! We will have the same quality and depth of love for our spiritual family as our Father and His Son enjoy with one another. This call and invitation is to the church! And again, because it is Jesus' prayer, it will be answered!

Relational Closeness Means Family

To achieve this level of unity, we *must* become a family. When we say that God designed the church as a family, we don't mean that is simply *like* a family; it *is* a family. Family is God's design for His Church. The government of God is relational. God is a 'family Man', and family is how He does things.

"So now... you are citizens along with all of God's holy people. You are members of God's family. Together, we are His house... the cornerstone is Christ Himself. We are carefully joined together in Him, becoming a holy temple for the Lord. Through Him you... are also being made part of this dwelling where God lives by His Spirit." --Eph. 2:19-22

We are members of God's family! And as we do life and ministry together, we create a dwelling place for God. We are becoming God's house—the place where He Himself dwells! Again, this is another *staggering reality*. As we honor God and endeavor to become a spiritual family, He responds by choosing to hang out in our midst—to live in our community by His Spirit! Beloved, there could be no higher honor than for the God of the universe to choose to live among us.

Choosing Community
There are many today who claim to be Christians but who shun or avoid the church. In many ways, this is a 'trend' within Christendom in our day. It is almost chic to claim to be a citizen of the kingdom while disparaging any sort of real commitment to the local church (ie, the family).

Consider the rest of Psalm 68:6 ~

> "God places the lonely in families;
> He sets the prisoners free and gives them joy.
> *But he makes the rebellious live in a sun-scorched land.*"

The choice is clear. When we allow God to place us strategically into spiritual family, we experience the freedom and joy that comes with belonging. God breaks us out of the prison of loneliness! But when we resist God's plan for church families, we find that the fruit of our rebellion is a difficult life that lacks His full blessing.

Letting God Choose Your Community
So God *places* individuals into spiritual families. And what is the local church but a spiritual family? The word 'places' in this verse is also translated 'sets' and 'settles.' The Hebrew word is 'yashab' (יָשַׁב). It means to 'stay', to 'remain', to 'dwell', and to 'abide.' It is actually translated 'married' six times in the Scripture. What this literally means is that God handpicks the local church He would like you to be involved in! And then, He expects you to settle in, to plug in, to make a commitment, and to walk out life in that place and with that people.

Of course, we are always related to the larger body of Christ, His global Church. We have a worldwide family, to be sure! However, the idea and spirit of commitment to family has to be lived out in real space and time among a real people. I suppose it is possible to fool ourselves into believing that this intimate, highly relational connection is simply to the larger body of Christ without any local commitment. It is certainly a theological reality that we are one with Christ's body throughout the earth and throughout history. But in our experience, we are called to something much more practical. At the end of the day, we must allow God's plan for our lives to happen in a local expression of that global Church. It is the heart of God that we would learn how to become a spiritual family with a select, defined group of people, where people know us, we know them, and where we actually do life, ministry, and mission together. This group of people is bigger than our biological, natural family and smaller than our global, spiritual family. It is a local church family.

The call to become members of local kingdom churches is quite different than the nomadic, pseudo 'Spirit-led' church hopping and cafeteria-style attendance we see going on in increasing measure today. Where did we get the idea that this version of 'freedom' was Biblical? It simply cannot be supported in Scripture. It is an anti-family spirit, birthed from the world and from the enemy. Rather than building a house for God to dwell in, it destroys His house by dismantling the walls because of unstable, transitory, constantly moving stones that pull themselves out of the wall on any spiritual whim—leaving instability in their wake.

My colleague/friend/mentor Kris Vallotton recently wrote about this on Facebook:

> "Corporately WE are the Body of Christ. But saying "I" am the Body of Christ is like saying my big toe is the body of Kris. We are all a part of the family of God. Yet it's only when we are fitted and held together in covenant love with other Believers that we realize the full benefit of the Body of Christ. Many have reacted to religious control, hurt and/or disappointment, and become independent, unaccountable, unleadable Believers, marooned on the uninhabited island of isolation singing "we are one in the Spirit." Despite popular opinion, you were designed to find your place in the Body. Many proclaim, "the church is not a building!" That's true, but it is a family with fathers, mothers, sisters and brothers, who relate to us out of their various God given roles. Cutting yourself off from the rest of the Body will stop the circulation necessary for you to grow and thrive as a member of Christ."

For us to really see God's house built on the earth, we must allow Him to strategically place each one of us in the right family that He has for us. Jesus promised to build His church. In order to do that, He has to be given freedom and honor from His people to place us, the living stones, where He needs each of us to be. Because He is the builder, He determines where we belong on the wall.

Church Membership
Church membership classes, then, are not simply another program or an awkward attempt to squeeze commitment from people. When done in the right spirit, they are one of God's methods for creating commitment among individuals who are called to family. It is one of the ways we watch God 'place' individuals in families.

God uses these simple structures to help people hear the sound of their tribe. I liken it to a tuning fork. When you hear the sound of the right tuning fork, it is the sound of alignment that is calling you in and on. A clear trumpet sound, a tuning fork—these are the kinds of devices God releases into the atmosphere so that His people can pay attention and end up in the church family God has for them.

Changing Churches
I need to address the issue of changing churches, because it is the cause of many problems in the Western Bride. Obviously, there are seasons in all of our lives. And these seasons can, at times, involve changing churches. Not every house is equally healthy. Churches that are stuck in old ways of thinking (that we somehow own people and that we deserve their unquestioned allegiance regardless of how dysfunctional our leadership style may be) will continue to decline, as people naturally seek out healthy kingdom churches. In such cases, the Lord may indeed call us out of one place and into another. After we have followed God's due process of prayer, waiting, receiving godly counsel, checking our hearts, reconciling over any issues we may have, and so on, He may lead us into such a transition.

But I think it happens far more often than God intends. What we see too much of is Christians in the West who leave churches on much smaller grounds. Countless Western Christians, called to local church A, will far too easily migrate to church B down the street because they like the worship better or because there is an opening to serve in their particular gifting. What we're not grasping is that these things miss the point. That would be like swapping spouses because someone else cooks better or decorates the living room better. Our commitment to local churches must run deeper than this if we expect to see the kind of revolution God wants to bring. When we see a deficiency in our local church, we must learn to pray and to become part of the solution. To change churches at that point simply reinforces the consumer mentality in both God's people and the leaders of churches.

And too often, to cover up the shallowness of our decisions to abandon one family for another, Western Christians over-spiritualize such decisions, blaming the Holy Spirit for so many things He never said or initiated. It is staggering how often the Holy Spirit has to silently take responsibility for our immaturity. We use Him a lot.

Sometimes, what people call the leading of the Spirit is really just offense that has not been dealt with in a healthy way. In any family, even great ones, there are going to be hurt feelings, misunderstandings, letdowns, and unmet expectations. These are not reasons to leave a spiritual family! These are opportunities to deepen our relational love, as we humble ourselves and learn how to dialogue with each other in healthy ways.

Remember the tuning fork we talked about? Often the sound that first drew us to the church God has for us can become distant and difficult to hear because of pain, disappointment, and disillusionment. And frequently when believers no longer hear the sound, they assume it is 'time to go!' But really, much more often than not, our hearts have simply gotten out of frequency. We've grown overfamiliar, or distant, or wounded. And these moments, which happen more than we may realize, become the true tests of family. While I would be the first to discourage blind, uninformed family loyalty, I also would strongly encourage a much more powerful display of healthy loyalty and honor than what we see now in the church in the West.

Keep in mind that there is a staggering number of broken homes in the West. Most Christians come from broken, dysfunctional homes. So I think it is safe to say that we are going to need to relearn some heart standards and skills that are required to function in healthy family structures. So many of these issues can be solved as we begin to understand family leaders (ie, fathers and mothers) and family members (ie, sons and daughters) and what it means to be family. We need to ask our Father God to give us fresh eyes to see His design for family among imperfect people trying to do life and ministry together.

Let's begin to unpack some of these truths, both from a leadership and a membership perspective.

FAMILY DYNAMICS

Every family has dynamics or ways of operating. Spiritual families are no different. As Christians, we want to take our cues on what is normal and healthy from Scripture. God has intentions for our family dynamics.

Apostolic Communities

To summarize what we saw in the previous chapter, God is raising up spiritual families that are apostolic communities, which we are calling *kingdom churches*. These kingdom churches operate under an apostolic ethos. They are led by apostolic leaders or at least have the regular influence of apostolic ministry in their midst. The culture of these churches is apostolic. They are characterized by the nine primary traits of an apostle mentioned in the previous chapter. Of course, God doesn't simply want to raise up and release apostles. He wants the *entire church* to be apostolic, communities that are missional in their orientation. Here is a summary list of the kinds of things we see in true apostolic communities:

1) transformed lives and people coming to Christ
2) leaders who plant new churches as expert builders
3) supernatural power in signs, wonders, and miracles
4) significant time in prayer in private and in public
5) preaching and teaching to the lost and to the saved
6) servants who focus on ministering to and blessing others
7) stewards who give away & unfold the mystery of Christ
8) spectacles who bear the stigma of misunderstanding
9) spiritual parents who father children and churches

If every member of every church laid down every title and position they had and focused solely on becoming a living demonstration of these nine apostolic traits, we would be on our way to revolution! In America, we are continually seeking new ways to *organize* our way into revolution. But it's about becoming, about embodying the realities of the kingdom. These traits are the heart and essence not only of all kingdom leadership but also of all kingdom people!

Strong Leader, Strong Team

Some years ago I was in a meeting where Jim Goll introduced the term 'apostolic team ministry' (ATM for short). Although I never heard Jim teach on this subject beyond the introductory comments in that meeting, I always sensed in my heart that he had captured in a phrase something very significant for our understanding in the years to come.

Someone has said, "You cannot strengthen the weak by weakening the strong." As the church is experiencing a radical shift in many of its paradigms, there is often an unconscious "dumbing down" of leadership and strongly gifted people. Because we desire the priesthood of every believer so strongly, we must be especially cautious of devaluing strong, healthy leadership. If you have a strong leader and a weak team, you have the same old pattern of overly controlling leadership that dominates. Equally true is the fact that if you have a strong team but a weak leader, you have a committee! (And they certainly don't exist in the Scriptures.) I believe there is coming a healthier model of strong leader and strong team, where everyone on the team is honored and valued, no one feels intimidated, and leadership is present but it functions in life-giving ways so everyone stands shoulder to shoulder and advances together in strength.

More Authority, Less Control

Kingdom churches experience more authority but less control through their leaders. As the Lord continues to restore apostolic authority to the church, we may begin to hear news of modern-day Ananias and Sapphira moments! When Peter spoke to this couple in Acts 5 about their deceit, he was operating in spiritual authority from heaven. It wasn't about church or structure or politics or control. It was about the kingdom authority Peter carried in the Spirit to discern what was needed for the moment and to pronounce God's temporal, corrective judgments within the church. Think about that. Peter spoke, and people died! But the result of Peter's use of authority was not others bowing down before him. Instead, more than ever, believers fixed their eyes on God as "great fear seized the whole church" (v. 11). In fact, even unbelievers and God-seekers were affected with a holy reverence for God and His people (v. 13). The final result of seeing kingdom authority expressed through the church was that more and more people believed in the Lord, and the company of believers grew (v. 14).

When kingdom authority functions in the church, the result is reverence, respect, and repentance. Control is not needed in such an environment.

Everyone's eyes are on Jesus, the atmosphere is filled with holiness and the fear of the Lord, and humble submission and godly honor are the only logical heart postures of everyone in the church. There are no superstars in kingdom churches. Instead, there are like-minded people who have entered into covenant relationship and who have chosen to walk together in love. Leaders are those who simply occupy a role and fulfill a ministry that is no less than or greater than anyone else's. There is so much mutual honor and heart-felt appreciation for one another that the fear of control dissipates. Perfect love casts out fear! When there is tension over leadership, I am learning to call out to God for more love! I believe we need greater love to walk in greater authority and more Biblical realms of leadership.

A Fluid Model
Kingdom leadership and membership have more curves than square edges. There is more overlap, more shared responsibility, and it is derived from a more fluid rather than static model. Leadership structures are depicted best not by a pyramid, where top-down authority works best, but by a flock of birds, where leadership changes hands based on the objective, or by a network, and where true partnership occurs. It's about team and mutual submission versus command and control, and yet leaders do, in fact, guide and govern. It's about servanthood in the context of partnership and mutual honor. Kingdom leadership always empowers rather than disables the unmediated priesthood of all believers. Any leadership model we embrace must accomplish this.

FAMILY LEADERS

To become family and to walk in healthy family dynamics, we must recognize the family structure. And in order to see His intended structure, we must first learn to see those whom God has made leaders of the family.

Understanding Leaders
As kingdom churches emerge with a strong emphasis on the priesthood of every believer, mutual submission, self- government, and so on, the nature and role of leadership must change to fit this new wineskin. This change will be especially tough for pastors who do not have apostolic gifting. Pastors of existing institutionally-oriented churches are already beginning to feel the tension of a paradigm shift (and the accompanying loss of power). In the past, there were always those to blame for this

tension--the rebellious crowd that is always bucking authority. But now, the massive shift that is occurring is so widespread, it is so pervasive, that it cannot be dismissed with such shallow analysis.

An entire generation of new leadership is taking shape! Those who have been leading under an older, modernistic framework will soon have a very important decision to make: (1) Will I hold my ground, remain unwilling to change, and vilify those who are calling for change? (and eventually leaving 'my' church); (2) Will I see my role as pastoral while also recognizing the need for apostolic leadership on our church, and make needed changes? or (3) Will I allow God to transform me into a new kind of apostolic leader--even though I don't quite know what that will look like?

The role of a leader in a kingdom church is different from what church leaders have been trained to do. Kingdom leaders are not primarily managers, controllers, pulpiteers, priests, or encyclopedias (with all the answers). Rather, kingdom leaders are those who pray, impart, and model. They are catalysts and voices who help create opportunities and who articulate God's heart. My favorite definition of leadership is found in Psalm 78:72, where King David is described:

"He shepherded them with integrity of heart; with skillful hands he led them."

David was a leader of both heart and skill, of character and talent. Clearly, David wasn't perfect! He struggled with lust, he committed adultery and murder, he was an absentee father who failed to bring needed correction. He ignored the Holy Spirit and disobeyed God at times. This recounting is not meant to lower the standard of leadership today! But we must also see with God's eyes when we look at His designated leaders. David, a man after God's own heart, was God's chosen leader. And even though David did wrong things, he did more things right. God saw something in David's heart that endeared Him to David. And God loved and defended David so much that He named His own Son after Him—'Son of David.' What love and honor God has for this imperfect leader!

Responding To Leaders

I believe this is how we need to be toward leaders. They are simply not perfect. They have weaknesses, flaws, and areas where they get it wrong. We've acknowledged that there have been many church wounds and disappointments at the hands of imperfect leaders. Even though that is tragic but true, we must learn to recognize the leaders God has placed in our lives. As much as we love the priesthood of all believers and the mutuality of the body of Christ, we must also learn to truly embrace God's plan for leadership in our lives.

Just as there have been church wounds at the hands of leaders, there have been many human wounds at the hands of parents. But parenting is God's design. Even though there are good and bad examples of parenting, God doesn't give us the right to throw parenting out the window! He works on the parents to love their children well (eg, Eph. 6:4). And He works on the children to honor and submit to their parents (eg, Eph. 6:1-3).

Similarly, God has called each of us to find the leaders He has placed in our lives for our own good. Paul strenuously pleaded with the Christians in Corinth to recognize him as their spiritual father and authority figure— not so he could do them harm, but so that he could build them up and be a blessing to them (see 2 Cor. 10:8, 13:10).

Coming Out Of The Caves

It is a basic Scriptural principle that every believer is meant to be part of the sphere of a local church. Psalm 68:6 tells us clearly that God sets individuals into families. Every believer is meant to be part of a local church family. The goal of Biblical spheres of authority should not be to rule or lord it over anybody but to serve the church and to equip the saints. Likewise, the goal of each believer should not be to act independently but to walk in mutual submission and to minister interdependently in concert and partnership with others.

Here is one of the things that God is doing today: He is calling millions of people out of the caves of Adullam, the caves of hiding and fear and protection, back to the castle. David spent a good part of his life in the cave with 400 mighty men. These men had issues. They were desperate! In debt, discontent, dissatisfied with life, and stressed out. But they had one thing going for them (besides their fierceness!)—they were loyal family men. Aside from the one time when they were going to stone David (!), they were incredibly loyal guys. And there would come a time when they would finally have the opportunity to move from the cave to the castle.

This is God's desire and design for untold millions in the West who have opted out of any form of church expression. God is calling for David's mighty men to come out of the caves and into the castle! The coast is clear, and it's time to rejoin a functional, Biblical community that includes elders and leaders and the five-fold ministry expressions of Ephesians 4. Perhaps you know someone like this, or perhaps we're describing you! In either case, would you help the Lord by getting the word out: it's time! It's time to move from the cave to the castle. It's time to occupy our place in the community and to start becoming part of the solution. It's time to build kingdom churches by being members of the family and by recognizing our need for mentoring relationships.

Mentoring Relationships

Deep within each of us is a God-given need to love and to be loved, to feel significant in our impact upon others, while at the same time allowing others into our lives to help us grow and become all we are called to become in Jesus Christ. This need can be addressed in mentoring relationships. Mentoring relationships occur in all 'directions.' There are those relationships where we are mentored by someone else. There are those relationships where we are actively mentoring another person or small group of people. Finally, there are those relationships where each person 'mentors' the other in a peer-level way.

Kingdom diversity is preserved best when we honor the intergenerational dynamic of Biblical family. This dynamic allows mentoring relationships throughout the church, whether aided by the structure of a formal discipleship system or simply encouraged and celebrated as they occur naturally. Either way, mentoring relationships of spiritual fathering and sonship provide the Lord an opportunity for divine 'matchmaking', where God uses the one to strengthen the other.

We need all types of relationships in our lives in an ongoing way, much like the stones in a wall are surrounded by those stones above, to either side, and below. When we mentor someone else, we are helping that person  become a disciple of Jesus. We are pouring ourselves into them, teaching them what we know, and holding them accountable in their desire to become more like their Master. When we see success in our efforts and genuine growth occur, we are like 'proud parents.' When we have peer-level mentoring relationships, we mutually benefit, as Proverbs 27:17 indicates: *"As iron sharpens iron, so one man sharpens another."* We also need the other kind of mentoring relationships where we receive spiritual help, input, and accountability from a caring person who has something to offer us.

Spiritual Fathers And Mothers

Far too many believers walk around with an ache in their soul as they look longingly for a spiritual father. This longing is right! We are called to have spiritual fathers, just as the Corinthian Christians had Paul (1 Cor. 4:14-17). But to know what we're looking for and to know what to expect, we have to understand the roles of fathers and sons, of leaders and members.

When it comes to impartation from spiritual fathers, more is caught than taught. This is why building an intergenerational church full of models is a worthy kingdom goal. People in kingdom churches will rise to the call to live lives worthy of imitation. Paul boldly said, "Follow my example, as I follow the example of Christ" (1 Cor. 11:1). But did you know that at one point, Paul even went so far as to tell people just to imitate him? Listen to the bold exhortation coming from a mature veteran in the faith to a church struggling with basic maturity issues:

> "Even though you have ten thousand guardians in Christ, you do not have many fathers, for in Christ Jesus I became your father through the gospel. Therefore I urge you to imitate me. For this reason I am sending to you Timothy, my son whom I love, who is faithful in the Lord. He will remind you of my way of life in Christ Jesus, which agrees with what I teach everywhere in every church." --1 Cor. 4:15-17

This intergenerational mentoring is not gender-specific. Aquila and Priscilla, a husband-wife team, pulled Apollos aside and mentored him in his understanding of the gospel (18:26). Paul referred to himself as both a spiritual father and a spiritual mother to the Thessalonians (1 Th. 2:6-12).

Part of the apostolic reformation that is occurring in our day has to do with the love of our Father God flowing through us to one another. God is truly turning the hearts of His people back to a proper apostolic fathering dynamic that will be healthy and appropriate, free from control but with great love that finally removes the orphan spirit from the church in the West and causes us to cry and call out, "Papa! Papa! I am loved by my Father!" (cf. Rom. 8:15; Gal. 4:6).

Walking as fathers and sons is always first and foremost a heart issue. It requires a prophetic work of God to turn our hearts toward fathers and sons. We need to ask God for a heart revelation so we can trust again (Mal. 4:1-6). This revelation comes not only through spiritual encounters but through loving human examples of fatherhood and sonship in our lives.

Becoming A Spiritual Father. A spiritual father (non-gender) is all about helping those in his sphere of influence to reach their God-given potential, to fulfill their destiny, and to finish well. Spiritual parents not only display the characteristics of basic spiritual maturity and victory, but they know God in a way that makes others hungry. Spiritual fathers spend time with children, modeling life. They encourage their children by calling out potential and destiny. They prophesy and encourage freely, and they often function as cheerleaders. They are not passive but take the lead in the relationship, fighting for their children, jealous for their success. A father makes reasonable demands on his children, calling them higher and to a place of excellence. He is not afraid to bring needed correction, but he is also ready to forgive. When a father doesn't know something, he freely admits his own weaknesses and walks in the freedom of personal vulnerability. He accepts misunderstanding as part of the cost of fathering and pushes past it for the sake of the well-being of his sons.

Becoming A Spiritual Son. Tired of dominant leaders, many Christians misuse the verse where Jesus says not to call any man on earth "father" (Mt. 23:9). In this same passage, Jesus says not to call anyone on earth "teacher." But Ephesians 4:11 plainly tells us that there are teachers in the body of Christ, and Paul the Apostle, under the inspiration of the Spirit, calls himself a teacher on at least two occasions (1 Tim. 2:7; 2 Tim. 1:11). Is Paul in violation of Jesus' warning? I don't think so. Jesus was addressing the motive of the heart. He was denouncing the pharisaical use of titles, not the proper use of words to describe Biblical functions. In the same way, Paul called himself a father and others he called 'sons.' This is good and right, because it describes not a title given from a false motive, but rather a functional relationship that gives life.

A spiritual son (or daughter) is someone who willingly receives life and help from a spiritual father or mother. It is important that we understand our need to be both fathers/mothers and sons/daughters. When we are younger, both in age and in the Lord, we can have many spiritual parents who will provide a mentoring role in our lives, but we are spiritual fathers to few or none. This is good and right! The need for such mentoring is much greater than when we are seasoned, mature, and occupying a significant fathering role ourselves.

The Apostle John describes a progression in the faith where one becomes a father in the faith, and the implication is that the role of being a son is no longer his primary role (1 John 2:12-14). It is doubtful that the Apostle Paul had a spiritual father in his life toward his latter years, or that the Apostle John, on the Isle of Patmos, was a spiritual son to anyone, although he carried that heart. Still, it is best, when it can happen, that we all, at whatever age, receive mentoring, fathering, and mothering, from significant people in our lives. Whether we are receiving from a spiritual father or mother or not, there are heart attitudes within sons and daughters that we need to cultivate--what the Bible calls the "spirit of sonship" (Rom. 8:15) rather than the spirit of slavery/servitude.

One way to discern the heart and activity of sons is to contrast them with mere servants. (To be clear, being a servant is usually a good thing! But in this comparison, we are making a clear distinction between what it means to be a son versus what it means to be a servant in the house and as we relate to the father and the family.)

Use this next paragraph as a spiritual gauge to discern where you are on the son---servant spectrum:

> Sons are faithful to build the house, while servants are looking to build a ministry. Sons put the family first and use the language of 'we', while servants put issues first and use the language of 'me' and 'they.' Sons inherit, because they are secure and free from anxiety or pressure. Servants take, seeking their own, always pushing early for the blessing. Sons feel ownership in the house, and therefore it is natural for them to take responsibility. Servants live like temporary residents in the house, so they resent being asked to take responsibility. Servants avoid by blaming others or making excuses. Sons honor and protect fathers and find it easy to submit to authority, while servants continually challenge fathers and authority and struggle with submission. They feel that they know better. It's not wrong to question, and truth is valued in healthy families, but sons are honoring even in their questioning, whereas servants have no problem throwing others under the bus. Sons allow love to cover a multitude of sins, while servants expose weakness, especially in spiritual moms and dads. Sons delight in their fathers, and therefore they are glad to rally people to fathers. Servants rally people to themselves, often displaying an 'Absalom' spirit, causing people to turn away from leadership by winning their hearts to themselves. Servants are often the cause of church splits due to their orphan spirit. Sons have puppy feet! They are teachable. Servants, however, arrive at the house fully grown—at least in their own eyes. You

can spot a servant immediately because they are trying to show everyone what they know. Servants are defensive when they are corrected, because they are afraid of rejection. But sons are correctable, because they are secure in their father's love.

OK, how did you do?

HOW TO BELONG TO A LOCAL CHURCH

It all starts with belonging. The hurts in the church, the rebellion in society, the awareness of the kingdom's priority and prominence, our own internal issues, the freedom and joy of dreamers, the emphasis shift to the marketplace and to the mountains of culture, the availability of amazing worship and messages online--whatever the cause or combination of causes, one thing is certain: Far too many Christian believers don't belong anywhere! As in the days of Judges, 'each one does what is right in his own eyes.' This statement is not a point of bragging; it is a point of conviction. God wants us connected, belonging to a legitimate, local Christian community where there is apostolic authority, elders, connectedness, and family.

Paul said something so interesting in 2 Corinthians 10. After clearly communicating in his previous letter to the Corinthians that he was merely a servant and no big deal (cf. 1 Cor. 3:4-7), he then goes on in his second letter to more or less promote himself as their apostle and spiritual father. Listen to this paraphrase of 2 Cor. 10:7-18:

> "I may seem to be boasting too much about the authority given to us by the Lord. But our authority builds you up; it doesn't tear you down. **So I will not be ashamed of using my authority.** You may think I'm overstating the authority He gave me, but I'm not backing off... We aren't making outrageous claims here. We're sticking to the limits of what God has set for us. But there can be no question that those limits reach to you. **God does a lot within the boundaries He has given us, boundaries which include you, by the way. We are not reaching beyond those boundaries when we claim authority over you...** Nor do we boast and claim credit for the work someone else has done. And we don't go into other's territory... We boast only in the Lord."

Beloved, in this revolution that God is bringing, in the midst of all the things He is changing, He has not discarded belonging. And He has not discarded family and fathers. Now more than ever, He wants us to belong to a local spiritual family with all the Biblical components that He

Himself considers part of what it actually means to be the church. There is a Heavenly blueprint, a design authored by God Himself, that calls and woos and draws us to spiritual family, to spiritual fathers and mothers, imperfect as they are, so we can learn to walk in love.

So, what does love look like for a local church? What does it actually mean to really belong?

Relationship & Friendship

First and foremost, family is about doing life together. We dwell together and share experiences. We enjoy each others' company and spend time together. We do a variety of things together, often centered around food, involving work and play, having 'down time' at home and enjoying shopping and recreation outsides our homes.

Spiritual families are the same. The church isn't defined by its programs but by its relationships. Doing life together as a spiritual family is important. It is part of what defines us and makes us a family. Because we are part of the larger body of Christ, our relationships can span multiple churches and even states and countries! We have relationships all over the world. But at the same time, there ought to be a real sense that our priority is on our local, tangible spiritual family—ie, the kingdom church that we primarily identify with and do life with.

Attendance & Participation At Family Gatherings

In our family (the Perrys), as our kids were growing up, we had dinner times and family times. These were staples for us...not because we thought they defined what our family was about. But simply because that's what families do. Families spend time together. They eat together, regularly, consistently, showing up on time, participating in game nights and so on. Part of belonging is 'showing up' for family gatherings. We'll look at this more in the next chapter.

But there is a pendulum swing even in this, isn't there? I sometimes see natural families, friends that I admire, spend lots and lots of time together as natural families, doing all kinds of activities. And who could fault them? After all, isn't natural family what it's all about? And yet their attendance and participation in their spiritual family—ie, their local church—is so hit-and-miss. It seems like a huge Biblical blind spot to see the value of spending consistent time together as a natural family but not to walk out that same value with our spiritual family.

Jesus seemed to place spiritual family above natural family, the same way He placed the kingdom above all else. In a particularly poignant passage, Jesus's family came to visit Him. One would think that He would drop everything! After all, family has to be the highest-ranking priority in God's kingdom, doesn't it? And yet, Jesus' response is telling:

> "While Jesus was speaking to the crowds, his mother and brothers came and stood outside because they wanted to talk with him. Someone told Jesus, 'Your mother and brothers are standing outside and want to talk with you.' Jesus answered, 'Who is my mother and who are my brothers?' Then he pointed to his disciples and said, 'These are my mother and brothers! Anyone who obeys my Father in heaven is my brother or sister or mother.'"
> ~ Mt. 12:46-50

What should we think about this? Certainly Jesus isn't trying to devalue or marginalize his own mother and brothers! No, this isn't about devaluing natural family; it's about elevating the value of spiritual family. One thing is certain: God wants us to invest in our spiritual family through the most precious commodity we have--time! To be a healthy kingdom person, we must be with our spiritual family.

Becoming a family is first of all about 'attendance' (ie, showing up) *and* participation. Isn't it depressing when you have a family member 'show up' for a meal but not participate? They're either on their cell phone or otherwise distracted. They're just not present--and that's just a bummer! As the church, we've been called to a kind of attendance and participation that looks like we actually love and value each other. That means consistency, being on time, and getting involved! Those two actions of attendance and participation help define who we are within the family, because people know that we vote with our feet. Let's vote for family!

Serving

Every family has 'family chores.' There is a wonderful emphasis in the body of Christ right now of trying to insure that every person reaches his or her destiny. This is a good thing! But there is also another reality that we've largely forgotten or lost: we exist for others. Our destiny isn't for us, any more than our spiritual gifts are for us. They are for others. And so, it is only right, it is only appropriate, that everyone who is part of the family of the local church serve.

Finding a place to serve is easy when you have the heart of a servant (we're using the term 'servant' in a good way in this section!). If your highest dream is personal greatness, then you will find most jobs in the church beneath you. But if your goal is to display the heart of Christ who was a Servant, then fitting in and serving is easy!

And of course, any healthy, truly apostolic church deeply desires to see each member find his or her true kingdom fit in ministry and to be serving in a way that brings life, utilizes gifts, and fulfills destiny. This is our deep desire at Everyday Church, where we have tools in place to help people find out who they really are and what they've been created to do. We never do this at the expense of relationship. We always tell new people, "You're more important than what you can do for us." Still, though, we all want the same thing—every believer functioning in his or her perfect, God-given role within His body and within the local church. Serving is a definite way to communicate our membership in the family and our commitment to the family.

Giving

The 'give-and-take' of family includes the give! Part of what it means to belong to a church is to give financially. Whether you believe in Old Testament 'tithing' (which is 10%) or New Testament 'giving' (which is 100%) or both (which is 110%!), giving is part of the fabric and nature of family. The church is called to give and to give generously.

Jesus told us plainly that where our treasure is, there our heart will be also. There is a correlation between those who give and those who love the church. People who tend to avoid giving to the local church also tend to have trouble remaining committed and 'into' what God is doing through the church. They either give nothing, very little, or they give most or all of their gifts outside the local church.

And giving is a practical way to honor the church and its leadership. Learning to give and to trust leaders with our money is not a foreign concept to Scripture. It is modeled and called for all through the Old and New Testaments. In Acts 4, where the early church was clearly flourishing and walking in God's favor, people were giving the proceeds from real estate sales to the church in Jerusalem. This probably included very large sums of money! And what did they do with all that money? How did they actually give it? They *laid it at the apostles' feet!*

I believe in good stewardship, and I think it's important to make sure that what we're giving to is a responsible, godly ministry that handles money well. But at some point, faith is involved. The reality is that we're not called to get all our ducks in a row before we give; we're just called to give. Period. Oh, that the current church in the West would get a vision for true, Biblical giving!

Loyalty

I don't think it's possible to claim to be part of a family without loyalty. Every family needs loyalty, or else the family itself would implode through infighting, abandonment, and betrayal. After all, in the family structure, we usually know the worst about each other. We have the potential to cause each other the most damage.

That's where loyalty comes in. I'm not talking about codependent relationships, where we tolerate major dysfunction for years without so much as a peep. No. Loyalty is much better and higher than that. But loyalty is the place of friendship that allows us to 'cover a multitude of sins' (cf. 1 Peter 4:8). It is a deep commitment to one another through thick and thin—'for better or for worse!'

Our loyalty to God and to His kingdom is also expressed horizontally in kingdom churches on several fronts. We are loyal to one another, to our leaders, to our shared mission, vision, values, strategies, and structure. We are loyal to honor and protect what God is doing in our midst, and so we are loyal in our speaking and our actions.

Accountability

When we belong to a good family that cares about us, we will need to 'check in' frequently. On some very busy days, my wife and I may not have the opportunity to talk for most of the day. But on most days, we send little texts or call one another, making sure that we let each other know where we are and what we're doing. Same with our daughters. Good families have a pulse on what is happening with each person at any given time or season.

Spiritual families work the same way. Accountability was designed to be voluntary. It shouldn't be just the pastor's job to check in with everybody. It is the responsibility of each family member in a local church to voluntarily be accountable, to report in, to let people know when we'll be out of town, and so on.

Conflict Resolution

A big part of family is fighting! I don't mean that to sound worse than it is—it's just true. Families (that are honest) will admit that they disagree with each other. Sometimes a family member speaks or acts poorly, and they get in trouble with the rest of the family! Sometimes a family member needs to be confronted for various reasons, and there cannot be the risk that every time someone is confronted they threaten to leave the family. And yet, this is exactly how many Christians in the West behave! When confronted (or when anticipating confrontation), they bolt. We must have grace in correction, whether we are giving it or receiving it!

Someone once said, "Marriage is the garden in which love grows." Observing the 50% divorce rate in America, I'd say that we're not letting much blossom in our marital garden! The same can be said for the church. We need to recognize that the church is the place designated by God in which love is meant to grow. We can only grow into the love that Jesus spoke of in John 17 if we learn to love one another deeply, even fervently, from the heart—as we are commanded to in 1 Peter 4:7. And this has to happen through conflict.

People like Danny Silk and others have deftly taught us how to disagree agreeably. How wonderful to have teachers like him! But the bigger issue is this: Will we allow the God-ordained instrument called 'the local church', and often those who lead it, to address the remaining areas of growth needed in us? Will we allow the instrument of God's Divine surgery, the very scalpel of God, to be our brothers and sisters, and our leaders, imperfect as they are, to help us get rid of our own cancers of self-protection, of defensiveness, of dishonesty, of hidden sin and shame? Will we say 'yes' to God's plan for a church that sharpens one another, as iron sharpens iron?

Beloved, we are called to become members together in kingdom churches! Membership is God's idea, whether formalized on paper or not. We are already members of the body of Christ on the earth:

> "The body is one and yet has many members... God has placed the members in the body just as He desired. God has composed the body... so that there would be no division, but that the members would have the same care for one another." --1 Cor. 12:12-27

Now it's time to really walk out kingdom membership on earth with one another in local kingdom churches!

Chapter Nine
Kingdom GATHERINGS

"Jesus spoke to them about God's kingdom and gathered them together in Jerusalem [to empower them and send them out]." --Acts 1:3-8

John Wimber used to tell the story of going to a church funeral. A mother church was closing its doors, and all of the sons and daughters were gathering to say goodbye to this great church. Years before, this church had been very large. And the leadership of this church had made a commitment to always give away and send out their best. So leader after leader and team after team was sent to various places to plant churches and to do missions work. They sent people and finances all over. They did so much sending, in fact, that the church had grown very small, lacking in resources. And, by necessity, it was time to close the doors. John recounted to us, with tears in his eyes, how person after person came to that 'funeral' service to commend this church for being a sending church. And John said to the Lord, "Lord, if I ever get to lead a church or a movement, I want it to be like this."

The church in Jerusalem was like that. It was the ultimate gathering and sending place. So was Antioch. In fact, when we survey the early church in the book of Acts, we see a rhythm of coming together and going out, a gathering and scattering dynamic that is very compelling.

The Western church used to be like this, too! Many years ago, the Western church was also a leader in sending. We sent missionaries around the world. But then, somewhere along the way, we lost our way. We began to focus so much on church growth that the highest goal in many churches was to see how big the church could get. And for those numbers to go up, sending had to decrease.

*"Therefore **go**! Make disciples of all nations, baptizing them...*
and teaching them..." --Mt. 28:19

It is very exciting that the Church in the West is hearing again the call of Jesus to go. The church huddled is again turning into the church mobilized. God's people in the West are growing restless with platform-driven Christianity, mostly confined and mostly defined by the default setting of gatherings. We are bored with meeting after meeting, where much is talked about but little is actually done. As one song goes, *"You're not some dead god who lives in a building..."* God said this first in Isa. 66:1 ~ *"What sort of house you could build for me?"* Christianity was never meant to be an indoor sport! The world and the church are bored with the same thing! Good riddance to the days of the immobilized church focused on itself through repeating services.

The holy discontent we've spoken of earlier in this book is producing more churches without walls. Kingdom churches are made up of missional people who are not meeting-centered. These fiery missionaries are keenly aware that they are on a holy assignment from God to infiltrate society with the gospel of the kingdom. Their Biblical center is not platform ministry but everyday Christianity lived out in our homes, among our neighbors, at work, school, and in the marketplace. Jesus modeled a life on the streets and out among the people. His ministry was an effective model for all who live under the New Covenant and who want to see a holy invasion.

As this holy emphasis on organic Christianity continues to build into a tidal wave of nameless, faceless believers bringing the gospel of the kingdom to every facet of society, we will find ourselves rejoicing more in the church 'scattered' than in the church 'gathered.' This voluntary and purposeful scattering will enable more people to hear the gospel and meet the King than if we had stayed together and simply enjoyed our meetings.

Don't get me wrong. Meetings in and of themselves aren't bad. The early church had lots of gatherings. In fact, the early church in Jerusalem collectively met together every single day, both in smaller contexts (houses) and in larger venues (the temple courts)--see Acts 2:46 & 5:42. Paul later recounted a similar gathering dynamic in Ephesus, where the assembled church gathered in houses, to facilitate smaller groups, and outdoors, evidently where larger groups of Christians and unbelievers could gather (Paul calls this "publicly" in Acts 20:20). The early church clearly gathered often, though gatherings didn't define them.

Gatherings are not the problem, per se. In fact, gatherings are Biblical when in their proper proportion. While the "go ye" command is primary in kingdom churches, there is a secondary call to gather together as the people of God for encouragement:

> "Let us not give up meeting together, as some are in the habit of doing, but let us encourage one another—and all the more as you see the Day approaching." --Heb. 10:25

Again, it's about a recipe, not a pendulum swing. The ratios need to change, to be sure. But we needn't throw away key ingredients! Some of Christ's Bride have become so disenchanted with meetings that they've just stopped obeying Hebrews 10:25! That's not the answer. Kingdom churches are balanced and dynamically fluid. They enjoy a wonderful balance of coming and going, of gathering and scattering. Creating this dynamic is the assignment given to kingdom servants:

> "Then the master told his servant, '**Go out** to the roads and country lanes and **make them come in**, so that my house will be full." --Luke 14:23

This verse captures the dual "go ye, come ye" mandate given to the church. The church mobilized is the army, seeking and saving the lost, one person at a time. Those individuals are then brought into something--the house of God. While this "house" in Luke 14:23 is spiritual and doesn't in any way imply a building, the term "house" does speak of a large community of people ("that my house may be full"). As we've seen, Psalm 68:6 declares that "God sets the solitary in families." The church gathered in community simply represents the family, into which God brings the solitary.

Kingdom churches are sending churches. In this chapter, we're going to look at gatherings, but any discussion about gatherings must be in this context of sending.

The Church Is A Group Of People

Most believers understand that the Church universal includes all who trust in the Lord Jesus Christ alone for salvation. While each of us is 'the church', a local church expression is partially defined by its gatherings. A viable expression of church happens whenever believers come together, even "where two or three come together" in the name of Jesus (Mt. 18:20). But there are also components that define the church besides coming together. That same passage of Scripture in Matthew 18, which earlier deals with correction, tells us that there are certain matters to be told to the church (Mt. 18:17). This text implies that there was a recognized and defined group of people to whom these matters could be told. A similar dynamic is described in Acts 14, when Paul and Barnabas returned to Antioch from their missionary journey and wanted to give a testimony to their sending body:

> "On arriving there, they gathered the church together and reported all that God had done through them and how he had opened the door of faith to the Gentiles." --Acts 14:27

Whether large or small, what is commonly called the local church is, in fact, a defined group of people that make up a subset of the larger body of Christ called the universal Church. Although limited in cases of extreme persecution, *part of what it means to be the church is to gather*. And, since this is true, the subject of gatherings has great significance for those attempting to build kingdom churches with excellence. What are we to think of gatherings? How often should we gather, and for what purposes? How do we meet as local expressions of the church in small and larger contexts? What about the church in the city, or the church in a region? And what 'family' lines should and shouldn't be drawn at this time in order to build with a new set of kingdom eyes? These are the kinds of important questions that are worth reconsidering as we build kingdom churches.

GATHERING CONTEXTS

For as long as I can remember, a primary litmus test for being a committed Christian has been faithful attendance at a Sunday morning church service (or whenever the church has its main service/services). Nevertheless, there is an increasing boredom and restlessness in the hearts of many of God's people with these services, well-intentioned though they are. While pastors are exerting effort to encourage people to 'show up' at these services, more and more Christian people are growing disinterested in and even ambivalent towards attending Christian gatherings-- and especially the Sunday service. To be sure, some of these restless ones struggle with structure in general and have problems with commitment and authority. Yet there are others--sincere, godly, submitted, committed believers--who feel that something is missing, though they might have trouble articulating what that is. Confusion comes because they know there are good things happening in these services, and they feel guilty for not being more excited about what they are experiencing.

There are a few key complaints that are repeatedly leveled at the main service/services, which we are calling 'the Sunday morning service.' Here are five primary complaints:

The church is IMPERSONAL. As a service grows and becomes larger than a hundred or so, this complaint is increasingly heard. People come and attend an event, but inside they are hungry for relationship. Therefore, the longer they sit and listen, filing in and out of a building each week, the longer they start to feel disconnected, especially as the church grows.

The church is a 'ONE MAN SHOW.' Many Christians understand that God has given them spiritual gifts. They know there has to be more than one person in such a large crowd that has something to say, and yet we only usually get to hear from the same one person over and over. The church is longing for the body to be the body, where we get to see many gifts in operation and many people making contributions. Sitting in a pew on Sundays seems to perpetuate a version of consumer, spectator Christianity, and many Christians are finding themselves less willing to perpetuate this.

The church is BORING. Because we design services to contain certain elements, they quickly become predictable. This tends to breed boredom and frustration, as people pretty much know what is going to happen. The surprise is long gone, and so is expectancy. Once a person has been a believer for several years, this boredom increases, because they have now heard hundreds of sermons often on the same topics or scripture texts, sung the same songs hundreds of times, and greeted thousands of people over the years. The sheer repetition alone can cause boredom, and coupled with the predictability, boredom is pervasive. People sometimes come to church services more out of duty than delight, and many can't wait until it's over.

The church lacks POWER. As more and more of the church is getting in touch with God's presence & power on a personal level, they expect to see and feel the same in gatherings. Many believers are having experiences with God, and when they come to 'church', they expect to have continued experiences with God. For a variety of reasons, many services tend to lack power and experience. People don't encounter God in services the way they want to.

The church is too INWARD. Once a church reaches a comfortable level, either in size or in vibe, and the founding or majority members are satisfied, there tends to be a lack of desire or effort to reach out to new and lost people. The sad result is that over time the church doesn't seem to care as much if anyone new shows up. For many visitors, going to a new church is like breaking into a high school clique, and fewer believers are willing to do that in church.

For these and other reasons, the Sunday morning church service (or its equivalent) has become a dividing line for a growing segment of Christians in North America. People are less willing to simply show up, be quiet and behave. This quiet revolt speaks of the need to take another look at gatherings from a kingdom perspective.

Having said that, it must also be stated that Sunday morning church services have become the perfect scapegoat for all that is wrong with the church in North America and the West! In any organization, often the most visible elements become universally responsible for the problems of the whole, because they are easiest to see and point the finger at. While God is revolutionizing many aspects of His church, not all of what He is doing is aimed at the Sunday services. Often, what's wrong in the Sunday service is simply a symptom of what needs to change in the overall vision and expression of the local church. The issues at stake are larger and deeper than simply reformatting church services to be more interesting, inclusive, or culturally relevant.

Gathering God's people together is a Biblical practice, modeled and encouraged as part of both the Old and New Covenants. But that is not the end of the story. Assumptions about gatherings have been passed on from generation to generation of churchgoers, resulting in mind-numbing repetitiveness and, at times, a cool detachment from the vibrancy of New Testament Christianity. The paradigms and practices we've built our churches around are currently subject to adjustments by the Holy Spirit. As my colleague Gary Goodell says so eloquently, "Permission has been granted to do church differently in the third millennium."

Changing The Center

Dare I say it? Sunday morning services in particular have become *an idol* in our church expression in the West. I am not advocating the removal of all Sunday services. Rather, I am definitely advocating the removal of their centrality in our thinking and practice. While weekly Sunday services can be convenient to have because of the cultural expectations in the West, we don't actually need these services to accomplish our mission of bringing the gospel of the kingdom to humanity. Nor do we need them to accomplish our mission of changed lives. Even though Sunday services are culturally convenient, they are also incredibly labor-intensive, and the effort put into many Sunday services across America is not always worth the results. Sometimes our Sunday services are underwhelming. Can you imagine a highly impacting, growing church in North America without a Sunday service (or its equivalent)? I can, because they are emerging in many places. Furthermore, Sunday mornings are becoming a great time to either gather as house churches or, better yet, for believers to spend time with unbelieving neighbors and friends for the sake of evangelism!

So, a growing number of God's people are beginning to embrace the value of the church scattered over the church gathered, and this is causing us to question our gatherings. For those of us who are used to thinking of and defining the church in terms of its gatherings, this shift, while easy to talk about, is much more difficult to embrace and to put into practice--especially for church leaders.

Let's face it. Regardless of rhetoric to the contrary, the center of most churches in the West is the platform that is used at our main service/services, whether that is Sundays, Saturday nights, or Tuesday nights. For centuries, we have been developing platform-centered church life. Because we have been putting so much emphasis on the Sunday service and other gatherings, we have developed a built-in consumer mentality that is now coming back to bite us. The value shift from the church gathered to the church scattered is a difficult one for paid professionals to make. We have made a large part of the job of the senior pastor (and the staff) to provide a fantastic service for the people, filled with great worship and dynamic preaching containing amazing alliterations and excellent exegesis. And once pastors do that, plus some counseling and some leadership development, what else is there time for? I know pastors who spend 20 hours a week on their Sunday message. Is this really what Jesus had in mind when He decided to build His church?

At some point, the platform is no longer adequate to be the center of organic church life, and a values shift must take place that redefines how we view and practice gatherings. The focus and attention of the church is moving from 'come ye' to 'go ye', and our identity is shifting from the church 'gathered' in meetings one or two days a week to the church 'scattered' in the marketplace, living courageously for Christ everyday and viewing the mobilized church scattered throughout the community as our most consistently valid expression of Christianity, far more important than church services.

Beginning in Acts 8:1, with the onset of the persecution of the church, we get a Biblical glimpse into the value of the church scattered: "On that day a great persecution broke out against the church at Jerusalem, and all except the apostles were scattered throughout Judea and Samaria." But because the early church in Jerusalem kept the focus of the church outward and missional, when the involuntary scattering occurred in Acts 8, they didn't miss a beat.

"Those who had scattered preached the word wherever they went." --Acts 8:4

The very next story in the narrative describes Philip being led by the Spirit into the streets to preach the gospel. Later in the story, he speaks with the Ethiopian eunuch. Philip leads him to the Lord, baptizes him, and then Philip gets transported to another town where he preaches some more, all the while rejoicing! This is not the behavior of a man concerned with when he was going to go to his next church service! This is a kingdom man who lived among an outward, missional people.

The effectiveness of the gospel multiplied exponentially when the church was scattered. The gospel went from a single city (Jerusalem), to places such as Phoenicia, Cyprus, Antioch, Pontus, Galatia, Cappadocia, Asia, and Bithynia (Acts 11:19; 1 Pet. 1:1). Modern-day examples, such as the house church movement in China, provide ample evidence that the church scattered, without the benefit of a platform-driven model of church life, flourishes.

Kingdom churches embrace each individual as a priest of the Lord. Therefore, there is great confidence in the church scattered. Kingdom churches value the church scattered over the church gathered, because it is as the church is scattered that we can model Jesus and impact society. We named our church 'Everyday' for this very reason—to emphasize that it's about a lifestyle.

The church gathered, when considered central to the definition of the church, becomes a holy huddle, irrelevant to the society around us and inward in our orientation. When the gathered church is considered central, our money and efforts reflect this thinking, and we are then forced to pursue larger buildings and staffing to accommodate the larger gathered crowd. The work required to pull off our gatherings can tax God's people to the point where our services are getting in the way of the church scattered. It's not about a particular size church but rather a focus on Sunday services or other large gatherings that become the sum total of the church's experience and effectiveness for most people in the church.

By contrast, when the value of the church *scattered* is central, with a focus on the kingdom of priests, all church gatherings take a step down in importance. We can only reasonably consider how to come together when the backdrop of the church scattered is in place and visible in the discussion.

It is evident in both Old and New Testament times as well as through early church history that God's people gathered in a variety of settings, depending largely on the level of persecution: indoors and outdoors; in living rooms, synagogues, temple courts; on mountains, in caves, in valleys; in prayer meetings and preaching services; with and without food present; in upper rooms and catacombs; and so on. With the exception of a few prescriptive passages, such as 1 Corinthians 11-14, the New Testament essentially contains descriptive rather than prescriptive language about gathering contexts. Therefore, there is a lot of liberty for kingdom churches to meet wherever and whenever! Other factors come into play that call for wisdom, discernment, and Holy Spirit 'intuition' (skills also required for good fishing!), such as what works best culturally and geographically.

Two Primary Biblical Contexts

The church has gathered in the two primary New Testament contexts of smaller groups and larger assemblies at various times throughout history. For example, before 1960, small groups were not very popular in the U.S., but since the charismatic renewal began in the early 1960s, small home meetings have now become a standard context for many churches in the West. Whether you call them small groups, cell groups, G12s, house churches, or some other name, collectively they represent one primary Biblical context. We use the term 'microchurches', because we consider these spiritual families to be smaller churches.

Of course, in addition to these smaller settings, the church gathers in larger contexts. In the early part of the book of Acts, this gathering place was either at the Temple or outdoors in crowds. Today, these gatherings are often called 'Sunday services' or 'celebrations.' The early church clearly gathered in both of these primary contexts:

> "Every day they continued to meet together in the temple courts. They broke bread in their homes and ate together with glad and sincere hearts" --Acts 2:46

> "...all the believers used to meet together in Solomon's Colonnade." --Acts 5:12

> "Day after day, in the temple courts and from house to house, they never stopped teaching and proclaiming the good news that Jesus is the Christ."
> --Acts 5:42

> "You know that I have not hesitated to preach anything that would be helpful to you but have taught you publicly and from house to house." --Acts 20:20

Some well-meaning but misguided folks are espousing the idea that the large gathering is the problem—ie, that we should only have house meetings. But I love the way God designed it—house to house and larger gatherings. It's a good design! And it works.

We all know that the church doesn't consist of a worship service one day a week, but of a people who walk with God in the midst of their ordinary, everyday lives. We are the church! And we are learning to *be* the church, carrying God's presence and power wherever we go and whatever we find ourselves doing. Then, when we gather at various times during the week, there is great joy in His presence as we enjoy each other and share together in a way that edifies & equips one another.

Purpose Of Gatherings

So why do we go to church services, anyway? It's a good question! Even though we are focused on *being* the church rather than *doing* church, there is still great value in being together in larger corporate settings.

To Express Family. We talked about this in the previous chapter. Families gather.

To Worship Together In The Company Of The Saints. In Ps. 35:18, David declared, "I will give you thanks in the great assembly." We can always worship God on our own. But there is a unique dynamic released when we are together. It is good and right to bring our offering before the Lord in the great assembly.

To Encounter God In The Company Of The Saints. Jesus said that when we gather together, He is in our midst (Mt. 18:20). Since God is omnipresent, this statement by Jesus is an invitation into another place of encounter that we are not able to access on our own.

To Be Strengthened In Christ. When the body comes together, we experience the fullness of gifts in operation, which releases the fullness of strength. 1 Corinthians 12 speaks of the vital necessity for all the gifts to be in operation when we come together. Further, when the five equipping gifts of Eph. 4:11 are released in the assembly, the church is edified and the saints are equipped for ministry. Preaching is a powerful, God-given tool to strengthen the church, modeled extensively by Jesus, Paul, and Apollos. And mutual ministry happens when we are together, which is a God-ordained dynamic for great strengthening and encouragement.

To Help Others Come To Know Jesus. When the early church gathered, the result was that people invariably became Christians! As the church experienced God's power, the lost were attracted and saved, from Pentecost in Acts 2 onward. Paul instructed the charismatic Corinthian church to gather in a way that helped the unsaved come to know Jesus Christ (1 Cor. 14:24-25). This is still a worthwhile reason to gather.

GATHERING CONTENT

So when we gather, what do we do? What makes up the content of our meetings? The answer is both Biblical and practical. Each gathering may have a different purpose, so to give a uniform answer for all gatherings is impossible. A relational gathering will have different content than a prayer meeting. In this section, I want to primarily focus on larger gatherings, but let's take a quick look at the content of smaller gatherings.

Gatherings In The Home

At Everyday, when we were first determining the content of our microchurches, we looked primarily to Acts 2, where we see the very first example of a home fellowship. In v. 42-47, we see that the believers studied the apostles' doctrine, they had fellowship, they broke bread, and they prayed. But there are more than 4 components. Studying the apostles' doctrine was easy enough, as the equivalent today is Bible study. Fellowship could include any number of things, such as social/relational time and 'one another' ministry. Breaking bread could include both dinner and communion. And prayer could include both intercessory prayer and ministry prayer.

After thinking and praying about this list, our formation team agreed that it would be difficult to accomplish all these things with any degree of quality in one night. There were just too many components. So we decided to have alternating formats with different components on opposite weeks. So in our microchurches, during one week we focus on Bible, Intercession, and Worship. During another week we focus on Dinner, Bodylife, and Groups. I think there is liberty in determining what components a kingdom church would like in its small group gatherings. This basic structure has worked well for us. (If you would like to find out more about our microchurch format, feel free to connect with us via our website: www.everydaychurch.com.)

Larger Gatherings

There are some key Biblical principles given to us that help us define the purpose of our larger meetings with much more clarity and help us discern what is meant to occur in gatherings of kingdom churches. Let's look at four principles that are essential to consider when preparing for and building great kingdom gatherings: (1) Biblical Participation; (2) The Role Of Preaching; (3) Planned Spontaneity; and (4) The Dwelling Place Of God.

Biblical Participation

There is a strong Biblical basis for more participatory gatherings than we have grown accustomed to. Ready for a short Bible study? These practical guidelines are given to us in 1 Corinthians 14. The context of Paul's discourse to the church in 1 Corinthians 11- 14 is captured in the phrase "when you come together", which is referenced 4 different times (11:18, 20, 33; 14:26). This is a passage of Scripture that is definitely instructive on gatherings, with much to say about participation. Let's take a fresh look at Paul's insights regarding Biblical participation in kingdom gatherings.

Our Basis. The basis for more participatory gatherings is woven throughout 1 Corinthians 14. Paul is indicating the involvement in the gathering of more than the worship leader, the announcement person, and the speaker. He not only says 'everyone' but then mentions various contributions. Paul repeatedly emphasizes multiple contributions during gatherings:

> "I would like *every one of you* to speak in tongues, but I would rather have you prophesy." (v. 5) "If an unbeliever or someone who does not understand comes in while *everybody* is prophesying, he will be convinced by all that he is a sinner and will be judged by all, and the secrets of his heart will be laid bare. So he will fall down and worship God, exclaiming, 'God is really here among you!'" (v. 24-25) "When you come together, *everyone* has a hymn, or a word of instruction, a revelation, a tongue or an interpretation." (v. 26) "Two or three prophets should speak, and *the others* should weigh carefully what is said. And if a revelation comes to someone who is sitting down, the first speaker should stop. For you can *all prophesy* in turn so that *everyone* may be instructed and encouraged." (v. 29-30)

Our Purpose. The purpose for participatory gatherings is two-fold: edification and evangelism. Our first reason for mutual contribution is for the benefit or edification of the whole church. Our goal is not simply self-expression [which is childish thinking, v. 20]. Paul always subjugates self-expression to the test of mutual benefit. In other words, it is not enough to have people contribute in a church gathering simply because they want to, or because they feel stifled. The goal and purpose is always for the greater good of the church. These contributions are for the benefit of others.

> "For anyone who speaks in a tongue does not speak to men...but everyone who prophesies speaks to men *for their strengthening, encouragement and comfort.*" (v. 2-3) "He who speaks in a tongue edifies himself, but he who prophesies *edifies the church*...he who prophesies is greater than he who speaks in tongues, unless he interprets, *so that the church may be edified.*" (v. 4-5) "Now, brothers, if I come to you and speak in tongues, *what good will I be to you,* unless I bring some revelation or knowledge or prophecy or word of instruction?" (v. 6) "Since you are eager to have spiritual gifts, try to excel in gifts *that build up the church.*" (v. 12) "You may be giving thanks well enough, but the other man *is not edified.*" (v. 17) "For you can all prophesy in turn *so that everyone may be instructed and encouraged.*" (v. 31)

Our other reason for mutual contribution is for the salvation of lost people. Paul also puts evangelism above self-expression when he says in vv. 24-25:

"So if the whole church comes together and everyone speaks in tongues [which is generally for self-edification, v. 4], and some who do not understand or some unbelievers come in, will they not say that you are out of your mind? But if an unbeliever or someone who does not understand comes in while everybody is prophesying, he will be convinced by all that he is a sinner and will be judged by all, and the secrets of his heart will be laid bare. So he will fall down and worship God, exclaiming, 'God is really here among you!'"

Read in context, Paul is clearly saying that our purpose for the priesthood of all believers practiced in gatherings must include our desire for lost people to come to Christ. Our expression of gifts must be mindful of those with us who don't know the Lord. This principle would apply to any size meeting.

An exciting truth in this verse is that the multitude of gifts flowing in a church gathering is used by God to bring salvation to lost people! Perhaps our evangelistic efforts have been hindered because we've required one person (the pastor) to use all the gifts to help people get saved. Praise God for the day when we see unbelievers coming to our gatherings and finding Jesus because He is so clearly seen and heard through the prophetic contributions of so many of His people!

Our Guidelines. Guidelines speak of both what we release and how we evaluate what we've released in gatherings. We then use these Biblical guidelines to determine how to administrate participatory activity in our gatherings. We want to release all Biblical gifts of the Spirit, in their proper context, given through godly people filled with the Holy Spirit and in relationship, within the Biblical guidelines He has given us in His Word. There are specific gifts listed in 1 Corinthians 14:26 as appropriate for participation:

Singing: A song offered to the Lord that builds up those who hear it. I would include dance & the arts here. This song could be planned (with music, on stage) or spontaneous.

A word of instruction: This is not a full teaching, but a word. It is like a prophecy but from the Scriptures to instruct and encourage all who hear it.

A revelation: This could be a word of knowledge, word of wisdom, dream, vision, picture, or impression. Given clearly and appropriately, this can be powerful.

Tongues with interpretation: Tongues is worship in another language from man to God. It is not prophecy, but a word of praise to God. In the church, it must be accompanied by interpretation. [This does not prevent individuals from singing or praying in tongues softly within a church gathering. The guidelines apply to when the attention is purposefully on one person who is 'giving' a tongue for all.]

Especially prophecy (v. 1, 3, 24-25): Of the gifts listed, Paul singles out prophecy (speaking to others on God's behalf) as the most important and useful gift in church gatherings. He encourages us to eagerly desire to prophesy (v. 1). This would include general prophecy (v. 3), which involves speaking God's heart and mind (i.e., His present Word) for individuals and/or for the group gathered so that people are strengthened, encouraged, and comforted. This builds up the church! It would also include specific prophecy (v. 24-25), which involves speaking from God to another the 'secrets' of a person's heart (who may not know the Lord) so they can either come to Christ or be convinced of God's wonderful presence among us. It includes words of knowledge (i.e., 'secrets' revealed). This builds up the individual and in some cases causes the pre-Christian to repent and be saved!

Our Evaluation. And then there is evaluation. Once we understand the potential for powerful good that a release of God's Spirit in a gathering can be, we must also see the unfortunate potential for damage. Like a powerful river, there needs to be banks to steer or direct the 'flow' so that the power is used for God's purposes and not to distract or even damage the body in any way.

Few people feel safe when there are no guidelines and no facilitating leadership, especially when it comes to 'open' sharing that has a spontaneous element in larger gatherings. Thus, evaluating such activity is vital, since we are aiming for quality (i.e., beauty & excellence in worshiping Jesus Christ) as well as quantity (i.e., many people making contributions). In fact, we are commanded by God to 'judge' the contributions of others (1 Cor. 14:29). To judge here, or 'weighing carefully' (NIV) means 'to separate thoroughly, to discriminate, to call in question; to discern, to think, and to conclude.' The idea here is not to be judgmental, but to use discernment as you listen to others speak. As thinking, feeling people trying to learn how to release multiple contributions in a gathering, we want to help gently guard the quality of those contributions by using Biblical measurements to evaluate and give feedback. Here are the kinds of questions we use to evaluate:

Did it strengthen? "All of these must be done for the strengthening of the church." (v. 26) Our standard for evaluation is whether or not the church is being strengthened. If it was revelation, was it accurate and fitting? If it was song or dance, did it draw attention to Jesus? If it was a word of instruction, did it help the majority of people in the room?

Was it for the whole church? "...so that everyone may be instructed and encouraged." (v. 31) Some things are meant to be shared with a close friend. Some things are meant to be shared in a home and/or a small group setting. And some things are meant to be kept to oneself. We want to have things shared in their context that are meant for the whole church that is then gathered. This could include a prophetic word for an individual that blesses the entire church upon hearing it, or someone might have a word of knowledge that leads us to pray for a group of people within the church. As long as the whole church that is gathered is built up, it is appropriate.

Was it decently and in order? "Everything should be done in a fitting and orderly way." (v. 40) Biblically and practically, it means following the rules and rhythm of the gathering. If there is an atmosphere of joy and celebration, a rebuking word about repentance probably wouldn't be in order. Following the theme that seems to be established by the Spirit is important here and requires sensitivity. If there have already been a few prophetic words and the facilitator is closing that time, another prophetic word might not be in order. Further, it helps to ask, is the contribution fitting with the philosophy, heart, and people of the church? Common sense, courtesy, and consideration work well here to help us find balance in these things, as well as making sure we are in relationship with each other.

Was it done in love? "Eagerly desire the greater gifts. And now I will show you the most excellent way." (12:31) Sandwiched between 1 Corinthians 12 and 14, the two greatest chapters on spiritual gifts in meetings, is 1 Corinthians 13, the greatest chapter on love. To exercise spiritual gifts in love means that our motive is truly to bless others rather than draw attention to ourselves. It also means that we are not easily offended if others do not receive or appreciate our gifts or if we need gentle correction about the use of our gifts. The opposite of loving contributions are those done out of "envy and selfish ambition" (James 3:14-16). These contributions create confusion and potentially invite trouble from the enemy! (cf. James 3:16) It is important that our contributions are from a heart of love than from a lesser motive.

Now, before we immediately qualify this message of participation as only applicable to small groups and home meetings, we'll want to notice that no such qualifications are given in the text. The city of Corinth was a large, thriving city of around 500,000 people. Paul spent a year and a half there investing in the church. It is possible, of course, that the church in Corinth was a house church. At least thirty people are mentioned by name as part of this church, and if we imply family members we end up with perhaps eighty people mentioned or alluded to. Often house churches were conducted in homes with large courtyard areas, where up to eighty people were accommodated. If this was indeed the case, then the Corinthian church was slightly larger than the average church in America (which is seventy). However, the size of the church in Corinth is not clear. Some Bible teachers believe, based on circumstantial evidence, that the Corinthian church could have been several hundred or even several thousand people. What is clear is that large gatherings can (and should) include at least some expression of Biblical participation as outlined in 1 Corinthians 11-14.

The Role Of Preaching

On the other side of the coin, and equally evident in the Scriptural model and mandate of kingdom expression, is the place of one person preaching the Word of God to a group or crowd of people. Some who advocate egalitarian participation as the only legitimate activity in gatherings seem to have forgotten or ignored the many Biblical examples and exhortations towards Biblical preaching. They see preaching as some sort of "old wineskin." In light of the thousands of sermons many of us have heard, we might find ourselves agreeing with those Gentiles who found preaching to be a foolish activity! (1 Cor. 1:21) Still, preaching and teaching have a powerful anointing and blessing from God and ought to be part of what happens in our gatherings. One person talking to the many is modeled and encouraged over seventy times in the New Testament:

Jesus preached and taught continually, from the beginning of His ministry (Mt. 4:17) to the very end (Acts 1:3), even going so far as to say that this is why He had come (Mark 1:38).

The disciples were commissioned by Jesus to preach and teach (Mark 3:14), and they preached everywhere (Mark 16:20).

The early church taught and preached to the lost (Acts 8:4) and to the believers (Acts 14:35). They preached in larger meetings in the public arena and also in the smaller context of home meetings (Acts 20:20). Paul talked so long to the Christians that someone fell asleep and fell out the window (Acts 20:7-11)! He actually spoke through the entire night from dusk to dawn--one person speaking to the many. When in Ephesus, Paul taught the believers day and night for three years (Acts 20:31).

The pastoral epistles of 1 and 2 Timothy, which are highly applicable to every church today, reveal a strong exhortation to publicly read, teach, and preach the Scriptures (1 Tim. 4:13; 2 Tim. 4:2) in church gatherings, even going so far as to say that preaching and teaching is part of the job description of at least some of the elders of the church (1 Tim. 5:17).

The balance of participation and preaching/teaching is one of the challenges we face in having Scriptural gatherings. As we're thinking about gatherings, there is another important factor to consider.

Planned Spontaneity

I have both read of and spoken personally with church leaders who typically plan Sunday services down to the minute. They believe strongly that God has led them to have the kinds of meetings that are orchestrated with excellence, and for them, this means excellent planning. This is especially common in both orthodox, liturgical churches and in seeker-sensitive churches.

I have also read of and spoken personally with church leaders who believe that a meeting has no value and is clearly not led by the Holy Spirit if it is not completely spontaneous. In their minds, to plan for a service is to leave out the Holy Spirit. This is especially true in smaller, independent, Pentecostal and charismatic churches and in renewal churches of any denomination.

Of course, the Bible really teaches both of these perspectives. Proverbs 16:9 is an example of how the Scriptures embrace the dynamic kingdom tension of both of these realities: *"In his heart a man plans his course, but the LORD determines his steps."* The original Living Bible says it even more clearly: *"We should make our plans, counting on God to direct us."* The alternative to choosing either only planning or only spontaneity is to take the best of each of these mindsets and combine them for great effectiveness. A friend of mine calls it being smart and Spirit-filled! I call it "planned spontaneity." Kingdom churches that experience planned spontaneity can enjoy the best of the power of planning and the joy of spontaneity. And this combination of Word and Spirit, or planning and spontaneity, of preaching and participation, is the dream of many in kingdom churches.

To that end, let's look at four principles that are especially applicable to those who are leading or facilitating a kingdom gathering:

Spirit-Led Thematic Planning. As the leadership team of a kingdom church seeks God together, we sometimes discern overall themes and seasons that will impact our planning and preparation. Like the pedals on a bicycle, God may be "pushing" on a particular theme or emphasis, such as family, outreach, prophecy, or healing. We can honor Him by leaning into these Spirit-led themes while also allowing room for the Lord to orchestrate the elements of our times together in a way that release His theme. We can set sail for our destination while allowing the wind of the Spirit to determine our exact course to get there.

Prayer First. Regardless of the format or purpose of any meeting, most gatherings in the church in the West are thin in the area of praying about the gathering ahead of time. Every time that we gather ought to have been first bathed in prayer. It is a holy activity to assemble people in the name of the Lord Jesus Christ. Prayer expresses our dependence on God to do what only He can do. The results we are looking for must come from heaven, whether it is a gathering aimed at winning lost people, strengthening the church, or both. *"Unless the LORD builds the house, its builders labor in vain"* (Ps. 127:1). As we prepare for gatherings, we are discerning from the Lord the purpose of the gathering. What does He want to do? Heart preparation must take precedence over strategic planning. Preparation means that the people who will be leading or facilitating the meeting have gone before God to prepare their hearts, to listen for His instruction, and to wait in His presence. Much of what passes for pre-service prayer in our churches is simply a quick request for God to bless what we are doing. There must be a context where God can speak to us and lead us, in real time, even to the point of speaking to us to lay aside part or all of our agenda and to do something different, even spontaneous. Of course, God's leading can be entirely in the planning stages, and then we simply execute His plan. But even when I have prepared a specific Biblical message that I end up preaching, the prayer before our gatherings has been used by God many times to influence, fine-tune, and clarify the message God has given me.

Spirit-Led Default Setting. It is important to prayerfully determine among your leadership team what elements you believe God desires in your gatherings. It is not unspiritual to have a default setting for the elements of your gathering. These can include worship, preaching, announcements, offering, ministry, intercession, meals, communion, videos, open sharing, testimonies, etc. Because not every meeting can accomplish every purpose, it is OK, both Biblically and practically, to plan gatherings, as long as there is sensitivity to the leadership of the Holy Spirit during the planning times.

Prayer During. In the midst of any meeting, leaders (and the entire assembled community) must learn the gentle art of sensitivity to the Holy Spirit and flexibility on our feet. This does not come naturally to most people. Why is this essential? Because for Jesus to be Head of the Church, and for the Holy Spirit to truly lead us, we must be subject to the leadership of the Spirit and the Headship of Jesus "on the spot", in real time. In other words, God's leading in our lives cannot be relegated to only when we are planning the annual preaching calendar. He must also be Lord of the actual gathering itself. We instruct people to live "moment by moment by Jesus" and to allow the Lord to lead them spontaneously into encounters with lost people in the marketplace. We must practice this same level of spiritual sensitivity to God in our gatherings. In Acts 10, Peter was in a situation where the Lord made him pay attention "on his feet." In the middle of his message to a group of God-seekers, the Holy Spirit fell and interrupted his sermon (Acts 10:44). Peter quickly recognized what was happening and switched gears, turning the meeting into a testimony time and a baptism service (vv. 46, 48). This is the kind of sensitivity needed in our churches and among our leaders.

Jesus instructed us to be willing to leave the ninety-nine to go after the one. I believe this is true even in our gatherings. There are times where God will ask the many to wait patiently while He diverts His attention on the one. He modeled this all the time.

The Dwelling Place Of God
Ephesians 2:22 tells us that the church is becoming a dwelling place in which God lives by His Spirit. This reference to a corporate dwelling is an invitation from God to His people to create a place where He can dwell in our midst, and because this reference of the church is plural, this involves our gatherings.

> "This is what the LORD says: 'Heaven is my throne, and the earth is my footstool. Where is the house you will build for me? Where will my resting place be?'"
> --Isa. 66:1

As living stones, the collective body of Christ in a given place and sphere make up the house of the Lord. God is expressing His desire to be with us as a place where He can live and rest. He is looking for people who will create a dwelling place for His Person and His Presence.

This has everything to do with our gatherings. If the first commandment is to have first place, then our gatherings must honor the Person and Presence of God ahead of anything else--not in theory, but in practice. He is church. The Holy Spirit is a gentle Dove, recognizing when our agendas take priority over His Presence. The Person of God must be honored at every single one of our gatherings more than anyone else's person or presence. His Person is our first priority, ahead of even equipping or evangelism.

FACILITATING GATHERINGS

What can we learn, then, about facilitating gatherings in kingdom churches that include the best of planning and spontaneity? We close this chapter with 10 applications that summarize how to have gatherings in a more Biblical, powerful way:

1. **We gather best when we've been scattered most.** If the culture of the people who are gathering is outward, then the gatherings are that much sweeter.

2. **We don't get hung up on our gathering environment.** Jesus gathered people around a stinky fishing boat. Surely it's OK for us to gather in a gymnasium, a living room, a bar, or wherever it works best. Facilities facilitate...period.

3. **We don't get hung up on our gathering size.** Let's not fixate on whether the entire Church is supposed to adopt a cell/house church model, or whether megachurches are good or bad. This is shallow thinking. Let's focus on why we're gathering and encountering God and each other. Let's gather big and small and in between, for the sake of a lost world desperately in need of Jesus!

4. **We discern God's purpose of each of our gatherings.** Why are we meeting? What are we trying to accomplish? This is key. Other things will fall into place as we understand God's heart and His agenda for our time together.

5. **We come prepared to participate at every gathering.** Everyone ought to come as though you will participate--and then do it! Even when there is a main speaker, there are still opportunities to bring our offering and to lean into what God is doing.

6. **We expect the Spirit to lead us.** We wait on God before and during our gatherings to discern His direction, because His agenda is always best!

7. **We expect the unexpected.** We believe in the creative, spontaneous nature of God to be expressed in the assembly of the saints!

8. **We have a track to run on.** Planning is good, not fleshly! God is a planner! Be liberated to hear God during the preparation stage, not just on your feet!

9. **We evaluate what we're doing.** We have no sacred cows. We're not afraid to take a hard look at what's working and what's not--and then improve. Even a prophet only sees in part, so we must be learners in process.

10. **We bathe every gathering in prayer.** We're more about preparation than planning, because we know that God can do a whole lot more than we can. People are gathering to see Jesus, not us, anyway! So we bathe it in prayer, counting on His leadership, knowing that He loves people more than we do, and He wants to be with us!

Chapter Ten
Kingdom ADVANCEMENT

"The kingdom of God is like a mustard seed--the smallest seed you plant in the ground. Yet when planted, it grows and becomes the largest of all garden plants, with such big branches that the birds of the air can perch in its shade."
--Mark 4:30-32

The kingdom of God cannot be stopped! It is expanding throughout the earth at an incredibly rapid rate, and it is picking up speed. This is the time for the church to stand up and lift up her head, because Jesus' return is drawing near! (Lk. 21:28) We are closing in on the end of an era, and the end will be better than the beginning!

God seems to always start small, and then when things look like the can't get any worse, they do! But then, over time things get bigger quickly. In the investment world, this is known as the 'J-curve.' Creation began with light, Jesus began in a stable, the feeding of 5,000 began with a few loaves and fishes, and the church began in an upper room. Jesus compares the kingdom to a mustard seed. It is pitifully small. Yet because of the exponential quality of the kingdom, it grows and spreads until it affects everything around it. The kingdom of God, when planted, yields results that are much larger than would seem possible. This is why the prophet tells Zechariah not to despise the day of small beginnings. When the kingdom of God is at work, the possibilities are exponential.

An example is the Muslim world. For centuries, the Church was mostly hopeless when it came to reaching Islamic people with the Gospel of Jesus Christ. Yet today, thousands of Muslims are having sovereign encounters with Jesus Christ. God is breaking through this culture with the Gospel, and many Islamic people are coming to know Jesus as their Savior. The work of Iris Global and other missions movements are seeing amazing things happen in Islamic countries in Africa--including entire villages being saved in a day! The hour we are living in is absolutely remarkable. Thank you Jesus.

The question isn't whether or not God's kingdom will advance and accelerate—it is and it will! The question is whether it will happen in our geography, where we live, on our watch. Our heart as those who build kingdom churches is not only be part of what God is doing but also to accelerate it. We want to partner with Him to see radical kingdom advancement. In order to be a catalytic people, we need to understand the factors that cause kingdom advancement to happen and to accelerate. In this final chapter, we're going to look at some of these catalytic factors that release supernatural acceleration in kingdom advancement, whether that is in local churches, businesses, cities, regions, or nations.

FULLNESS

> "And you have been given fullness in Christ,
> who is the head over every power and authority." --Col. 2:10

The first principle of advancement is fullness. Kingdom churches embrace fullness, and when we build with fullness, we unlock exponential possibility. Having only part of the kingdom, only part of our inheritance, a little bit of unity, a whiff of power, a smidgen of diversity...these things will never do. There is a generation rising that must have fullness! They insist on it, and this is a trait of the people of the kingdom of God.

Jesus models fullness for us: "For it was the Father's good pleasure for *all the fullness* to dwell in Him." (Col. 1:19) Because we are re-presenting Christ in the world today, it is essential that we walk in the fullness of Christ. As He is, so also are we in this world. We are called to be people of fullness. And we've been *given* fullness!

Fullness is intended for us as individuals and also as communities. When it comes to fullness in churches, a mentor and friend of mine likes to say, "I want to build a church that runs on all eight cylinders." I love that! Why settle for a church that is excellent at worship and poor at discipleship? Why embrace a paradigm of church life where we can be prophetic but not evangelistic? Kingdom churches "run on all eight cylinders." This is Biblical and right. Because we have been given fullness in Christ, fullness is our inheritance and our birthright.

Fullness stretches us and calls us higher. It is easier to walk without fullness (and settle) than to embrace the fullness of the kingdom. The scope and reality of the kingdom is huge, and fullness is Biblical, because it originates in the Person of God.

The Fullness Of God

One of the most captivating prayers in the New Testament is found in Ephesians 3, where Paul describes the content of his intercession for the church in Ephesus. He asks God for strength and power for his friends. He cries out for them to have faith and love and the ability to grasp a fresh revelation of the love of God. And then, in verse 19, he tells us why he is praying these things: *"...that you may be filled to the measure of all the fullness of God."* To think that God's people could be filled with the fullness of His own Person is amazing. In 2 Cor. 13:14, Paul gives one of my favorite benedictions in the Scriptures: *"Now may the grace of our Lord Jesus Christ, the love of God [the Father], and the fellowship of the Holy Spirit, be with you all."* The fullness of God involves the Father's love, the lavish grace of Jesus, and intimate friendship with the Spirit of God. Some churches focus on the Father and His love. Others focus on the Person of Christ. Still others are all about the Spirit. Kingdom churches embrace the fullness of the Person of God as revealed in Father, Son, and Spirit.

Fullness Of God's Word

In Colossians 1:25, the apostle Paul describes his assignment from God to His Church when he says, "I have become its servant by the commission God gave me to present to you the Word of God in its fullness." Paul was committed to the fullness of God's Word. He essentially declared the same commitment to the church in Ephesus when he told them, "I did not shrink from declaring to you the whole counsel of God" (Acts 20:27). From parenting to praying for the sick, we want to build kingdom churches that declare to people the whole counsel of God. Paul was committed to fullness in his teaching. He understood the dynamic kingdom tension in building a people of the Word and a people of the Spirit. In some churches, only certain topics are "spiritual," while other meat and potatoes subjects are not exciting enough to give attention to. Not so in kingdom churches. They provide a balanced diet with all the nutrients of God's Word. Being radical does not mean being incomplete. Fullness in God's Word is right!

Fullness Of Maturity

We are called to be fully mature in Christ. To see that happen, we need *all* of God's people using *all* of their God-given gifts and serving to *all* of their God-given potential, so that we can all reach a place of maturity that releases the fullness of Christ in our midst.

> "It was he who gave some to be apostles, some to be prophets, some to be evangelists, and some to be pastors and teachers, to prepare God's people for works of service, so that the body of Christ may be built up until we all reach unity in the faith and in the knowledge of the Son of God and become mature, attaining to the whole measure of the fullness of Christ." --Eph. 4:11-13

The causal link between the five-fold ministry and fullness is striking:

Five-Fold > Saints Equipped > Saints Serving > Church Edified >
Unity > Know Christ > Maturity > Fullness

As we understand the importance of the five-fold ministry, we begin to operate in who we are and honor these gifts among us. The five-fold expression of apostle, prophet, evangelist, pastor, and teacher results in the people of God being equipped and prepared to serve. This preparation is what releases the saints to serve and minister. As God's people serve, the church is built up and edified. As we are built up, we become unified and we know Christ better. As that happens, we grow up and become mature. And as we become mature together, we experience the ultimate completion: the fullness of Jesus Christ!

Fullness Of Equipping

Each of the five gifts listed in Ephesians 4:11 must be operational in kingdom churches in order for us to reach a place of fullness in Christ. This is why we must give heed to the growing cry of the people of God for churches that embrace all aspects of what is called the 'five-fold' ministry gifts of Ephesians 4:11. People no longer want to build a church around the primary gift or gifts of the senior pastor. This is not a devaluing of the pastoral role but rather an elevating of the five-fold ministry. More importantly, it's just not Biblical to do so. It isn't fullness, and it doesn't produce maturity in the people of God. Rather than just a teaching church, or just a prophetic church, or just an outward church, people want it all--and they should! This is how God has 'wired' His people. We can and should want fullness of maturity through the balanced expression of these five equipping gifts.

The text in Ephesians is clear, using "kai" (and) as a means to group these five equipping roles. This means that in order for the body of Christ to experience true fullness of maturity, we must build churches where all five of these gifts—apostle, prophet, evangelist, pastor, teacher—are working together and in the same community to edify and equip the saints. This is God's plan. Ephesians 1:22-23 tells us that the church is the fullness of Christ. When the body functions together in fullness, we see a literal, physical expression of the fullness of God.

As we build leadership teams, we must think and plan and pray and recruit through the lens of the five-fold ministry. One of the best examples I see in the U.S. is Bethel Church in Redding, California. The senior leadership team of that church includes all five functions. Bill Johnson has given the pastoral leadership of the local church to his son, Eric. But the five-fold senior leadership team is still in place, surrounding Eric and providing the strength and balance for the church to continue to grow and prosper. At Everyday, we have been working hard to raise up five-fold leaders. And, we have watched with joy as God has been answering our prayers, bringing world-class leaders to complete our leadership team.

HONOR

"Honor all people, love the brotherhood, fear God, honor the king." --1 Pet. 2:17

Honor is another catalytic agent in kingdom advancement. There is nothing that will accelerate the move of God and create exponential increase more than honor. Conversely, a lack of honor seriously impedes God's kingdom. To honor is to release life. It is to recognize God's beauty and glory in another and to express what we see by way of encouragement and deference. My friend Paul Manwaring in his book, What On Earth Is Glory? gives us a great explanation:

"Honor is both the desire and the ability to recognize glory in others. (Kabod, the Hebrew word for glory, is translated 'honor' 32 times in the Old Testament.) Whenever I recognize in someone or something the attributes, nature, or power of God, I am beginning the journey of honoring...

The cross is the supreme revelation of honor. At the cross, Jesus showed us how much He valued every man, woman, and child... He valued all of us above His own life... The honor Christ paid for us at the cross established the pattern of honor that defines the way we are to treat one another. The journey of honor requires first that we learn to value one another according to the value Christ has given us, and second that we learn to show that value as Christ did, by treating them as more important than ourselves."

We don't simply honor others because they deserve it, because sometimes people haven't walked honorably themselves. But we honor them because we our honorable. When we honor others, we choose to recognize the value they carry, even if they aren't able or willing to see that value themselves. Honoring others is part of what it means to be like God. And when we honor others, we honor God.

Honoring Our Differences

The kingdom of heaven is like a net that *caught all kinds of fish* (Mt. 13:47). The Greek word for 'caught' here in Matthew 13 is most often rendered 'gathered' in the rest of the New Testament. In the book of Acts, in particular, the word 'sunago' (συνάγω) refers to the assembly of the saints. Anyone who has been part of a local church for any length of time knows that the church gathers 'all kinds'!

Much of the church in the West sees this as a negative truth. The opposite of diversity is uniformity, and frankly, from a management standpoint, churches are easier to 'manage' when uniformity is promoted. A key principle in the church growth movement is the intentional effort to minimize diversity by focusing on homogeneous groupings. Evidently, studies show that churches grow bigger when you weed out the ones that aren't like you.

But this kind of thinking has a big price tag. Wherever the goal of the church is growth rather than the kingdom of God, kingdom diversity will suffer. Over four decades ago, Martin Luther King, Jr. declared eleven o'clock on Sunday mornings to be the most segregated hour in America. The church growth principle of homogeneous grouping hasn't helped change this sad reality. While we enjoy stereotype churches because they're easier to grow, and conforming Christians because they're easier to manage, God has always delighted in diversity.

With the exception of a few notable churches sprinkled here and there that already walk in great diversity, the majority of churches in the West have yet to experience the joy (and tension!) of kingdom diversity. We have enjoyed a shallow kind of unity based on conformity, homogeneous groupings, and a vibe of cool and comfortability that suits us. But we're not supposed to be building this thing for us! According to the Lord's prayer in Matthew 6, heaven is meant to touch earth in every aspect of life. God is now calling us to see heaven touch earth in the realm of diversity. The church is meant to reflect heaven, which reflects the heart of God. The kind of church standing before Him in heaven is quite diverse:

"After this I looked and there before me was a great multitude that no one could count, from every nation, tribe, people and language, standing before the throne and in front of the Lamb..." --Rev. 7:9

We know, for example, that here on earth, the animal kingdom separates and groups itself according to its own kind. But the kingdom of heaven displays what is possible under the rule of God. Twice, as Isaiah prophetically describes heaven, he speaks of diversity in the midst of unity: the wolf and the lamb, the leopard and the goat, dwelling together in unity (cf. Isa. 11:6; 65:25).

This diversity in the midst of unity pleases God. Part of the reason I believe God delights in kingdom diversity on earth is because where there is true diversity, Biblical unity is unexplainable except through the power and presence of the Holy Spirit. The outpouring of the Holy Spirit in Acts 2 brought together people from 15 different nations and regions of the Middle East to hear the gospel--people diverse in ethnicity, language, and culture. Undoubtedly, some of those 3,000 people who joined the church in a day were made up of from among this diverse crowd of people.

But we mustn't assume that the heart of kingdom diversity is achieved when we have people from a variety of racial backgrounds attending our services. In some places, this just isn't feasible, because the ethnicity of the geography means that the church will draw from a uniform demographic. In fact, a church can be made up of people from mostly the same racial and socioeconomic backgrounds and still embrace and practice kingdom diversity. While I believe we must continue to break down racial and socioeconomic walls in order to experience diversity in these realms, this is not the only way to model diversity. There are other dimensions of kingdom diversity that every church can embrace.

Recognizing and embracing our differences is essential in order for us to depart from 'one-size-fits-all' church life and to flow in diversity. Program-based design churches tend to count on uniformity, while kingdom churches are good with God's 'blended family.' To embrace a revival atmosphere that causes growth in every believer, kingdom diversity is our essential backdrop.

Honoring Unity

In the area where I live called the Central Coast, there is a pretty amazing work going on among the pastors. Pastors are meeting together and becoming friends. We take turns each month going to each others' churches, praying blessing on the host congregation and pastor while laying hands on one another as colleagues. We're enjoying semi-annual retreats together, and we are cheering each other on.

It wasn't always like this. In the past, the landscape of our region was similar to many other places where disunity, gossip, slander, mistrust, competition, and attack rule the atmosphere. We had a breakthrough largely due to the grace on our friend Tom Demaree, who came to our area 'in the fullness of time', when the conditions were ripe for breakthrough, as a catalytic 'outsider'. He led us in some worship and exercises designed to knit our hearts together in love. I recommend his ministry to cities and regions looking to grow in unity.

Where there has been a breakthrough in the realm of unity, it is our job to maintain it. Paul tells us in Eph. 4:3 be "diligent to preserve the unity of the Spirit in the bond of peace." Through the Cross every barrier has been removed, and unity is available to all of us. Our job is to maintain unity—to protect what we've been given and to keep investing in unity by being real and vulnerable and humble with one another, always responding with trust and respect and honor as we are honest together. It is honorable to walk in the unity Christ died for.

Demonstrated Unity

Walking out unity can look like a lot of things. It looks like friendship as it begins. Relationship is always the foundation of unity. And when relational love and trust are in place, we can go farther. In our region, we have quarterly all-regional events. Some of our pastors engage in pulpit swaps to create understanding. Sharing the responsibility for conferences and events helps the believers in a city or region to see a visible demonstration of unity. Joint ministries in a city or region are another great example of demonstrated unity, as well as regional gatherings just to come together.

When we were in Akron, Ohio planting a church, we heard about a pretty amazing work of unity in Cleveland. Some pastors there agreed that they wanted to work together to do a ministry school rather than each do a separate version of pretty much the same thing. So after much prayer, they asked one of the local pastors to consider stepping down from his pastorate so he could run this school. You can read the full story at: http://www.harvestnet.net. We can go farther into kingdom advancement when we demonstrate our unity in practical ways.

Kingdom churches love the whole church. They have made a decision to avoid self-preservation, which leads to comparison, envy, hoarding, and competition. Instead, kingdom churches believe that the kingdom truly does come first. With a kingdom orientation, there is nothing to gain and nothing to lose. There cannot be competition, because there is nothing to compete over. We genuinely want other individuals and churches to succeed.

This heart of unity allows us to embrace one another without sizing each other up. Jesus' prayer will be answered! There will be unity. The only question is whether or not we will be included or replaced. Lest you think that statement is harsh, remember what happened to the unbelieving Israelites when they wouldn't go into the promised land. God replaced them, every single one, with a brand new generation of people who would obey Him. God is currently replacing leaders who will not embrace the call to unity. He is raising up new leaders and building new churches that will truly embrace unity, even at their own expense. It is foolish to think that only some will pay a price. Everyone pays a price for unity. Everyone has to die to at least some aspect of their dreams and plans for true unity to take place. But wherever unity truly happens, it releases incredible multiplying power.

Honoring Protocol

Protocol is not an exact term you can find in Scripture, but it is definitely a Scriptural concept. Protocol has to do with *how things are done*. It is the fine art of understanding how to read between the lines and how to follow the law of love (cf. Rom. 13:10) as we apply God's wisdom to situations. Love frees us to intuitively know what to do in a given situation. The love of God as our motivation, mingled with God's wisdom, results in kingdom protocol. When we recognize and walk in God's protocol in a given situation, we are walking in the place of honor.

Perhaps the best example of protocol is found in Solomon. The Lord gave such wisdom to Solomon that when the Queen of Sheba observed the protocol of his house, she was stunned:

> "When the queen of Sheba saw with her own eyes Solomon's wisdom--the palace he built, the meals at his table, the seating of his servants, the attendance of his waiters and their attire, his cupbearers, and his stairway that went up to the house of the Lord—it took her breath away, and there was no more spirit in her." --1 Kings 10:4-5

God has ways of doing things. It is said of Moses that He knew God well enough to actually know God's ways. That means that Moses understood how God thinks! Israel is not given high marks like Moses. They only knew God's deeds. They didn't perceive His real heart behind His actions.

"He made known His ways to Moses, His acts to the sons of Israel." --Ps. 103:7

Discerning the heart of God and the ways of God is a key to kingdom acceleration. Anything less doesn't represent His kingdom very well. At times, I have been guilty of not honoring protocol, and at times others have violated our sense of protocol as well. We do this in the body of Christ, perhaps more often than we realize. The challenging part is that the 'rules' of protocol are not clearly spelled out in Scripture, so there is room for disagreement. But we want to be sure that the Lord is leading us. It is our responsibility as citizens of the kingdom to make sure we do not run roughshod over others in God's kingdom, all in the name of exercising our liberty but ignoring the still small voice of conviction that would point us to a better, more excellent way of love.

People may convince themselves that their hearts are right,
but is the Lord convinced?" --Prov. 16:2, 21:2

When we plant churches, we must consider existing works. Existing ministries must be open to new churches, and church planters must be sensitive to avoid causing undue stress on existing ministries. We must have a win-win mentality as the kingdom expands. If an opportunity presents itself to us and we have the opportunity to advance our ministry, but in the process it costs another ministry, kingdom protocol requires that we rethink our plan. When senior pastors or pastoral staff members of churches leave one church and either start a new church or join the team of a neighboring church in the same geographic area, this can become a serious protocol violation.

We talked briefly in chapter 8 about individuals changing churches. Protocol among pastors means that when people come to us from other churches, we grieve more than we celebrate. We should never find our strength as churches in transfer growth but especially not when the people 'growing' our church are from other churches in the city or region. We want to be quick to send them back to their previous church, trying to ensure unity and graceful exits. Sometimes the most appropriate thing we can do when someone from a church down the street shows up at our church is to immediately call his or her previous pastor. This creates accountability while modeling unity for the larger church in our city or region.

In the chapter called 'Kingdom Membership', we touched on the idea that God has really called people to specific congregations. When that happens, a true spiritual father and mother will 'adopt' that new person and begin to treat him or her like a son or daughter. The real pain for all of us who care for people is that when someone comes to our church and commits, telling us that God led them there, our hearts as shepherds begin to become attached to that person. As spiritual dads and moms, we love them like our own children, enfolding them into our hearts and involving them in our lives. If they then leave for no apparent reason (other than preference or minor conflict that should be reconciled), and then on top of that if they don't bother to actually dialogue about it, it feels like a violation of protocol. It seems to me that the protocol of loyalty demands more from people.

These kinds of protocol issues are not always crystal clear. Nor does everyone agree on what protocol means. But if we're going to see kingdom advancement in our churches, in our cities and regions, we must honor each other as best we can. Sometimes that means that we don't exert our full rights in deference to another. Sometimes it means that we need to go back and reconcile with people that we have violated.

> "If you are worshipping and there you remember a violation against a friend, abandon your time of worship and go immediately to make things right with your friend. After that, you can come back and work things out with God."
> --Matt. 5:23-24

Honoring Uniqueness

God's kingdom advances when we embrace each others' uniqueness rather than try to copy it. This may be one of the final frontiers for church leaders to overcome, but we're getting there!

The other day I was at our monthly pastors' meeting where I heard my friend Ron repeat a conversation he had that week. He was asked by someone in his congregation, "Why don't we have 'Celebrate Recovery' at our church?" Ron answered, "We *do* have a 'Celebrate Recovery' ministry. It meets down at 'New Hope.'" I *loved* Ron's answer! It is so very kingdom. More than that, it honors uniqueness. Ron was trying to help this member of his church recognize that there is one church in the region, and that his church, New Life, wasn't obligated to reproduce every ministry in the area when there was already an effective version of that ministry functioning somewhere else. He could simply get behind it and bless it, enjoying the fact that his church had a ministry where they could send people!

What unique ministry have you been called to in your city or region? What about your church? As churches and leaders in regions start to recognize our unique contributions, there will be less jealousy and competition. Instead, we will see more cooperation and recognition as we cheer each other on.

Honoring City And Regional Development

I believe a primary issue we face today in seeing city and regional revival is learning how to steward the growth and transfer of leadership within the city or region. I believe the Lord has a flexible wineskin for city and regional government that moves and flexes depending on the situation. Here are some scenarios that deserve our prayerful consideration:

Apostolic Prominence. There is a move of God in every city and region toward apostolic prominence. He is highlighting apostles and desiring their honor. Many churches are led by Eph. 4:11 pastors who lack apostolic leadership. Biblically, pastors have an equipping role in the body of Christ and have been gifted by God to train the saints in the ministry functions of listening, counseling, prayer, inner healing, deliverance, relationship, shepherding, and care. While these functions are extremely important, they are not the best gift mix to lead a community of faith significantly larger than a home fellowship (unless the person has a strong leadership gift as well). The crisis of pastors leaving the ministry is a testimony to this fact. They are not built for the job they are being required to do.

Every kingdom church and ministry needs apostolic DNA in its leadership. How this occurs is secondary. Sometimes, an apostle leads the church. In other cases, an apostle or apostolic team plants the church, turns it over to elders, and then visits periodically. Sometimes, there is an apostolic network of churches where each church is led by a spiritual father & mother (elder couple) and the apostolic team cares for these leaders and churches.

We will continue to see the development of 'apostolic centers' as a viable expression of apostolic ministry in cities and regions. These centers not only provide local pastoral care but also regional and global ministries that build and bless translocally. And apostolic function means more than just planting churches! Some years ago, the Lord visited Lauren Cunningham, founder of YWAM, and the late Bill Bright, founder of Campus Crusade For Christ, with very similar revelations of what is now commonly called 'the 7 mountains of culture.' Dr. Lance Wallnau and others have done a great job teaching on these arenas where God wants to break in with His kingdom. Apostolic prominence will include the leaders within these spheres.

New Church Dynamics. God must be the one who starts churches, not man. If people collectively decide to start a church on their own, without the heavenly mandate, I believe the church itself is out of order. Will God use it? Yes. Will God bless it? If the gospel is being preached, yes, He will bless it. But, as with everything else in the Christian life, the good is the enemy of the best. In this freewheeling era of spiritual entrepreneurship (and I am hugely in favor of spiritual entrepreneurship!), it is important for us to know that we were "sent" versus we "went!" Sending is modeled continually in the book of Acts, a loose handbook for church planting. Of course, we are first sent by God, but even Barnabas and Saul, whom the Holy Spirit clearly sent, were commissioned by the other leaders at Antioch. When they had preached the gospel and planted the church, they reported back to the leadership there in Antioch.

I believe apostolic ministry should be involved in the birthing process of every local church. Apostles started churches in the New Testament, and apostles released other ministry roles, such as elders. In places where churches are rapidly reproducing, apostolic ministry can partner with the local 'pastor', elder or team to birth the church and turn it over right away to local, indigenous leadership.

House Church Scenarios. Clearly, house churches are growing in popularity in the West, as they should. House churches are a refreshing alternative to many larger traditional churches that have become institutional in their orientation. I believe house churches work best when they are led by a couple like Priscilla and Aquila (1 Cor. 16:19) who serve as spiritual father and mother to their flock. This is eldership in action, defined by function rather than as a position on a board.

Because house churches are relatively small and are usually focused on shared leadership, any of the five equipping roles (apostle, prophet, evangelist, pastor, teacher) could also lead/facilitate a house church. As long as there is reasonable care and 'one another' ministry, the type of gifted person leading the house church is not as mission critical. The important thing is that the flock is cared for while remaining connected to something bigger than itself so that apostolic influence is constantly injected in the DNA. House church networks are emerging as a viable model of church life. These networks provide the best of all worlds in that, the leadership of the church is eldership, but the network has apostolic influence.

Community Churches. The average and most common church size in America is somewhere around 70 people. Why is this so? I believe a primary reason is because for centuries, we have built churches around the pastoral gift almost exclusively. Good pastors (with lots of energy) have an ability to effectively care for around 70 people. If the church gets larger than that, people begin to lose touch with the pastor. And when they no longer feel connected to the pastor, often they leave to find something that better meets their needs.

Over the coming years, I believe many community churches will change the way they operate. As more and more senior pastors of community churches are quitting the ministry due to unfulfilled expectations and burnout, I believe many community churches will either (1) change from pastoral to apostolic leadership and grow; (2) join forces with another church; or (3) disband. Many leaders who were originally created to be apostolic and who have settled for pastoral roles are currently being called by God to make a shift from pastoral to apostolic. This move of God will revitalize the community church scene, and we will see fresh releases of apostolic authority coming on seemingly stalled community churches.

MegaChurches. My observation is that almost every growing megachurch is led either by a highly gifted evangelist, an excellent teacher, or more often an anointed apostle. It would indeed be rare for a true prophet (and I love prophets!) to be a megachurch point person because they're usually too vertical (and combative!), and true pastors (and I love pastors!) usually don't lead megachurches because they're not wired for the pressures of hundreds or thousands pulling on them.

Nearly every healthy, growing megachurch has multiple layers of leadership that involve all or nearly all of the New Testament leadership gifts. Whatever gift the senior leader has, usually he has surrounded himself with complimentary gifts on his staff. There are also usually designated elders and small group leaders, so the church is flowing in most of the essential gifts in the New Testament. A great megachurch is incredibly valuable.

City/Region Leadership. When you combine these various kinds of churches, along with other ministries, kingdom businesses, and influencers from the various mountains of culture, you get a more complete picture of kingdom leadership in cities and regions. Citywide and regional eldership begins to emerge. An apostolic council can emerge, made up of those apostles of megachurches, along with apostolic church planters and others who have apostolic authority in a region. The equipping ministries of Ephesians 4:11 become translocal consultant gifts and servants to the churches in the region as they exercise their function and equip the saints for the work of ministry, sometimes through city or regional ministries, such as houses of prayer, training schools, healing rooms, prophetic companies, and so on. As walls between local churches continue to fall, we will see new city and regional networks emerge.

THE POOR, THE LOST, THE NATIONS

True devotion to God means that as laid-down lovers our eyes are on the poor, the lost, and the nations. At Everyday Church, our commitment isn't merely 'every member a minister' or 'every member a leader' but rather 'every member a *missionary*.' We want the people in our church to see themselves as true missionaries, sent by God to a people group.

When we planted the church in the Mid-West, we agreed to practice a model of "seek, soak, and go!" We would gather on Sunday mornings to seek God's face in worship. Then we would wait before the Lord and pray for one another, soaking in God's presence and power. And then we would break into teams and go to the 'projects.' We took church to the poor, ministering love and hope to the hearts and practical needs of God's 'chosen' people (cf. James 2:5).

When we moved back to the Central Coast of California, we were greatly concerned, because we knew that the "poor" in our geography were not as prevalent, and yet ministry to the poor was so central to our mission and heart. My friend David Van Cronkhite says, *"We need the poor more than they need us."* This is true! Now, in our geography of abundance, we are finding new ways to serve the poor. We are learning to *'stop for the one'* in our geography! I have been so proud of some of our young adults who have actually purchased homes in poorer neighborhoods in order to love their neighbors better. A large part of our vision is to become an apostolic center helping resource effective ministries to the poor. Serving the poor is not an optional ministry. It is central to our mission (Luke 4:18) and central to what it means to know God (Jer. 22:15-16). God is turning the attention of the church in the West on the plight of the poor. Even movie stars have been jumping on the bandwagon! God accelerates revival on those cities and regions that prefer the poor.

Acceleration happens through sending! If our goal is church growth, we will find it difficult to truly release people. But when we give away our best to seed the nations of the earth and in particular to reach the poor of the earth, our kingdom impact is exponentially increased, and God is well-pleased.

SIGNS, WONDERS, AND CHURCH GROWTH

> "For the kingdom of God is not a matter of talk but of power." --1 Cor. 4:20

In 1984 I went to a life-changing conference called 'Signs, Wonders, and Church Growth.' It was modeled after a course John Wimber taught at Fuller Seminary. John taught us that wherever the supernatural is occurring regularly, the church is growing.

For kingdom advancement to occur in any significant way, power is required and is not optional. Kingdom churches are filled with the reality and demonstration of the power of God. The very essence and nature of God's kingdom is power. It is complimentary to Romans 1:16, where Paul proclaims that the gospel is the power of God to salvation for everyone who believes. Clearly, Paul is not talking about a gospel of mere words. The gospel of words has power, but the kingdom doesn't come through talking heads. Raw power is part and parcel with the gospel. Anything less is Biblically suspect and is to be avoided:

> "There will be terrible times in the last days. People will be lovers of themselves...lovers of pleasure rather than lovers of God--having a form of godliness but denying its power. Have nothing to do with them."
> --2 Tim. 3:1-5

Surveying the landscape of churches in the West, it is clear that many church leaders have been holding onto a worldview of power as optional, or worse yet, as something that is suspect. All too often our greatest strengths become our greatest weaknesses. Because God's power is dynamic, unpredictable, and sometimes even 'messy', those who work the hardest to be Biblically accurate and theologically sound are often the worst offenders at ignoring and avoiding the Biblical reality of the power of God. In short, we have been trying to build New Testament churches marked by kingdom reality without New Testament power. The lack of power in the church in the West has become embarrassingly obvious.

When I became a Christian in the seventies, I was told by my mentors that God wasn't in the "power" business any more. Demonstrations of God's power were theologically relegated to the validation of Jesus' ministry and to the first thirty years of the early church. After that, I was told, we had God's written Word, and there was no longer a need for supernatural displays of God's power. When I offered examples of people I knew or had heard of who were recently healed of diseases, I was summarily corrected that either (a) the people weren't really sick to begin with; (b) it was a fluke and we shouldn't expect such things; or (c) something other than God's power had healed them--usually medicine, coincidence, or even the devil (which made no sense).

As I grew in my Christian faith, studied God's Word more, had more experiences with God's power, and prayed more effective prayers for others, I noticed that my power- challenged friends had a more difficult time defending their position of powerlessness. As communication and testimonies have become more globalized through the internet and better travel, this position of powerlessness is becoming all but indefensible. It was only later that I would realize that this worldview is entirely unbiblical. Power is part and parcel of the nature and activity of kingdom people and kingdom churches.

It is alarming that a still significant (but shrinking) part of the North American church doesn't make room in their theology for the power of God as normative. But what is more alarming is the stunning absence of power in churches that do embrace a theology of the supernatural! Over recent decades, we have been able to bluff our way through with only a tacit nod towards power, but now, the power of God flowing through His people in China, South America, Africa, and other places is providing an 'in-your-face' mirror to His people in the West. It is time to build kingdom churches unashamedly filled with the power of God!

Radical Dependency

People in kingdom churches exhibit a total commitment to being continually filled with the Holy Spirit. Many older Christians wistfully remember that when they were new believers, they would just "follow the Spirit!" This is where many great stories came from--those early years of following God. Somewhere, many of us tried to grow up, and we forgot about the childlike essence of the kingdom. This new generation of churches and leaders are exhibiting a radical dependency on the Holy Spirit. "Immerse me, Spirit of God! Fully possess me, precious Holy Spirit!" are the kinds of prayers being prayed today by a people absolutely convinced that whatever we do and say and build and plant must be authored, birthed, led, protected, and sealed by the wonderful Spirit of God! These ones, fully committed to the written Word of God as their foundation, realize that it is possible to diligently study the Scriptures and miss the Person of Jesus, just like the pharisees did (Jn. 5:39). We must radically depend on the Holy Spirit.

The Stigma Of Power

How many churches in the West are ashamed of what the Holy Spirit may do when He touches people? How many churches in the West, seeking to be respectable, have grown uneasy with and ashamed of God's power demonstrated in regular (and unusual) ways in and through people? We hedge our bets, we qualify Him, we make excuses for God, and we explain away any demonstrations of power. Rather than shy away from power, the apostolic nature of kingdom churches expects demonstrations of power as normative:

> "My message and my preaching were not with wise and persuasive words, but with a demonstration of the Spirit's power, so that your faith might not rest on men's wisdom, but on God's power." --1 Cor. 2:4-5

As incredible as it may seem, Paul teaches us here to rest our faith on God's power. That makes power pretty important. Notice that Paul establishes the causal relationship between kingdom power and the Holy Spirit when he calls it "the Spirit's power."

The Power Of The Gospel

The causal link between the Holy Spirit and power was previously made by Jesus when He said in Acts 1:8--"You shall receive power when the Holy Spirit has come upon you..." It is the Holy Spirit that releases the

Divine reality of the power of God. This power allows us to truly be witnesses of an evidential Christianity, a God who is alive and not dead, who is active and not passive, who is passionate towards humanity and not listless, bored, or disinterested. Jesus came out of the desert, a time of temptation and testing, full of the power of the Spirit. He was ready for action because of the power of the Holy Spirit. We, too, must be completely filled with the Spirit and His power to impact a world for Jesus Christ, armed with the Word and the Spirit.

The Glory Of God

In the Old Testament, there were frequent occurrences of the weighty glory of God descending on the people and their gatherings like a thick blanket. To think that because we are under the New Covenant we would not experience this is backwards thinking. How much more, now that we have the indwelling Holy Spirit, should our gatherings be characterized by the manifest Presence and Glory of God! 2 Cor. 3:18 tells us that we behold God's glory with unveiled faces. The apostle Paul tells us in Ephesians 2:22 that we, the people of God, are being built together to become a dwelling place of God in the Spirit. This means that it is God's intention to live among us and to demonstrate His powerful presence and His beautiful nature in our midst. May the weighty glory of God fill our homes, our cell groups, our house churches, our celebrations, our prayer meetings, and every place where two or three are together. He is in our midst!

STEWARDING THE PROMISES

Finally, any city or region that will steward God's promises well will see advancement. Kingdom people (and by extension kingdom churches) are pregnant with promise! Jesus loves to create an atmosphere of surprise and anticipation. It is our job to steward that atmosphere of expectation in our hearts. The promises of God are "yes!" and "amen!" Many promises await us as we steward them through prayer, expectation, and action.

The Promise Of Immeasurable Increase. One of the primary reasons the Western church has lost its surprise, spontaneity, and power is because of our propensity to measure everything. We count people, dollars, empty chairs, full chairs, small groups, parking spaces, minutes on the clock, graduates from our programs, and so on. In Luke 6:38, Jesus tells us that our measurements will come back to us, one way or another. The law of measurement is this: whatever measurement we use will be measured to us. This is both a promise and a warning.

It's not exactly the actual numbering of things that is the problem (although sometimes it is, as in the case of David numbering Israel). I can already hear the arguments of wise stewards proclaiming loudly that we're just being responsible with what God is giving us. Yes, stewardship is a real responsibility before God. Certainly we must balance our checkbooks, plan wisely for enough space for meetings, and so on. But the heart reality of kingdom measurements has to do with the fact that the kingdom is so incredibly powerful and explosive, it cannot be encompassed by mere human observation and recording.

For years we trained our pastors, church planters, and leadership teams to count everything in sight as part of good stewardship. But I think we've missed a key principle that can significantly limit our thinking and reduce our experience. God wants to take us beyond measurements! The benediction in Eph. 3:20 assures us, "Now to him who is able to do immeasurably more than all we ask or imagine, according to his power that is at work within us... "

God is able, but are we able to embrace the infinite ability of God? If He can do more than we could ask in our most fervent prayer times or imagine in our most liberated times of daydreaming, then we are only limited by our current measurements. Truly, we are measured, and therefore we receive, according to the measurements that we use. If we build churches around our common understanding of measurements, then ultimately, we will never know the raw power and potential of God working within us and through us. The term "immeasurably" can be defined as "incapable of being measured; broadly: indefinitely extensive." The intense burden that has been on the leadership of the church in the West will finally be lifted as we understand and are liberated by kingdom measurements into a multiplication mentality.

The Promise Of Multiplication. Multiplication is a dynamic reality that we experience as we build His kingdom. In Leviticus 26:8, God promised multiplication when He told His people: "Five of you will chase a hundred, and a hundred of you will chase ten thousand..." This spontaneous dynamic of the rapidly expanding kingdom was lived out in the early church on numerous occasions as the church rallied together. For example, after the apostles and the congregation came together to commission seven men to oversee the food ministry, there were immediate results: "And the word of God increased; and the number of disciples multiplied..." --Acts 6:7 (KJV)

God can grow things through addition or through multiplication. Because we are living in the eleventh hour before the return of Christ, and because we want to redeem the time before us, kingdom churches are focused on multiplication, not simply addition. Addition occurs as we each do our part, but multiplication happens when we come together.

The Promise Of Massive Harvest. The light shines brighter as darkness increases! As we walk in the presence of the King, those who don't know Christ experience God's presence and respond. We will see more and more people coming to Christ as the people of God exude the holiness of our King. As the church begins to embody the kingdom and become again living epistles known and read by all men, as believers begin to "outlive" their unbelieving contemporaries, the contrast between those who know God and those who don't will again become evident. There will also be increased supernatural expressions of healing, words of knowledge, prophecies, miracles, and signs and wonders released in the marketplace as believers walk in the presence and power of God and begin to take risks again for the sake of the King. Many more people will come to Christ as they see and experience an evidential Christianity and a God who is clearly alive and present in a holy, mobilized people.

There are thousands of believers who have come to know Christ but have abandoned the church. Now is the time for these ones to reestablish fellowship with a local body of believers. The last decade of deconstruction that caused many believers to grow disillusioned with the church is over! God allowed thousands of us to see what is wrong so that the dismantling of the ship called the church in Acts 27 would take place. But read the story. Paul said, "Unless these men stay with the ship, you cannot be saved." This is not the time to jump ship on the church. Only if we all stay on the ship together and go through the process together, first of deconstruction, and now of reconstruction, can everyone live. While the ship of institutionalism is being run aground and destroyed, we are all meant to grab hold of our piece of the ship and go safely to shore. There is safety in going through this transition with the people of God, not away from them.

This is not the time to hide in the cave like Elijah, thinking we're the only ones! God has been doing a major, global work in the church in the West. Now, God is building new kinds of churches with new kinds of leaders, and He is refitting existing churches and leaders with a fresh kingdom paradigm. The net result is that the church is becoming safe again. The Father's heart is being released in an increased way so that a generation can come to Christ and so many prodigals can find their way home. When Joseph fled to Egypt to protect Mary and Jesus, the Lord spoke to him at the right time that it was safe to return. In the same way, the Father is saying to many that it is "safe" to return to fellowship with the local body of Christ. Those who remain prodigal after this window of grace will have more difficulty returning and are in danger of hardening their hearts.

The Promise Of The Canopy Of David. Among other things, David's tabernacle (or tent) was characterized by a stunning absence of the veil around the holy of holies. This powerful prophetic picture speaks to us of an intimacy with God available to every believer. When Jesus died on the Cross and the veil of His flesh was torn, so was the veil in the temple. We have unrestricted access, both as individual believers and as a corporate temple of the Lord, to the most intimate places in God available on earth. The promise of the restoration of the tabernacle of David is about this radical intimacy expressed through wholehearted, extravagant worshippers. Over recent years, we have identified with many metaphors as the Church--house, hospital, school, army, etc. But the Bridal metaphor will take highest prominence. As the church finds her identity as the Bride of Christ, intimacy with God will then lead to increased fruitfulness on earth. This radical shift of attention from works to the Person of Jesus changes everything. The Ephesian church that received correction from Jesus in Revelation 2 was working very hard and holding the line on doctrinal purity. But somehow, they had left their first love. There is a strong bridal call being issued forth from the heart of Jesus Christ to His Church. We will continue to become a people who are confident in God's love for us and His gracious friendship. Each believer will become a literal "house of prayer" on the earth!

The Promise Of The Power Of Love. Many waters cannot quench love, because love is stronger than death. Nothing can separate us from God's love. God's love is the most powerful reality in the universe. Kingdom churches build through the culture of God's love. One church I know has declared the following mission statement: "That we may walk in God's love and then give it away." Love will always find a way. We will see arguments solved and tensions reduced by love. Love settles arguments! When we don't know the way forward, we must call out to God for more love. The increased love of God is the answer to our challenges as we move forward to build kingdom churches together. Jesus prophesied that in the last days, the love of many would grow cold. Love will be the defining characteristic of true kingdom churches. The love of God will become more prominent because it will grow so thin outside of the kingdom. As darkness increases, the culture of God's love will shine brighter and brighter from God's people.

The Promise Of Possibilities. In the years to come, encouragement will become a more and more important ministry. Everyone is carrying around two buckets--one with gas and one with water. We will learn when to pour from which bucket. God has put little fires in people's hearts. It was said of Jesus, "A smoldering wick he will not snuff out." In the same way, the church will become more skilled at calling forth destiny in one another. This atmosphere of grace will empower the church to live out of her true identity. The palette of creativity will emerge even more as individual believers begin to express their love for God in more spontaneous and creative ways. New sounds in worship will emerge. New kinds of churches will be birthed. Church without walls means that the wineskin of the church will truly be simple, flexible, and supple in the hands of the Master. We will be blown away by the creativity coming through the body of Christ, and the net result will not simply be self-expression, but a tidal wave of people coming to the Lord Jesus Christ. It will be impossible to orchestrate and barely able to be chronicled. Like a river, our choice will be to watch or jump in.

The Promise Of New (& Beyond) Structures. Currently, many Western churches are still scrambling for the latest and greatest gathering methodology. But how we gather is really not a wineskin. As of the writing of this book, Sunday morning meetings may still be quite central in many churches while becoming a bit passe with some, and in some places the movements of G12 and house churches are still "hot." But look out! God is still using all kinds of contexts! Many of our African brothers and sisters are gathering mostly in relatively large meetings and sitting in rows on the ground or in chairs while one person does the speaking. Traditional Bible schools, crusades, and platform ministry are still popular. The techniques, structures, and gathering contexts they use are not keeping the dead from being raised, blind eyes from opening, food being multiplied, and thousands from coming into the kingdom! As this revolution grows, we will find that many have been barking up the wrong tree! How we gather is really actually not a wineskin. It is a context. The new wineskin is the paradigm and culture of the kingdom, and the wine is extravagant devotion to a Person and the wine of His love in our hearts and lives and families. A kingdom revolution among a people in love with their King compelled to go to the lost--that's it!

The Promise Of A Prepared Bride. Intimacy with God produces urgency among God's people. We will see an intensity and fervency among these kingdom priests who live everyday as walking revival. A forerunner spirit will emerge as Christ's return hastens and people prepare themselves for the wedding feast of the Lamb. The return of Christ will begin to occupy the thoughts of most believers much more often than is the case today. The Spirit and the Bride will truly say, "Come quickly, Lord Jesus!"

The Promise Of Revolution! A nameless, faceless generation will emerge, not because of the abolishing of leadership, as many have thought, but because everyone else will "step up." When there are so many living radically for Christ and serving Him with all their hearts, and as kingdom churches deemphasize title and position and focus on function and commonality in Christ, it will be hard to tell who the "leaders" are, except by the fruit of their lives and their kingdom impact. Even then, it won't really matter, because the entire body will have reached a place of maturity, expressing the fullness of the measure of Christ in their stature. We will see the priesthood of every believer in our lifetime. And we will see this priesthood expressing themselves in like-minded communities called "kingdom churches." And it will be glorious.

ABOUT THE AUTHOR

Mark Perry is the senior leader at Everyday Church, a growing regional apostolic center on the Central Coast of California. Everyday is also a church planting movement, planting microchurches throughout the Central Coast and in other parts of California.

Mark also serves as director of Iris Central Coast under the leadership of Rolland and Heidi Baker and Iris Global.

Mark Perry has been building kingdom churches for over 35 years. He has served as an assistant pastor, senior pastor, church planter, and church consultant. Mark & his wife have enjoyed starting successful churches and successful businesses.

You can contact Mark for speaking opportunities at:
mark@everydaychurch.org

www.everydaychurch.com
www.everydaymark.com